THE MOTHER, THE POLITICIAN,
AND THE GUERRILLA

# The Mother, the Politician, and the Guerrilla

**WOMEN'S POLITICAL IMAGINATION IN THE KURDISH MOVEMENT**

*Nazan Üstündağ*

FORDHAM UNIVERSITY PRESS   NEW YORK   2023

Visit us online at www.fordhampress.com.

Library of Congress Cataloging-in-Publication Data available online at https://catalog.loc.gov.

Printed in the United States of America

25 24 23 5 4 3 2 1

First edition

*To my mother and best friend, Ayşe Üstündağ*

# Contents

# THE MOTHER, THE POLITICIAN, AND THE GUERRILLA

# Introduction

What to do, how to move, in such a world wherein your resistance against violent conditions — resistance as prayer meetings or protests, resistance as simply wishing to breathe — produces the occasion for violence?

— ASHON T. CRAWLEY, *BLACKPENTECOSTAL BREATH*

Historical catastrophe, then, is not a final moment in a historical period, or a single event within time. Rather, it is the repetitive constitution of death worlds in which lives are erased and in which forms of domination exist, in which the human is "superfluous" over a long historical period. So, when from this ground of historical catastrophe the living corpse asks the question, "And what about the Human?" he or she does not begin by turning to the objects of their labor, nor seeks recognition in the ways that Hegel outlines in his Lord and Bondsman dialectic in the Phenomenology of Spirit; I suggest instead that attention is turned to practices of freedom.

— ANTHONY BOGUES, "AND WHAT ABOUT THE HUMAN? FREEDOM, HUMAN EMANCIPATION AND THE RADICAL IMAGINATION"

They were the children of the rebellious mountains that gave birth to the sun. Their lives; colorful like a very very old tragic saga, the song of a dengbej, the song of birds that falls on the dawn. One side always blue, green; one side always grey and foggy. Their language maternal and poetic. They were defeated. But they did also defeat.

— SAIT ÜÇLÜ, *GÜNEŞ ÜLKESINDE DIRILIŞ: AMARA BIRINCI KITAP 1. CILT*

Life is sudden, deep and momentary. Especially in Kurdistan. Like the
tune of a pipe.

— BERJIN HAKI, *KAVALIN EZGISI*

"By resisting here we are opening a space for politics," a woman guerrilla I
met in Cizre told me.[1] She was in her early twenties and had come to Cizre
from the mountains surrounding the city with three of her friends. When the
first publicly announced peace talks between the Turkish state and Kurdistan
Workers Party (PKK) ended in 2015, Kurdistan youth opened up trenches in
their neighborhoods to protect themselves from the raids by the Turkish police
forces.[2] With the assistance of guerrilla teams located near city centers, they
also mined these trenches and equipped themselves with arms. Meanwhile,
in several Kurdish cities, local assemblies that were created during the peace
talks as (extralegal) bodies of governance parallel to state bureaucracy had
declared regional autonomy.

Cizre was one of the most organized among the "trenched" cities. I was
in Cizre with the Women for Peace Initiative — an initiative we had founded
in 2009 to struggle for peace in Turkey between the state and Kurdistan
Worker's Party (PKK). Our visit aimed at showing our support for the people
in the town, especially the women, who had experienced an eight days' long
around-the-clock curfew imposed by the state in order for the security forces
to raid the neighborhoods where the trenches were dug.[3] Twenty-two people
had died during the raids. Despite the losses, the mood in Cizre was high;
security forces aided by special counterinsurgency squads brought from the
capital, Ankara, and equipped with tanks and drones had failed to enter the
neighborhoods because of the resistance shown by the people and the armed
youth. The woman guerrilla continued: "They want to annihilate us. We can
only push for politics and peace by showing that we will not be annihilated."

Once we left her quarters, I contemplated with a friend, who lived in Cizre,
why we were so moved by her and her friends. He said, "Because they are like
stray puppies, and so loving towards each other." While there was some truth
to that, this did not explain why everyone else also felt so much love for them,
following their orders even though they were so young. I thought to myself
that the people regarded them also as warriors and prophets, leading the way
to a much-anticipated free future with their very flesh. After a moment of
silence, my friend added, "They inspire people to be their best."

Soon the trenches and the declarations, both acts of sovereignty on the
part of the Kurdish opposition, unleashed an even greater violence from the
Turkish state surpassing that of the 1990s, when various counterinsurgency
tactics had traumatized the whole region. Overall, around-the-clock curfews

in "trenched" neighborhoods lasted for more than six months, and Turkish counterinsurgency squads killed hundreds of civilians, youth activists, and fighters, demolishing buildings and infrastructures, which reduced the insurgent cities to rubble.[4] After a second curfew in which state forces destroyed entire neighborhoods in Cizre, displaced thousands of people, and burned alive more than one hundred people (including the resisting youth, politicians, nurses, and other supporters who were waiting for a ceasefire and ambulances in three basements), I frantically searched through the pictures of dead bodies on the Internet that counterinsurgency accounts posted to find out whether the woman guerrilla we met was among them. She was. Face down, lying on the ground, her flesh exposed.

The Kurdish people witnessed numerous atrocities at the hands of the Turkish state. What differentiated this last wave of violence and increased its terror was that — in addition to its intensity and scale — whereas before, the state tried to hide its destruction from sight and hence forced it upon Kurds to prove the occurrence of forced disappearances, displacements, and executions, now the destruction was being done in open sight as proof of the Turkish state's power.[5] During the curfews security forces regularly produced corpses for public viewing, both as they were attacking the trenched cities from afar and later as they slowly drilled their way into the resisting neighborhoods.[6] Videos and photographs of rotten, crushed, naked, and pulled-apart Kurdish flesh were leaked to the Internet, supplemented by images of captured bodies dragged from place to place. Acoustically, the noise of tanks, drones, and bombs displaying the superiority of the technologically advanced Turkish "Special Forces" accompanied the voices of insurgents who anticipated their own "corpsing" as they talked to Kurdish Television stations on their cell phones.[7] In the 1990s, seeing and hearing were unevenly distributed in Turkey, keeping the hope alive that if everybody would know what was really happening they would understand the truth of Kurdish oppression. Now, people saw the same pictures but were affected differently: Turks felt victorious and Kurds were horrified, making it almost impossible to dream a potentially just future of coexistence.

The spectacle of suffering and destruction was as much about confirming the proper role of Kurdishness in the order of things as it was about performing Turkish sovereignty.[8] As I have written elsewhere, Kurdish bodies that do not perform their own symbolic death by an absolute obedience to state law are made to pose face down on the pavement, testifying to the impossibility of surviving a free life in Turkey.[9] For the purposes of this book I want to remind us of three images of such "forced poses" that constituted a devouring "trauma of representation" for Kurds during the curfew and raids.[10] By the concept of "trauma of representation," I wish to evoke the difficulty and the obligation one feels to look at the reality of dead flesh and how this disrupts the fantasies invested in the human rights discourses and the ways in which resistance, power, and reconciliation are conventionally understood.[11] If imagination always involves "the image," "trauma of representation" causes imagination to be poisoned and imagined futures to be ruined. The following images played crucial roles in making it clear to Kurds in general and Kurdish women in particular that all of them had the potential to die like those in the images; their bodies were always open to the gratuitous violence of the state. The same photos rehabilitated Turks by restoring their narcissistic image without troubling them with feelings of guilt because no perpetrator was explicitly shown in them.

The first image belonged to Kevser Eltürk, a woman guerrilla known with the code name "Ekin Wan" who, after being killed by the security forces in August 2015, was dragged and left on a sidewalk for everyone to see. In a photo the security forces leaked to Twitter, civilian and uniformed men, whose presence and pose could be recognized by their legs captured in the shot, surrounded her body stripped of clothes.[12] Writing about photographs on lynching, David Marriott states, "The camera lens is a means to fashion the self through the image of a dead black man."[13] In Eltürk's case, too, those who photographed her fashioned themselves as sovereign Turks through the image of her dead and stripped body. This image also universalized the violence, sexism, and racism across the Turkish community and displayed the fact that law will always remain Turkish and patriarchal in Kurdish lands.[14]

The second image was a photograph of Taybet İnan lying face down on the street. A mother of eleven shot by Turkish snipers, she remained on the street for seven days while the crossfire between the Turkish armed forces and the armed Kurdish youth continued. Despite persistent demands by her family to stop the fire for a few hours so that her dead body could be taken off the street, central and local state authorities denied the ceasefire and her right to burial. Unlike Ekin Wan, Taybet İnan had not fought the Turkish state. Her crime, however, was as severe, because she claimed life in a zone where Kurds were condemned to death. Moreover, her failure to play her part in the racial genocidal order of the Turkish state by not leaving her home so that the state could kill the insurgents in more effective and less costly ways led to her inevitable corpsing.[15]

The last case concerns not an image but a text message and an emptiness to be filled by one's imagination informed by the horrors already witnessed. The public received news of the injury of three female politicians, Seve Demir, a member of the Party Assembly of the Democratic Regions Party, Pakize Nayır,

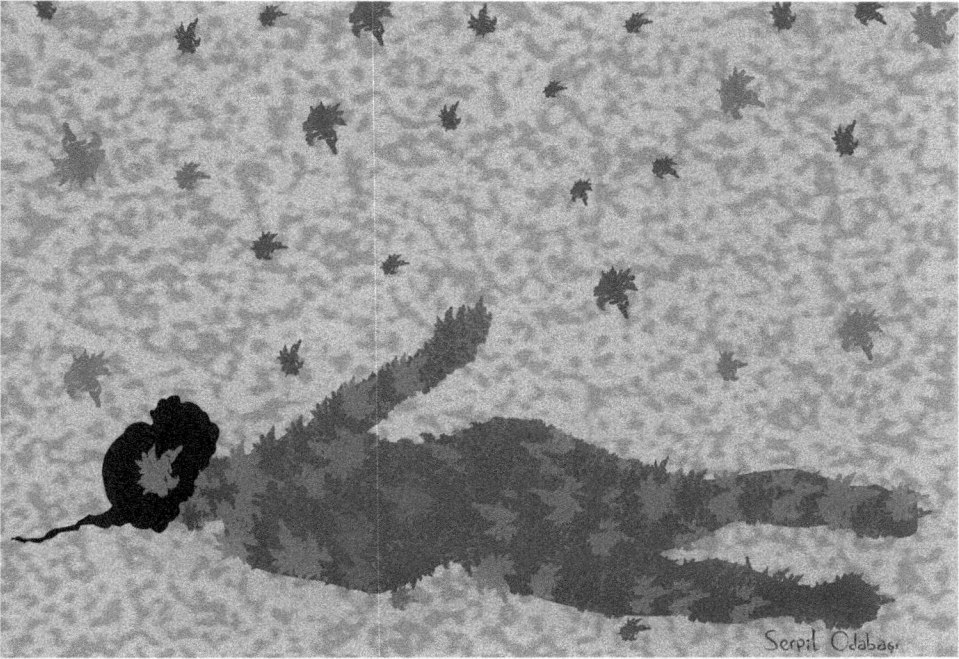

Figure 1. Ekin Wan drawn by Serpil Odabaşı

a member of the Free Women Congress, and Fatma Uyar, the co-president of Silopi People's Assembly, from the telephone call they made to a Kurdish MP asking for an ambulance. Fire from an armored vehicle shot by the Special Forces had hit them while they were trying to bring to safety the residents of a neighborhood the youth had left. Hours after this call, an ambulance was dispatched to pick them up, but it was their dead bodies that arrived at the hospital. While how they actually died after being able to phone was never clarified, rumors that Seve Demir was decapitated spread, linking the destruction and violence of the Turkish army to that of ISIS, against whom Kurds were fighting in northern Syria.

In his discussion of the wide distribution of lynching photographs in America, Ashon Crawley writes,

> The photographing, selling, buying, and mailing images of killed, swollen, burned, mottled flesh . . . were the instantiation of what Joseph Roach calls the "It — Effect": not only was black flesh made into bodies through discourse and material violence, but those bodies were

Figure 2. Taybet İnan drawn by Zehra Doğan

radically, unalterably . . . available to the public, what Roach calls
"public intimacy" that is "the illusion of availability." The It — Effect
of blackness is not the ruse of public availability but a violent performance that attempts to make It available, that attempts to furnish forth
It itself. In violence, making It available meant closing off objects,
silencing and shutting them up, it was to force enclosure, to create a
boundary, to produce, that is, a liberal subject, the possessive individual, through violence.[16]

Despite the spatial distances and the historical differences that distinguish our
cases, I find Crawley's analyses helpful for a framework to understand why the
counterinsurgency squads leaked the photographs of "corpsed" women and
men to the Internet. Violence and its display rob living flesh away from its
community, where it breathes, to capture and individualize it. They enclose it
and thereby ensure that the purity of the rest of the society is recovered while
at the same time performing the nonconvergence between the insurgents and
full human/citizen.

Crawley also argues, "Racial mob and lynching violence are confessions
of faith, declarations given about the desired interdiction of the capacity to
move, to be on the run, to have pleasure in blackness."[17] This book is an
inquiry into that which the Turkish state aimed at interdicting when it killed,
displayed, and spectacularized the flesh of women. What pleasures in Kurdishness and womanhood did the state want to unmake, and what visions of
potential futures did it want to prevent?[18] The book is also a celebration of
what still always remains and survives genocide and "onticide" and escapes
discipline and annihilation.[19]

My main argument in this book is that in the last few decades Kurdish
women in Turkey have been crucial actors in performing an "otherwise,"
pointing to potential futures and building a tradition of Kurdish and feminine joy in defiance. They have invented and occupied limits from which
to speak authentically, "reaching — with depth and breadth — inward and
outward."[20] They created public zones of contact and risked their lives, status, and respectability — in the sense of being recognized as proper women.
I claim that what they have produced is a "women's political imagination."
In the flesh of Kevser Eltürk, Taybet İnan, Seve Demir, Pakize Nayır, and
Fatma Uyar, what the state targets is this women's political imagination of the
Kurdish Freedom Movement. I discuss this imagination through the figures
of the mother, female politician, and female guerrilla, as it is the speech and
the flesh of these figures by which the Kurdish Freedom Movement practices
freedom and invents "a new genre of the human."[21] Such a praxis of freedom

and genre of the human challenge not only the Turkish state but also the very terms of the global racial patriarchal capitalist modernity on which the former's sovereignty rests. Before explaining what I mean by a women's political imagination and its praxis of a new human, however, let me say a few words on the Kurdish Freedom Movement from which this imagination emerged.

## Kurdish Freedom Movement

The Kurdish people are one of the largest stateless populations in the world, and with the exception of the Iraqi Kurdistan Region, have no recognized regional autonomy.[22] Divided among the states of Syria, Iran, Iraq, and Turkey, Kurds have suffered different forms of discrimination, injustice, violence, hostility, and repression in their respective countries.[23] In Turkey, "the Kurdish issue" has been one of the most pressing since the founding of the Republic in 1923 and has claimed more than 40,000 lives in the last three decades alone.

The Turkish constitution defines those who belong to the state through the bond of citizenship as "Turkish" and hence leaves no room for imagining ethnic difference within its territory. In other words, access to rights in Turkey can only be gained by pledging allegiance to the Turkish nation, whose sovereignty is guaranteed by the constitution. In such a framework, when Kurds claim even to exist, they are regarded as a national problem, posing a threat to and betrayal of the "indivisibility of the nation state." Although always remaining an ontological (who are we), epistemological (how do we know who we are), ethical (how do we relate to each other), and aesthetic (how do we perform and represent ourselves) problem, the Kurdish conundrum keeps taking different shapes in the life of the Turkish state as it adapts to the different needs of the capitalist global politics and economy and responds to the various forms of Kurdish opposition and resistance.

In the initial years of the Republic, Kurds were primarily seen as a threat to the project of nationalist homogenization and centralization. Kurdish groups destabilized internal and external borders as they kept forming and reforming allegiances, loyalties, communities, and subjectivities that challenged Turkey's positivist, nationalist, and modernist imagination. Accordingly, early military and administrative authorities adopted violent strategies to intervene in Kurdish regions and destroyed existing ways of life, balances of power, ecologies, and communities. In response, religious and community leaders, elite families, and kinship-based tribes of Kurdistan have started numerous insurgencies against the Turkish state and faced extreme forms of state terror in return. The memories of the Dersim genocide (1938), the Ağrı massacre (1930), and the public execution of Şeyh Said (1925), all of which occurred in the first fifteen years of the Republic, are still alive in Kurdistan, building the cornerstones of the oppositional historical consciousness transmitted to every new generation.[24]

The two decades that followed these events were relatively calm in the region; the state sought to convert local leaders to its side while tolerating some minimum unruliness. In the 1950s Turkey heralded a new period characterized by economic growth, infrastructural construction, and expansion of communication networks enabled by U.S. aid. This was also a decade when Kurds, along with other groups in Turkey, became more integrated into the nation-state geography and global cultural currents. As a result, they started to voice their grievances in the idioms of Western ideologies such as equality, rights, and development. However, it wasn't until the end of the 1970s that a mass-based popular front of Kurds against the Turkish state was formed, when an increasingly urbanized and mobile Kurdish youth (along with their Turkish counterparts) came under the influence of Marxist, Stalinist, and Maoist ideologies. In 1978 Abdullah Öcalan and his friends founded the anticolonial armed guerrilla movement of PKK (Kurdistan Workers' Party), which from then on became a major player in Turkey's political field.[25]

The so-called low-intensity war between the Turkish army and the PKK has transformed bodies, lands, and relationships in Kurdistan into war zones for the last forty years.[26] During this time the state proved itself to be extremely resourceful in applying the newest counterinsurgency technologies, including surveillance, body searches, house raids, and checkpoints; mass arrests, torture, and imprisonment; and environmental destruction, economic discrimination, and regional disparity. It recruited paramilitaries and committed executions without trials and massacres.[27] It then classified these executions as collateral damage in the war against terrorism. It imposed bans on language and censorship on art and journalism. While it burned houses and forests, forcing millions to evacuate, it also carried out targeted operations to "disappear" politically significant actors. Meanwhile, Kurds have become masters of survival and reinvention both in military and civil arenas. Most importantly, the sheer bodily presence of masses in protests, police stations, hospitals, court houses, prisons, mountains, and associations and the demographically undefeatable excess of men, women, and children who refill each political position the state force is fixated to empty out with "perseverance" kept defying control and produced a particular form of Kurdish life in Turkey.[28]

In 1998, Abdullah Öcalan, the leader of PKK, was first forced to leave Syria, where he had lived since the 1980 military coup in Turkey; then he was kidnapped in Kenya with the collaboration of different Intelligence services (including MOSSAD of Israel, the CIA of the U.S., and MIT of Turkey) and handed over to the Turkish state.[29] After a quick trial he was sentenced to death; later, when the death penalty was lifted, he was sentenced to life without parole.[30] His imprisonment in an island prison, however, increased his influence as his ideas for a new paradigm of freedom, formulated in a series of five books, became widely disseminated.[31] Today, the Kurdish Freedom Movement is a loose political network that encompasses hundreds of organizations and millions of activists who struggle for decolonization and the rights of Kurds on the basis of the ideas of Abdullah Öcalan. It extends from Turkey to Iran, Iraq, and Syria and to Europe, where hundreds of thousands of Kurds live in exile as a result of political repression and prosecution.

In the new paradigm of the Kurdish Freedom Movement, democracy and autonomy have become widely circulating terms replacing nationalism and independence.[32] In his speeches and writings in the late 1990s and in his prison writings published in the early 2000s, Öcalan redefined the Kurdish struggle as one for democracy *within* the states Kurds live instead of being one for independence *from* the states that colonize them.[33] According to this view, the partitioning of Kurdistan, the separation of Kurds, and their status as minorities in four different countries should not be seen as an obstacle but as a strength "in fluidity," to be used for the purpose of developing democracy in the entire Middle East:[34] As a collectively organized movement, Kurds should push for democracy in their respective states while also proposing a model of governance in the Middle East as a transnational emancipatory project that brings together conviviality, local autonomy, horizontal organization, women's representation, and the establishment of an ecological life. The results of this imagination are already seen in the revolution that occurred in northeastern Syria in 2012.[35]

For the followers of the KFM the paradigmatic shift from independence to democracy involved both a transformation in political vocabulary and organization and a transformation in political subjectivities and sentiments.[36] The yearning for an independent and united Kurdistan constructed throughout 1980s and 1990s had to be replaced with a struggle for decolonizing "being," "truth," and "freedom" in the present. The nation of Kurds had to be reimagined as a multiethnic democratic nation with an irreducible diversity without a state. More importantly, the freedom of women has become central to the KFM's struggle, differentiating it from its predecessors and contemporaries.[37]

While Kurdish women first organized in the late Ottoman Empire, the creation of a mass Kurdish Women's Freedom Movement coincided with the emergence of PKK and was built from within the guerrilla organization.[38] Women joined the PKK in increasing numbers, drawn by Abdullah Öcalan. Against the discrimination they faced in the organization, they organized independently as an all-women army in 1993. Based on Öcalan's formulations, they have also developed a women's liberation ideology that revolved around the question of "who are we as women?" Through focused discussions and archeological and mythological inquiry, they aimed at rethinking and renaming the present from women's perspective. The women's liberation ideology had profound effects in PKK, as it commands women to separate themselves from patriarchal ways of being and engage in what is called an "endless divorce" from men and the definitions imposed by them on women.[39] Meanwhile, men are expected to kill the patriarchal "men" inside themselves. Both processes involve collective organization, education, and self-development through different means involving self-analysis, self-transformation, and self-mastery. Despite Öcalan's backing, women struggled immensely and painfully with men in the organization until the late 1990s, when they managed to have their autonomy accepted and gained power in shaping the politics and armed strategies of the PKK.[40]

Around this time, Kurdish women in Turkey were also being mobilized.[41] Forced disappearances, displacements, and the loss of their sons and daughters in the struggle led mothers in Kurdistan to make collective claims on the state and the public. Many women also participated in the insurgencies that took place in Kurdish cities in support of the guerrillas. Influenced by the women's liberation ideology, Kurdish women also formed associations to protest women's oppression and prevent femicide in the region in the early 2000s. Meanwhile, with the foundation of the first Kurdish political party in 1991, a different path of politicization opened for women. As the popularity of the Kurdish Freedom Movement increased and women's liberation ideology became more widespread, increasing numbers of women joined the political party and organized autonomously to exercise influence in its politics.[42] Currently, in the HDP, which is the latest among political parties that identify with the Kurdish Freedom Movement, there is co-presidency of a man and a woman, a quota of 50 percent women in all representative positions, and an autonomous women's assembly.

## A Decolonial Women's Political Imagination

This book's aim is not to chronicle this rich and powerful history of the Kurdish Women's Freedom Movement, which collects and keeps an extensive archive in the form of documents, diaries, and meeting notes to prevent erasure by the state and their own male comrades.[43] Instead, the book builds on and extends the argument that Ashon Crawley has developed in *Blackpentecostal Breath* to press "against the assumption about the narrativity of historical events to think through other lineages, other inheritances."[44] In that pursuit I follow images, figures, voices, echoes, and reverberations. I thereby also align myself with the self-definition of Kurds "as having a tradition of resistance" against History with a big H. I think alongside and together with this tradition, which Kurds have built through reiterating performances, to imagine how the political, the relational, the temporal, and the spatial can be rebuilt in ways that are liberating. I claim that, rather than a coherent history that follows the logic of cause and effect, what we find by following these other lineages and inheritances is a women's decolonial political imagination that informs the praxis of Kurdish women. I am interested in how this praxis of freedom links them to each other and to other women at other times and in other geographies (like Antigone, or the queer movement, or the Mothers of the Plaza de Mayo).

In the intersection of postcolonial, decolonial, and Black studies, I define coloniality in terms of a psychic and material violation that attempts to draw limits to imagination.[45] The Kurdish Women's Freedom Movement overcomes these limits and becomes a site of decolonization through two moves. The first is ideological and organizational. The Kurdish Freedom Movement defines Kurdistan as an "international colony" that has been central to the formation of capitalist modernity.[46] Dating the history of colonization back to the formation of Sumerian priest states in Mesopotamia, where Kurdistan is situated, the Kurdish Freedom Movement regards women as the first colony and sees the enslavement of women through the institution of patrilineal family as intrinsic to the formation of capitalist modernity. According to this view, today, this history of colonization continues through a Third World War, which is characterized by an attack on all social and communal forms of life.[47] Genocide, societycide, politicide, and femicide; the annihilation of people and their culture; the robbing of their means to reproduce themselves autonomously; the exclusion of them from politics by criminalization; and the systematic killing of women, in other words, are primary ways in which this war plays out. In the Kurdish Movement's thought, therefore, colonialism is an intrinsic part of capitalist modernity and, although having a specific form and history in Kurdistan, is a world system rather than being a specific property of single states. The Kurdish Women's Freedom Movement's overall goal is to build a comprehensive ideology, episteme, and conceptual apparatus as well as political and social organizations to lead a systematic decolonial struggle against genocide, societycide, politicide, and femicide. This struggle is informed both by the attempt to "restitute what has been destituted" in Mesopotamia by the formation of states (in Walter Mignolo's terms) and the tradition of democratic modernity that people all over the world have created by resisting against capitalism and its institutions. In this struggle, regaining autonomy from the state and accessing human ontology — by means of creating political visibility and power — from which Kurds have been excluded in a world system, where it is only through a nation-state that humanness can be represented, constitute the main strategies.

Secondly, having been colonized, dispossessed, and displaced, Kurdish people are condemned to craft a life out of the everyday racism and gratuitous violence they encounter and the nothingness they are reduced to. As stateless people, they have to "improvise" genres of living-in-common at the limits of the multiple laws that separate, regulate, and violate them. Their performances in "solo" or in "ensembles" work through the incongruence of their flesh with these multiple laws and the interval between the different epistemic categories imposed upon them discursively and materially.[48] Further, they have to find ways to situate their stories at frontiers in order for their stories not be captured by the given genres of modernity and to communicate that which is rendered incommunicable by laws of the state. The political tradition they build through organizations, political parties, and guerrilla squads is therefore also a radical aesthetic tradition that erupts frames of intelligibility. The decolonization of imagination that I talk about in this book by listening to voices, echoes, reverberations and by following images and figures is situated in the intersection between the totality of the ideology of the Kurdish Women's Movement and the performances of women in their singularities as they craft a life in the oppressive political circumstances in which they find themselves. It is here, in between a desire to form an ideological outside and the obligation to politically perform and link itself to the world and the word, that the Kurdish Women's Movement dreams its freedom dreams and improvises a new human, a new universality, and a new future.

Informed by Sylvia Wynter's and Frantz Fanon's thought, Anthony Bogues links radical imaginations of freedom with the question, "What about the human?" Citing Fanon's often quoted remark ("I should constantly remind myself that the real leap consists in introducing invention into existence"), Bogues argues that "Fanon is imploring us to engage in the work of the radical imagination to imagine anew what human life could be like."[49] The same quote from Fanon leads David Mariott to write,

> In the affirmation of invention as a moment of uncertainty, or radical
> undecidability, there is not only an affirmation of an ethics, but of a
> politics as the infinitely irreducible future that cannot be anticipated
> or known in advance, even though it always happens now, a happen-
> ing that cannot be easily subsumed under humanism or teleology.[50]

These two quotes together summarize what I want to accomplish with this book. First, what does human life look like when we follow the lineages of women who formulate a radical imagination? Second, how does Kurdish women's praxis at the limits of the political interrupt teleological history, thereby opening up new futures?

When the woman guerrilla I met in Cizre told me that her resistance opens the space of politics, what she meant was that the decisions she made on the ground disrupted colonial history, a history that either denies the Kurds' existence or describes them as already emancipated within the law of the Turkish state. She instead made visible the emergency rule under which Kurds are always living by turning her life into an exception. Although she is now dead, her lineage and heritage survive in unpredictable ways, and the future she opened still moves people in Cizre, especially women, to dream of freedom and other ways of being human. She also evokes a different political imagination because the way she does politics involves her very flesh. Even in her dead, most disfigured state, her flesh (and the flesh of all the dead) remind people of the form of life she/they lived that escaped existing phantasms of stateness, humanness, and historicality. The traces of their sentient flesh, their joy and their sorrow, the tone of their flute, in other words, are what survive genocide and transform the stakes of politics.

## Matter, Time, and Space as the Stake of Politics

In following the political imagination of the Kurdish women's freedom movement, I will use matter, time, and space as contours for this book. Three figures — namely, the Kurdish mother, the female politician, and the female guerrilla — will help me elaborate the performance of different temporalities that go against History and spatialities that go against enclosure and capture. I use the term "figure" in the way Sina Kramer conceptualizes it in reference to Antigone:

> I read Antigone as a figure in order to emphasize her position as ambivalently both within and without the space of politics, of representation, and of intelligible political agency. This ambivalent position is, I argue, the product of a constitutive exclusion. The figure of Antigone is produced as constitutively excluded. Constitutive exclusion describes both a structure and a process by which a system, symbolic, or body is constituted through the exclusion of some difference that is intolerable to it, and against which it defines or constitutes itself. This exclusion is, however, never entirely successful: that excluded difference remains within the body that has "excluded" it, continuing to do the work of structuring that body through its internal exclusion, but doing so under an epistemological block.[51]

The figures I take up here are similarly produced as the constitutive excluded of Turkey's political, representational, and intelligible space, and yet they transform, trouble, and threaten that space by unleashing a "force that renders that system of which they are yet a part unreadable and unthinkable."[52] My argument in this book is that the figures of the mother, the politician, and the guerrilla, their flesh and their voice, become the ground on which the radical women's political imagination of Kurdish women is realized. It is also through their performance that a feminine joy in defiance is produced against which the Turkish state is mobilized.

Images, speeches, bodies, performances, and the knowledge that the Kurdish Women's Freedom Movement produces challenge "the coloniality of the imagination, or the colonization of the imaginary."[53] What becomes imaginable when mothers, women politicians, and women guerrillas emerge as prominent figures in the Kurdish Freedom Movement? How, by occupying the limits of the legal, do these figures change the matter of politics? What I aim to capture by the term *matter* of politics is twofold: first how politics is practiced, with what organs, what movements, what flows, what loyalties, and what voices — in other words, how is politics given flesh? Second, by *matter* of politics, I refer to the questions of what is relevant to politics and what counts as political.

As Mendieta argues, "Colonialism [is] a practice of colonizing time," and "the decolonial imaginary aims to disrupt and shatter colonial and colonizing temporalities."[54] Therefore, a second theme of this book will be the different temporalities Kurdish women occupy, evoke, and conjure that work against "History." Some of these temporalities are maternal, others mythological. Sometimes they flow quickly, other times they flow slowly. Either way, they always build a countertradition of acting, sensing, and feeling.[55] It is the contagious performances, loose networks, a sense of collective destiny and labor, and shared troubles and passions shaped by lineages based on such temporalities that lead Kurdish women — to use another expression from Ashon Crawley — to rise to the "occasion of particular moments."[56]

It is not only in temporal terms that Kurdish women's political imagination challenges and disrupts the reproduction of the present as the future. When Kurdish women use the arena of politics, be it parliamentary, anticolonial, feminist, or civil rights, their practices question and destabilize the limits of the political. I conceptualize the space in which they are located as a space of the in-between. Different scholars have pointed to the ways in which in-between locations are fundamental to "introducing invention into existence." Lacan's concept of the limit, for example, which he attributes to the space Antigone occupies when she speaks her famous last words, is inspiring. According to

Lacan, situated at the limit between death and life, Antigone is able to articulate truth. One theme that runs throughout this book is the search for a limit, other than that between life and death, from which truth can be articulated.

If the word "limit" denotes not belonging to either (death or life), or belonging to both at the same time, the concept "threshold" and its chronotype are about crises. According to Kristeva, threshold "indicates a material process of differentiation and non-differentiation that refuses any unity of subjectivity or meaning and instead thrives on the transitive tensions and passions of concrete life."[57] At the threshold, contraries meet without reconciliation, giving rise to a creative openness. In this book I will use both "limit" and "threshold" as concepts that describe the performance of Kurdish women, since whereas "limit" gives me structural grounding for explaining the power of women's speech and flesh, "threshold" points to the agentive process by which the subject (the figure occupying the threshold) lets opposites bear on herself, thereby performing an openness toward radical possibilities.

Sylvia Wynter uses the concept "liminal" to describe the subjects that "conjugate alternative imaginaries that open a relationship to a world-otherwise."[58] These subjects are those that are "given over to death within a certain regime of human."[59] While Wynter has black people in mind when she conceptualizes the liminal, one wonders whether in the context of Kurdistan, women might occupy the same position, since it is the double operation of patriarchy and nationalism that give them over to death. While throughout the book I will not use the term "liminal" as often as "threshold" and "limit," this will be what I argue. The fact that it is Kurdish women rather than men who occupy and speak from the limit and threshold suggests that there is something in femininity that prevents women from belonging to one category and puts the system in crises. Grounded in a perspective at the intersection between women's oppression and the gratuitous violence directed against them by patriarchy and Kurdishness and the gratuitous violence directed against Kurds by the state, women struggle to delink themselves from both. They thereby engage in a creative rethinking of history, mythology, and cosmology as well as flesh, body, and voice to find ways to open the present to a different future to come.

Pointing to how women have been represented in contradictory stereotypes in history (Servant, Seductress, Lover, Saint), Alain Badiou defines femininity "with the logic of the Two, of the passing-between-two. This femininity is opposed to the strong affirmation of the One, of the single power, that characterizes the traditional male position and the oneness of the Name-of-the-Father."[60] Woman according to him is that "which subverts the One, that which is not a place but an act."[61] In the following pages we will see that the human invented and practiced by Kurdish women knows the world by occupying the liminal, the threshold, the limit, and thereby never obeys one law but is always in a position of negotiating contradictory laws in her flesh and speech.

## A Note on Concepts

Throughout this book I use the concepts of the real, imaginary, and symbolic, which I borrow from Lacan, who saw them "as the three most important categories, or registers" through which human experience can be mapped.[62] While "the real" for Lacan refers to the world before entry into language and corresponds to drive, the imaginary is about the representations with which we identify and recognize ourselves as separate beings from the world. The symbolic, on the other hand, involves language and becomes only possible by following the rules of communication and the Law of the Father in any given symbolic order. I am encouraged to transfer these complicated concepts to the study of the political and social by other scholars who have already done so in different critical traditions.[63] Most importantly, I am indebted to the late Begonia Aretxaga's usage of these terms in the context of violence, whose contribution to the field, I believe, remains greatly underappreciated.[64]

In a Lacanian framework, whereas the real is unrepresentable and hence always points to a lack in the subject from which a sense of loss, longing, and desire emanates, fantasies produced by the symbolic order promise fullness. These fantasies are, however, always unstable, as they are destabilized by the eruption of that which is excluded from language, the real. The very materiality of the body, the mortality that escapes language, is the insurance of this. The real is therefore associated with trauma and the sublime. The imaginary, on the other hand, is associated with imagination and ideology and how we imagine our relationship to and place in the world to be. Images play a distinctively important role in the creation of imaginaries, and images that dominate a culture constitute the kernel of any given "social imaginary."[65] Given the real and its eruptions, no social imaginary is ever complete giving rise to the social's demand of producing new images, concepts, and names for representing the unrepresentable.

In Aretxaga's framework, violence is one way in which the imaginary and the symbolic are destabilized and the real erupts in the social world, deconstituting fantasies and giving rise to trauma. However, what makes her work interesting is the fact that such violence can create a symbolic world of its own with its own images and communicative rules multiplying and sustaining itself through metaphors and metonyms that give rise to a new "Real" hidden from sight and made unrepresentable. Intramural violence within violent insurgencies against the state is the example she gives for this. In that sense Aretxaga is able to do justice to Lacan, for whom the Real has no content but is instituted by the symbolic order and its fantasies and hence is unstable, like the other two concepts.

By mobilizing the concepts Real, Imaginary, and Symbolic, this book aims at understanding the productive interventions of the Kurdish Women's Freedom Movement wherein psychoanalysis and politics meet. The violent and repressive conditions under which the movement unfolds lead the trauma of the Real to be ever present in the life of the movement. In the book I associate this Real with the voice of the mothers and the flesh of the guerrilla. The movement also is perpetually involved in the production of new images of identification, both because existing imaginaries are destabilized by the Real and because the movement gives rise to an unprecedented multiplicity of female public images as more women enter politics.

The Kurdish Women's Freedom Movement defines itself as a meaning making movement. They think that meaning making is a constitutive part of creating and discovering truths and attaining freedom. Therefore, the movement, rather than excluding the traumatic, forces the traumatic into language and tries to go after the unrepresentable by narrating, conceptualizing, and visualizing it. It therefore is always in the process of producing new norms that in turn give rise to new and comprehensive discourses, ideologies, and fantasies. Although I know that the movement is highly suspicious of psychoanalysis, I hope that in my usage, it will find it acceptable and joyful.

## A Note on Methodology

Thinking through Sylvia Wynter's "intertemporal, intergeographic, interhuman, co-relational, interdisciplined analytic refusal of colonial time-space," McKittrick et al. come up with the metaphor of rhythm to delineate Wynter's methodology and reading of the world and the word.[66] Rhythm, McKittrick et al. say, is "repeated and patterned (but not necessarily metered) sounds and/or movements" and "invites collaboration."[67] The texts we read have a rhythm; by bringing them together we create a new rhythm. The ethnographic field and the material we deal with have a rhythm, as well. And as we write about our material we tune in and out of its rhythm.

I find this metaphor particularly useful for describing the methodology of this book, since it is informed by so many different trajectories. Some of these trajectories are scholarly. Some are political, and others follow women's different lineages of friendship and care. I have traveled through Iraq, Syria, and Turkey's Kurdistan numerous times, sometimes to meet people, other times to discuss political issues; sometimes to do interviews, other times to give talks; sometimes to visit friends, other times to attend funerals, protests, and vigils. As I traveled through Kurdistan, its rhythm has always been *halay*, and this book is written in its rhythm.

*Halay* is a dance where multiple individuals hold each other's hands by their little finger, form a chain, and repeat the same sequence, composed of a limited number of moves. There are good *halay* dancers and ordinary *halay* dancers. Good *halay* dancers have not more space than the others, hence they have to use their own flesh, each organ, head, arms, legs, and their reverberations to improvise and perform the intensity they feel. Ordinary *halay* dancers, those who do the regular moves in a less intense manner, are carried in the chain; it is not the individuals but the chain itself that creates the aesthetic. In that sense *halay* is the performance of a universality given in the materiality of what Denise Ferreira da Silva calls "difference without separability" and incites individual improvisation as long as it occurs while holding the hands of others.[68]

I would like to think of the rhythm of this book and its content as that of *halay*, as *halay* grounds my thought in everyday praxis and "insists, in advance, that collaborative engagement is necessary to who and what we are." While writing this book I have held many hands: feminist psychoanalysis, critical theory, queer theory, Black studies, Black feminism, decolonial thought. I have danced with them following their rhythms. I danced jazz, disco, ballet with them. I sometimes stood all alone when I could not join their rhythm and watched them with envious eyes, trying to repeat their figures from afar. I could never stay long enough in any rhythm to learn it well enough because there was always the *halay* waiting for me. So, I always returned to the *halay* that I was dancing with my friends in Kurdistan. However, I am not a good *halay* dancer, either. As I carry with me all these different rhythms and as they give my flesh intensity and take my thoughts away from *halay* to other worlds, I miss my steps. For that I apologize to my Kurdish friends.

## Chapters

The book is composed of three parts and six chapters. Part I focuses on the figure of the mother. Mothers are crucial actors in the Kurdish political movement. While the study of the politicization of mothers in various contexts such as Argentina, Chile, China, Russia, and the Philippines during times of conflict has by now built a field of its own, these studies on mothers' movements with few exceptions remain locked in the question of whether mother's mobilization and activism is good or bad for the women's movement. In my chapters on motherhood, I shift the focus and ask instead, what fantasies of stateness are injured by mothers' political mobilization, and how are these injured fantasies then reanimated or replaced? At the same time, what new political fantasies are conjured up through mother's flesh and voices that enable the imagining of new futures?

In Chapter 1 I argue that linguicide and matricide — that is, the denial and destruction of the Kurdish language and the symbolic killing of Kurdish mothers — constitute the kernel of the Turkish state's genocidal law against Kurds. Inspired by the distinction that psychoanalysis makes between language and voice, I show that Turkey's war against Kurdish *language* has rendered Kurdish a *voice* and transformed it into something that is both more and less than a language: The ear of Turkish colonization listens carefully to Kurdish bodies to detect any echo that would link them to the Kurdish voice, and a wild suspicion over accents, words, songs, and sounds is unleashed in public. Meanwhile, among Kurds, Kurdish gains a surplus truth-value, and mothers as the main keepers and transmitters of the Kurdish language emerge as actors who have a privileged access to "the Real."

In the Turkish state's imagination, if Kurds want to enter the domain of law proper, they must dissociate themselves from the Kurdish language and Kurdish mothers. Based on my readings of ethnographic material as well as on cultural productions, where wild fantasies reveal themselves as real possibilities, I argue that the Turkish state is animated by a parthenogenetic fantasy of giving rebirth to the Kurdish people as Turkish citizens by erasing their mothers and their language as if they never existed in the first place. Finally, I also develop an explanation of why matricide is a constitutive feature of the fantasies of law and state: I argue that while killing Kurdish fathers destroys the alternative sovereign objectified in male bodies, killing mothers secures that there will be not even the possibility of the emergence of a discord with law at the subjective level: no mothers means no unsettlement that the "Real" imposes on the subject and transforms her into more than one: there is no cut in the body, no jouissance in language, and no void to be filled in the relationship between self and world.

Chapter 2 focuses on what happens when mothers take their grievances to the streets. Based on ethnographic material and the reading of the Sumerian myth Enki and Ninhursag and the Babylon myth Enuma Ellis within a framework of the Kurdish Movement's maternal thinking, I try to name some laws of the mother that are evoked against the colonial state when motherhood becomes public. I also argue that the public mourning women perform conjures a maternal time, and the incongruence of the maternal time with the historical time becomes a space where other ways of being and becoming human can be envisioned.

Part II of the book focuses on the woman politician. The figure of the woman politician is a complicated figure, since she is always already captured by law. She must improvise with her flesh and public speech performances and narratives to work through the interval between different commands that are informed by the laws of the state that individualize and what I have called the voice and the law(s) of the maternal that situate her in the entanglements of the *halay*. In Chapter 3 I hold the hands of feminist political philosophers and use the myth of Antigone to interrogate the different temporalities, limits, and thresholds Kurdish woman politicians occupy to do that. Here, I am also interested in the question of what happens when Creon does not die, Heamon marries another, and Antigone's performance is reiterated by other women. In other words, what about life after tragedy; how do women articulate spaces from which to talk about the truth? I show that by occupying the limits of the political, women politicians enact an alternative women's political imagination through their speech and perform the incongruity between the law and Kurdishness. Speech becomes a pure means without a foreseeable end, and, by making difficult (conscious or unconscious) decisions about what to say and what not to say, women politicians develop a Kurdish feminine form of life that can be cited and reiterated.

Chapter 4 holds the hands of black feminists to inquire into how woman politicians use their "flesh/body" to *show Kurdishness* and its troubles. While the women I discussed in Chapter 3 use the parliamentary floor or the press release to address a broader audience, the women I talk about in Chapter 4 transform the limit between flesh and body into a floor to address others, refuse the state, and perform autonomy for women and Kurds. This chapter argues that in the flesh/body and voice/speech of Kurdish women politicians, we are invited to bear witness to the impossibility of living under colonial conditions where the space between demands of peace and not forgiving and forgetting, legality and illegality, and the represented and those who represent forever shrink. Meanwhile, not only does access to human ontology that relies on such distinctions become increasingly unavailable to women, their flesh pulled by other flesh instantiates a different form of humanity.

Part 3 is about the figure of the woman guerrilla. Chapter 5 enters the life of the guerrilla through two questions they raise, which are "who are we?" and "how should we live?" Following the different answers they give to this question, the chapter traces how the woman guerrilla decolonizes being, truth, and freedom and how she enacts a humanness that occupies a revolutionary time and adopts friendship as a way of life. I argue that whereas decolonization of truth for the Kurdish women guerrillas entails finding new laws for their desire and forming new norms for women to cite, decolonization of freedom is engaging in mobile quantum entanglements of incitement, overture, and responsibility. Decolonization of being, on the other hand, involves transforming death and life into play in the sense of not owning it as a possession. Finally, the chapter also addresses the relationship between Kurdish people and the guerrillas and how the fact that the guerrilla occupies the limits between past and future and death and life makes it into a figure of the Real.

I am aware that I am occupying the limits of illegality when I talk about the guerrilla figure enthusiastically as a form of life and a different form of human. However, the opposite would not be possible. Occupying the world of Kurds, as many other insurgent populations, pushes one toward that limit, since the temporality and the spatiality they dwell in includes the figure of the illegal insurgent as the "Real" of their life-worlds. How the guerrilla homes that Real gives clues about how the world could be if it weren't for the nation state, capitalism, and patriarchy. It is impossible not to follow the passion of understanding this when it is exactly that passion that makes the pursuit of knowledge possible.

In Chapter 6 I focus on a speech by President Erdoğan, a letter by Abdullah Öcalan, a wedding, and a funeral to highlight the different understandings of peace that the Turkish state and the Kurdish Movement promote and how women figure into this understanding. I argue that for the Turkish state the future that is envisioned for Kurdish women is either death or a complete alliance with patriarchy through marriage. Hence, the figure of the public mother, woman politician, and woman guerrilla must be transformed into corpses and corpse images. The Conclusion of the book is a reflection on the main ideas that were developed in the book and a summary of the main components of the Kurdish Women's Freedom Movement's political imagination, which I claim intervenes in the world in the intersection of psychoanalysis and politics.

Finally, this book is my way of mourning the peace process when the figure of the guerrilla, the mother, and the woman politician were constitutive features of the symbolic world we were living in, where all felt possibilities increased. I became exiled from my country for taking part (along with many others) in that symbolic world and against those who decided that such possibilities must be foreclosed. The imagination itself, however, survived, and as much as mourning for what is lost, this book is a celebration of what remained: the joy of being an insurgent, or as Sadiya Hartman calls her, a wayward girl.[69]

# PART I

*Mother*

# 1
# The Voice of the Maternal

*Kurdish Mothers at the Intersection of
Linguicide and Matricide*

Women sing, men speak.

— KURDISH PROVERB

One of the most ancient people of the Middle East, the Kurds, have
survived without a state, without a written record, and without a
permanent home to settle in. In our culture everything is transmitted
through voice, words and the harmony of the rhythm. . . . The history
of our struggle with plunderers and usurpers is passed on orally from
generation to generation, through song, ballad and saga. Our history is
essentially based on human remembrance, especially that of women.

— ZEYNEB YAŞ, "LOST VOICES," IN *FEMINIST PEDAGOGY*

There is a vocal primitiveness to Kurdish because in Turkey it is not
used as the language of education, trade or even everyday life. The
patterning of sound, speech, thought, writing and reading is not as
widespread as in Turkish. Therefore Kurdish is a free language.

— MÎRZA METÎN, QUOTED IN JÎNDA ZEKIOĞLU,
"MIRZA METIN," IN *GAZETE DUVAR*

The sacred among women may express an instantaneous revolt that
passes through the body and cries out.

— CATHERINE CLÉMENT AND JULIA KRISTEVA,
*THE FEMININE AND THE SACRED*

For the core of the danger is the voice that sets itself loose from the
word, the voice beyond logos, the lawless voice.
                    — MLADEN DOLAR, *A VOICE AND NOTHING MORE*

Where shriek turns speech turns song — remote from the impossible
comfort of origin — there lies the trace of our descent.
                    — FRED MOTEN, *IN THE BREAK*

When I was doing fieldwork in 2002 in Esenyurt, a neighborhood in Istanbul populated by rural-to-urban migrants, I visited the house of a Kurdish
woman — whom I will call Meryem — to conduct a life-story interview with
her. Meryem was one of thousands of Kurds the Turkish military had forcibly
displaced from their villages in the 1990s, when it applied various counterinsurgency tactics against the Kurdistan Workers Party (PKK).[1] The military
had burned Meryem's house with everything in it and killed her husband
and brother-in-law during its siege of the village. After traveling from village
to village, from one relative's house to another and failing to find the support she needed, Meryem had ended up in Esenyurt — worlds apart from her
village — where her father had built a squatter house some decades ago when
he was working as a seasonal construction worker on the outskirts of Istanbul.
The house had two rooms, and both of these rooms were spacious, cold, and
unfurnished, typical of the spaces displaced Kurds occupied in the city. The
homes of middle-class dwellers in Esenyurt were often furnished with electric
appliances, dinner tables, matching curtains, couches, and ornaments sym-
bolizing the newly acquired status, domesticity, and dignity of its inhabitants.
The homes of the urban poor were also often cramped with objects — but
this time without context and apparent relationship to one another — mostly
remnants of unfinished or failed life trajectories. In sharp contrast to those of
both the middle class and the urban poor, the houses of recently displaced
Kurds struck visitors with their emptiness.[2] To the knowing eye, however,
this emptiness signified a nonmaterial form of abundance. Copjec writes,
"Someone dies and leaves behind his place, which outlives him and is unfillable by anyone else. This idea constructs a specific notion of the social,
wherein it is conceived to consist not only of particular individuals and their
relations to each other, but also as a relation to these unoccupiable places."[3]
Kurds in general and Kurdish women in particular endured the rapid and
relentless alterations of forced displacement and disappearance, extrajudicial
killings and war through their relations to such unoccupiable and unfillable
spaces. They turned emptiness into a statement of survival, resilience, and
mourning. In the city space of Esenyurt in the early 2000s, their unfurnished

houses exhibited their unspeakable losses in abundance: of people, of status, of community, and of home.

Meryem lived with her seven children. Two of them faced serious challenges. They had communication and learning difficulties and depended on wheelchairs. Another two, while still living in the house, had disconnected themselves from their mother completely. Meryem reported that they never contributed to the household budget, and they insulted her whenever "she meddled with their business." She suspected that both of them were involved with one of the gangs that had newly emerged in Esenyurt against the backdrop of the changing economic and political landscape.[4] Meryem's oldest daughter, Fatma, a teenager at the time, was her mother's "right hand," navigating her through the intricate bureaucracies of health, legal, and welfare systems, where they made various claims to collect assistance in money and kind and to receive compensation for their losses.[5] This daughter, who could speak Turkish without an accent, was in these institutions the logos of her mother: She moved her "from the infinitude of loss . . . into a finite and more governable economy of wants."[6] Meryem's suffering, on the other hand — çile in both Turkish and Kurdish,[7] which was reflected in her voice and body — informed Fatma's speech in such institutions as "the register of an economy of drives that is bound to the rhythms of the body in a way that destabilizes the rational register on which the system of speech is built."[8] Fatma often came close to begging, repeating her words tearfully, unable to become convinced that her testimony was enough to qualify her for the rights she claimed.

During my conversation with Meryem, Fatma was also present, and mother and daughter disrupted and inspirited each other, collectively orchestrating a unique grammar of witnessing — in a mix of Kurdish and Turkish — that addressed the Kurdish community, Turks, the state, and the global world all at once. While at the time I was doing this fieldwork I was interested in the subjectivities of these women, now, almost two decades later, I am interested in the place that the voice and the figure of the mother occupy in the Kurdish political imagination. How language, sound, and address are distributed between these two women points to the historically and culturally specific constitution of the Kurdish maternal while also displaying the ways in which the racialization and colonization of Kurds in modern Turkey shape the most intimate aspects of life.

In Esenyurt as elsewhere in Turkey, ethnicity is predominantly grasped and presented as an acoustic drama rather than a visual one, and it is the Kurdish speaking voice of the mother that inserts an uncanny sense of incommensurability into the otherwise tolerable cacophony of the urban soundscape.[9] This chapter is an inquiry into this voice and what survives the linguicide and matricide imposed on the Kurdish maternal in Turkey. In the introductory chapter to his seminal book *In the Break: The Aesthetics of Black Radical Tradition*, Fred Moten discusses Frederick Douglass's memoir on slavery, where an account of the screams of Aunt Hester beaten and tortured by the master is followed by a scene of slaves walking and singing. Moten writes, "I'm interested in establishing some procedures for discovering the relationship between the 'heart-rending shrieks' of Aunt Hester in the face of the master's violent assault, the discourse on music that Douglass initiates a few pages after the recitation of that vicious encounter, and the incorporation or recording of a sound figured as external both to music and to speech in black music and speech."[10] This relationship, according to him, is maternal and shows that "abjected Black maternity is a site of dangerous generativity."[11] In the radically different context of Turkey and following different procedures, I argue in this chapter that Kurdish maternity, too, abjected by both patriarchy and colonialism and the trace of the mother's cries and screams in the face of loss and violation, are generative of a discourse on Kurdish speech and language and build one of the essential blocks of Kurdish political performativity. Following the example of feminists who regard the mother-daughter relationship as a privileged site for investigating the life of the maternal in culture and psyche, I begin this chapter with the scene of my conversation with Meryem and her daughter.[12]

Before visiting Meryem, I didn't know much about her, apart from the fact that she was a relatively recent migrant from Kurdistan in dire financial straits.[13] After some everyday chatting over tea (facilitated by another Kurdish woman, who could speak both Kurdish and Turkish), my conversation with Meryem came to the reason for her migration. At that point Meryem started to sing a heart-wrenching lament while her daughter Fatma recounted their apparently many-times-rehearsed story in Turkish:[14] The year was 1993. The military commander of the region had come to their village a few days before and informed the villagers that they must either become village guards[15] and join the state's fight against the guerrillas or be forced out of their village, leaving behind their crops, animals, and belongings. The villagers refused to become village guards and were then accused of helping and harboring the guerrilla forces. It was nighttime when the soldiers returned and started searching the houses in the village, while repeatedly announcing that everybody should remain inside until their search was complete. Meryem's entire household was at home waiting for their turn. They were carefully listening to the noises from outside coming from their neighbors, whose searches were over and who were now slowly gathering in the middle of the village under the surveillance of the soldiers. When they heard shootings and the cry of one of their distant cousins, Meryem's husband went out with his brother to find out what was going on and to protect him from the soldiers. Soon afterward, more shots were heard. Meryem's husband and her brother-in law had not returned when the soldiers later came to Meryem's house, forced the rest of the household out, and burned down their house and their barn. The family walked to a nearby village that night. It was only then that they found out that both the father and his brother were killed. One of their neighbors reported that as he rushed out of the village, he had seen the bodies of the two men lying next to each other. In the early morning, Meryem walked back to the village with some of her male relatives to recover the bodies. For a day and night, they hid themselves from the soldiers and watched the bodies and the burning houses from afar. Once the soldiers left the village, they returned and buried the dead.

When Fatma finished the story, Meryem continued her lament. Without any hesitation Fatma took my tape recorder and held it close to her mother's mouth, to make sure that her voice was properly recorded.[16] When Meryem finished, Fatma told me that Meryem didn't want her lament to be translated, since it would lose all its meaning. "My mother says, if you were Kurdish, you would have joined her cries anyway whether you understood the lyrics or not," she added. With that remark, Meryem drew the boundaries of our communication, which she believed was taking place in the register of language but not voice.

Mladen Dolar states that singing "turns the tables on the signifier; it reverses the hierarchy — let the voice take the upper hand, let the voice be the bearer of what cannot be expressed by words. *Wovon man nicht sprechen kann darüber kann man singen*: expression versus meaning, expression beyond meaning, expression which is more than meaning, yet expression which functions only in tension with meaning — it needs a signifier as the limit to transcend and to reveal its beyond."[17] Singing, in other words, opens up meaning that systems of signification aim at closing. By unsettling seemingly stabilized signifiers, it reveals the gap between life and language, body and words. Meryem's singing also performs a political function. It contests the meanings of all the names that signify and try to fix her — Kurdish, villager, woman, widow, wife, and mother — and that are defined in relations of domination and violence over which she has little control.[18] The structural power of singing transcends these signifiers and reveals their beyond, as Dolar argues. This enables Meryem to perform the failure of these names to determine her subjectivity. It is here that the boundary is drawn between Turkishness and Kurdishness as subjective experiences. By stating that I would have cried with her if I were Kurdish — irrespective of whether I knew the language or not — Meryem makes clear that ethnic difference does not reside in linguistic difference per se. It rather resides in the differential tensions our voices have with signifiers and our bodies have with the Law.[19] It resides in the differential urgencies we feel to open up meaning and the tools we have at our disposal to do so.

Linguicide and matricide — that is, the denial and destruction of the Kurdish language and the symbolic killing of Kurdish mothers — constitute the kernel of the Turkish state's genocidal law against Kurds. Inspired by the distinction that Dolar makes between language and voice in his influential book *A Voice and Nothing More*, I contend that Turkey's war against the Kurdish *language* has rendered Kurdish a *voice* and thereby transformed it into something that is both more and less than a language: Kurdish has gained a surplus truth-value, and mothers have emerged as the main keepers and transmitters of Kurdish language who have a privileged access to "truth."

Feminist critique has already unraveled the multiple ways in which philosophy and common sense link the voice and the feminine and oppose it to the link between the word and the masculine.[20] Black studies, on the other hand, have pointed to the ways in which the violent repression of the maternal and its reduction to nothingness under conditions of slavery and its aftermath are linked to the reduction of black speech to noise.[21] In the Kurdish case, as well, "reducing" Kurdish to a voice through violence and repression involves the attachment of it to Kurdish women's excluded maternal bodies. In the Turkish state's imagination, if Kurds want to enter the domain of law (and the discourse of Man, as Sylvia Wynter would say), they have to dissociate themselves from the Kurdish language and their mothers. Using readings of a novel, a film, and a prison, I suggest that this is because the Turkish state is animated by a parthenogenetic fantasy of giving rebirth to Kurdish people as Turkish citizens by erasing their mothers and their language as if they never existed in the first place.

One way in which Kurdish political movements have struggled against linguicide has been by transforming Kurdish into a publicly recognized language with a standardized grammar that can be taught and learned. On the one hand, this form of struggle inevitably involves the dissociation of Kurdish from maternal bodies and possibly strips Kurdish from its more-than-language quality. On the other hand, the designation of Kurdish as the "mother tongue" of Kurds — that is, as the language that Kurdish mothers speak rather than that which is taught and learned in formal settings — anchors different and nonaligned fantasies of liberation and freedom in the flesh and speech acts of mothers.

On the surface it might seem that the emphasis the Kurdish movement puts on mothers is a replica of other nationalisms where the role of the mother as birth giver is celebrated and fetishized. My argument in this chapter is, however, that because the value that the movement puts upon mothers is mediated by the investment it makes in Kurdish, the attachment of the Kurdish movement to mothers takes a different shape. In the Kurdish movement the mother, rather than being a means by which the biopolitical governance of the nation is accomplished, becomes the starting point for envisioning and practicing a liberating psychoanalytical/mythical project and animates the movement's "freedom drive."[22] Chapter 2 will discuss this project and explain how the political imagination on which public space is grounded is affected when Kurdish mothers commune in a shared language and enter the political field as subjects in the light of this project.

## Conceptualizing Voice and the Kurdish Maternal

In his groundbreaking study on the voice, Mladen Dolar argues that voice is what is common to both body and language "without belonging to any" and is "situated at the limit of nature and culture, human and divine and the real and the symbolic."[23] The voice is the first manifestation of life (real) and provides one with the first experience of self-recognition (imaginary) while also being the means by which one acquires language and speaks (symbolic). At the same time, one becomes aware that one is not alone in this world and is always accompanied by the unpredictable presence of others through the voice of the mother, which provides the "first problematic connection to the other, the immaterial tie that comes to replace the umbilical cord."[24] Associated with the real, the imaginary, and the symbolic, as well as with dependency and otherness all at the same time, the voice, according to Dolar, "operates as a paramount embodiment of *objet petit a*" as conceptualized by Lacan: "the leftover, the remainder, the remnant left behind by the introduction of the symbolic in the real."[25]

*Objet petit a* emerges when the mother's body and the jouissance associated with it are forbidden to the infant. The infant must leave the sphere of "Real" in order to become a subject in language and the social world. *Objet petit a* denotes the feeling that something is lost in this process — a feeling that is retroactively created and instituted by the very symbolic order that seems to have caused the loss in the first place. As that which reminds the subject of its loss, *objet petit a* gives rise to desire, which "is structured around the unending quest for the lost/impossible jouissance" and aims at attaining an imagined original fullness. As Dolar puts it, *objet petit a* "does not coincide with any existing thing, although it is always evoked only by bits of materiality, attached to them as an invisible, inaudible appendage, yet not amalgamated with them: it is both evoked and covered, enveloped by them."[26] Desire at-taches itself to different things and bits of materiality as staged by politically and culturally constituted fantasies.[27] However, "when the object embodying the function is acquired then desire is fixed on another lacking object."[28]

Dolar's psychoanalytical approach, which conceptualizes voice as the par-amount embodiment of *objet petit a*, explains why in so many cultures the voice is endowed with a sacred power and why the singing voice is seen as capable of expressing what is inexpressible in language.[29] Voice evokes the "beyond" of the symbolic and generates a surplus meaning unrecoverable by words alone.[30] It denotes life "before" the entry into the law, which was sacri-ficed in the name of becoming a subject in language and promises access to a profound and original meaning that is erased when speaking in order to be intelligible.

Dolar reminds us, however, "that the singing voice" or "the singing in say-ing," that as he points out later, "might cure the wound inflicted by culture, restore the loss that we suffered by the assumption of the symbolic order," is nothing more than a fantasy grounded in the structural illusion that the voice is the bearer of a deeper sense:

> The time between hearing and understanding is precisely the time
> of construction of fantasies, desires, symptoms, all the basic struc-
> tures, which underlie and organize the vast ramifications of human
> enjoyment. . . . There is a temporal vector between the voice (the
> incomprehensible, the traumatic) and the signifier (the articulation,
> the rationalization), and what links the two, in this precipitating and
> retroactive temporality, is fantasy as the juncture of the two.[31]

Further, as voice evokes fantasies, obsessions, and pleasures, it might also perform a cut in the symbolic, a wound in the law, and make space for new fantasies to emerge. At different times and locations the unique voices of spe-cific figures, such as those of political and religious leaders, as well as the collective voice of "the people," animate cultural and political fantasies and arouse pleasure and fear. At other times a sigh, a scream, or an oral appeal heard in a public context might become a sign about law's failure to determine subjects and bind them to itself. Such noises/voices have the potential to vi-brate and reverberate bodies in unpredictable ways and to affect new psychic transactions.

The linguicide that the Turkish state directed to the Kurdish language re-duced the latter to a voice. The Kurdish language thereby was transformed into a space of trauma and enjoyment that can both destabilize and challenge the Turkish language. The Turkish state denies the claim that Kurdish is a language equal to Turkish and robs its capacity to signify by banning and devaluing it. It enforces Turkish on Kurdish as its signifier, as that which gives it meaning and without which it will remain unintelligible and noisy. On the other hand, the more Kurdish is categorized as senseless, lawless, and primitive, the more it becomes traumatic to the Turkish state as something that destabilizes it, reminding it of its less than full identity. The Turkish state obsesses itself with the Kurdish language, detecting and marking it, erasing it passionately and violently, circling around it like it's a prey and killing it over and over again. Meanwhile, for Kurds, Kurdish becomes an *objet-petit-a* that promises fullness beyond capture, "bearing the inescapable presence of the maternal."[32]

The argument that the maternal and the voice are psychically and culturally associated is not new. Many feminists have already shown that the feminine and the vocal are closely linked and have pointed to the excitements and fears that the feminine voice causes.[33] The unruliness and lawlessness and the seductive potential that the feminine and the voice are imagined to share is best exemplified by the figure of the Siren. In the myth of the Siren the feminine voice promises men limitless pleasure and drives them to their death, fulfilling the fantasy that both the voice and the feminine deceive and destroy; that they expose too much and that one is exposed to them too much.[34] The body of the maternal, on the other hand, rendered functional for patriarchy, transforms this intrinsic association between voice and the feminine. When emanating from the body of the mother in normal times, the voice promises soothing and calmness for men, a return to stillness and fullness. At other times, however—when she expresses the physical pain endured in pregnancy (making of life) and the emotional pain faced by the death of a child (taking life)—the voice of the mother operates at the limit of the symbolic and becomes unbearable. The Kurdish-speaking mother is then unbearable to the Turkish state twice: First, she breathes life into Kurdish and bears children on whose ears Kurdish will fall, turning them into ethnically *different* citizens. Second, when the state kills her children, she laments loudly, cursing the law under which Kurds must endure. In such a context, linguicide and matricide emerge as constitutive fantasies of the Turkish state that aim at preventing both the reproduction of Kurdishness and the mourning of its loss. In the Kurdish Freedom Movement, on the other hand, the maternal emerges as something that needs to be recovered, a trace in a fantasy of mythological origins.

## Linguicide, Colonial Democracy, and Decolonial Cacophonies

The linguicide of Kurdish has taken many different forms in Turkey: bans on speaking Kurdish in public spaces, prisons, and schools; denial of the existence of Kurdish as a distinct language with its own grammar, vocabulary, and history; naming it as an "unidentified utterance" in court and Parliament; changing place names from Kurdish to Turkish; preventing families from giving their children Kurdish names; and punishing those who speak Kurdish and/or listen to Kurdish music.[35] These policies aim not only at halting the transmission of the Kurdish language, but also at "eliminating" Kurdish identity itself, rendering abject the people who speak Kurdish.[36] Here, I don't use the term "abject" lightly: Turkish people often display disgust, shock, and horror when they hear the Kurdish language. In the last two decades such disgust has manifested itself in mobs beating, humiliating, and lynching Kurds who spoke Kurdish in public in predominantly Turkish-speaking populated areas.[37]

Testimonies, memoirs, novels, and academic studies document how the childhoods of many Kurds are scarred by the experience of linguicide.[38] In a policy report based on ethnographic field research published in 2011, Coşkun, Derince, and Uçarlar state that Kurdish-speaking children experience violence and stigmatization.[39] They try to keep quiet in school and keep their distance from public spaces even when they are brought up in predominantly Kurdish cities. The children interviewed express their frustration by saying that they "begin life with a 1–0 deficit" and that it is extremely hard — if not impossible — for them to ever become equal with children whose mother tongue is Turkish. To use the term that Jasbir Puar developed for talking about the Palestinian experience, these children feel they are "maimed" by linguicide; they experience having Kurdish as a "mother tongue" as a disability.[40] Linguicide "colonizes the psychic space" of Kurds, alienates them from themselves — as the Kurdish movement describes it — and makes them see their own voice and the voices in their family as obstacles to overcome and as "defects to be amended."[41] For Kurdish people, in other words, it is not the skin but the voice that becomes the object of self-loathing, and speaking Turkish with no accent is the "white mask" that they are forced to wear.[42]

Indeed, at least until the beginning of the new millennium, the pressures, restrictions, and bans on Kurdish in Turkey partially relied on the forced cooperation of Kurdish families. Many families chose to speak Turkish at home because their children would be stigmatized and face violence in school if they spoke Kurdish and be disadvantaged academically if Turkish were their second language. This was the case especially in city centers, where class mobility and national belonging through education remained a promise. As the Turkish language became associated with urbanization and education and Kurdish with the rural and the traditional, Turkish inevitably became an important symbol of modernity, progress, and knowledge. Meanwhile, Turkish words that signify things, movements, and affects constitutive of modern life entered the Kurdish language, imprinting Kurdish with a sense of anachronism.[43] In other words, a feeling that the two languages belonged to two different temporalities colored common perception of even those Turks who recognize Kurdish as a language while cultivating a desire among Kurds to speak Turkish.

The emergence of the Kurdistan regional government in Iraq, with Kurdish as its official language, has, however, brought Kurdish a new prestige and accelerated the process of the standardization of all its dialects, including Kurmanji, which is spoken in Turkey.[44] Also, after the forced displacement and mass political mobilization of Kurds in the 1990s and the politicization of speaking Kurdish thereafter, Kurdish became the voice of resistance and liberation. Kurdish slogans traveled worldwide and became symbols of freedom movements and women's struggles.[45] Still, the number of people who rely solely on Kurdish for everyday business and intimate conversations continued decreasing rapidly.[46]

Despite the effects of linguicide, Kurdish still remains the main medium for communicating with their mothers for 90 percent of Kurds, who report that they speak mostly Kurdish with their mothers, as compared to 60 percent who use some degree of Kurdish when talking to their fathers.[47] Many Kurds believe that Kurdish survived the Turkish state's linguicide thanks to women. Men regulate women's mobility and limit their relations with other people, which reduce the latter's need and opportunity to learn Turkish. Low levels of schooling and paid employment among women also keep them "safe" from the domination of Turkish in their lives. While some women learn Turkish from television, others are too occupied with housework and family care to spend any meaningful time watching TV.

People believe the second reason that Kurdish survived despite linguicide is the widespread passion Kurds feel for both traditional and contemporary Kurdish music.[48] The figure of the *dengbej*, individuals who accumulate and retell inherited stories of the past in lyrical and musical forms and thereby transmit culture and memory, is crucial in this context.[49] *Dengbejs* ensure that events, sensibilities, and affects that are violently written out by official history are regenerated through songs and poetry performed in communal spaces. They also reproduce the plurality in Kurdish (despite standardization of it by the production of a national grammar) by retaining the diverse accents, regional tones, and local syntax imprinted in songs.

Besides the *dengbej* culture, which relies on a face-to face transmission, historically, mechanically reproduced music has also played an important role in the survival of Kurdish against state-induced linguicide. Many Kurds I interviewed shared their anecdotes about how, in the 1980s and 1990s, under the most adverse conditions, Kurds kept their spirit and resilience by listening to songs released in other parts of Kurdistan or in Europe, which were then transported to Turkey's Kurdistan in cassettes hidden within Turkish covers. While such cassettes have become a means for archiving, teaching, and learning Kurdish, they also created a cultural intimacy among Kurds and a code for mutual recognition. Which songs you knew and enjoyed communicated your identity and political commitments to other Kurds without Turks knowing it.

Starting in the early 2000s and until the end of the peace process in 2015, Turkey's pending accession to membership in the European Union forced the government to remove restrictions "on linguistic and cultural rights for minorities."[50] Regulations that aimed at harmonizing Turkey's laws with those of the EU passed in 2002, and, as a consequence, broadcasting in languages other than Turkish and teaching Kurdish in private courses were permitted. Soon afterward teaching Kurdish as a foreign language in universities became possible, and in 2012 elective Kurdish courses were available in secondary schools. Despite these reforms, however, Kurdish remained unnamed and was lumped into the category of Living Languages.[51] Also, the demand of the Kurdish movement for the right to access "education in the mother tongue" never came to the table, which caused many Kurdish actors to remain suspicious of government initiatives and the Turkish state's newly found tolerance for diversity.[52]

Meanwhile, performing the nation's newly found multicultural sensibility, Turkish television channels have opened their frames to Kurdish-identified politicians, opinion leaders, artists, and singers. In the flourishing TV-series industry, Kurdish ethnicity and language captured audiences as exotic goods and enabled a shared imagination of new beginnings, where Kurdish could become a "color" in the Turkish landscape. However, even then, the Kurdish language in the mainstream media always remained a background "flavor," an expressive sound of worry, suffering, and hustle, which eventually was destined to be left behind as the heroes of the drama became famous, married across ethnic lines, migrated, and embraced a happy ending.

During this period, which was officially called the Kurdish initiative, and the peace process that followed it, Kurdish mothers also became momentarily visible. "Re-presented" by Turkish male politicians and TV channels, their tears and sighs were captured to make the argument that it was the new government of the Justice and Development Party, with its discourse of "democracy," "fraternity," and "service to people," that would end the pain that mothers suffered in the previous repressive regimes, where violent tactics and strategies of counterinsurgency reigned. Hunger strikes of Kurdish political prisoners and the mothers' struggle on behalf of them — mothers who mourned the continued killing of their guerrilla children and searched for their graves and the arrests of thousands of Kurdish activists, feminists, and (the so-called stone-throwing) children during this period however — barely made the news. In other words, Kurds in general and the Kurdish-speaking mother, in particular, with her cries and suffering, although appearing in the cultural and political realms, functioned "at the register of myth" and performed a colonial Turkish grammar where denial of difference was replaced by tropes of "partial recognition."[53]

The Justice and Development Party, committed as it was to neoliberalism, believed that the eventual erasure of the ontological danger Kurdish identity posed for the Turkish republic would occur through the magic of religion and market, which regulates not only value but also fantasy and desire.[54] However, at the same time, as the Kurdish language and Kurdishness enjoyed the "privilege" of becoming "freely" circulating goods to be sold and bought in the market, the Kurdish Freedom Movements' political ideals also found ways to resonate, giving rise to fantasies, desires, networks, and circulations that were neither predicted nor planned for by state actors.[55] Challenging the state's attempt "to make only some voices audible in the expense of silencing others" and delegate the Kurdish problem to an overcome past, Kurdish artists, activists, and politicians contributed to a "decolonial cacophony." Fighting for the right to make Kurdish political defenses in the court, using Kurdish slogans and singing Kurdish marches in public protests, but also pluralizing desires for a just present and stories of loss, mourning, and violence, they "publicly addressed them as ongoing" and refused to betray the multiplicity of Kurdish sounds, noises, and brokenness "by placing something far more legible in their place."[56] The increased number of Kurdish TV channels broadcasting from Europe through satellite ensured that Kurdish remained attached to an oppositional political sensibility rather than being transformed into a commodity to be bought and sold.

This period of relative opening gave the opportunity to Kurdish language activists, who were already investing passionately in Kurdish, to broaden their influence.[57] Municipalities run by Kurds adopted multilingualism as their main policy. Hospitals and other similar service-giving institutions followed. Universities started offering elective Kurdish courses, and Kurdish language schools opened. Fiction and poetry, grammar and vocabulary books in Kurdish flourished, and Kurdish became the medium of an emerging art scene dominated by documentaries, paintings, video installments, theater, and literature. Several music companies emerged that produced "ethnic music," mostly in Kurdish and Armenian, and publication houses printing and distributing memoirs of Kurds and Armenians became popular. Even conferences and lectures in Kurdish were no longer exceptional, pushing state authorities in the Kurdish regions to follow suit and give talks in Kurdish in order not to lose support among right-wing Kurds who conventionally vote for the ruling party.

Şerif Derince, an activist and a scholar of the Kurdish language, starts an article where he discusses whether broadcasting in Kurdish and Kurdish elective courses made any real changes in the way Kurdish people exercised their linguistic rights with the following anecdote:

> In a court case against Kurdish politicians and activists in 2011, the Turkish judge asked the clerk to write: "It is understood that the defendant spoke in an unknown language." This was the first time Kurdish was referred to as a language in Turkish court records. Previously, it had been recorded as "unknown sounds."[58]

I don't think any anecdote captures the spirit of the era better. Linguicide of the Kurdish language in Turkey had reduced Kurdish to being "a sound," a voice, rather than a language with a distinct grammar and vocabulary that could be learned and taught. Now, the Kurdish opening was providing the means to imagine that it was indeed a language, albeit only audible in certain places and certain ways. Still, this era was short-lived, and, with the resumption of the war between the Turkish state and the PKK in 2015, Kurdish became once again an ontological threat. Kurdish classes were canceled, multilingual banners banned, and speaking in Kurdish in court was once again categorized as unintelligible, as noise.

Differentiating voice and language, Dolar states that in its linguistic aspect voice is "what does not contribute to making sense,"[59] in its metaphysical aspect voice is dangerous, feminine, and other,[60] and in its ethical aspect voice escapes legality and instead addresses conscience.[61] From the Turkish perspective, Kurdish does not contribute to any meaning; it's just noise. Kurdish is located outside of the legal and the logical. It is the voice of the primitive and the irrational and can only be tolerated at the feminine margins of national space: as a lullaby, lament, a cry, or a scream whose echoes will quickly die down. For Kurds, on the other hand, it is the language of conscience, which has the potential of taking into account what is unintelligible to law and what connects Kurdish people beyond their political views, as Meryem's reaction to me reveals, where she notes that my not crying at her lament testifies to our belonging to different communities.

## The Echoes of the Mother Tongue

A post in April 2020 by the Twitter account @SerhadEyaletLordu, which is followed by tens of thousands for the archival knowledge it shares on *dengbejs* and on the true stories that inform their songs, reads, "Our first singers are our mothers, that is why they say women sing, men speak"[62] The Kurdish stage actor Mîrza Metîn, now in exile, on the other hand, and who couldn't speak Kurdish until very recently, describes Kurdish as a language, which he learned only later "with the love of an echo that had remained in his ear."[63] The echo here belongs to the voice of his mother, who spoke and sang to him in Kurdish when he was an infant. Kurdish, as he describes it, becomes a matrilineal song passed down from mother to child that the child carries in his unconscious, under conditions of linguicide.[64]

Yet not everyone welcomes this matrilineal song. Some Kurdish children, mostly girls, who are shamed on multiple levels by the racialization of Turkish society, "sacrifice" their mother and her songs in order to experience a feeling of belonging.[65] They gradually "forget" Kurdish, bond with their fathers, and try to separate themselves from their mothers with as little communication as possible.[66] They associate the body and the voice of the mother with the primitive and the backward and abject her, often until later in life, when they are politicized or become mothers themselves.[67] However, even in these cases Kurdish and Kurdishness find ways to speak through them, revealing the impossibilities of dwelling in and inhabiting the societal order as colonized subjects whose voice and visibility are violently repressed and strictly regulated. In order to elaborate this point, let me return to my encounter with Meryem and Fatma.

Right after Fatma told me that her mother didn't want her lament to be translated, she changed the subject and said that a couple of weeks before, she had entered the qualifications for the contest "Popstar Turkey" but wasn't accepted.[68] I had difficulty moving my attention away from the affective space of mourning that her mother had carved out with her voice a minute ago at the radical margins of Turkish public space to its newly and loudly emerging center that Fatma evoked. Fatma then asked me if she could repeat her performance and if I could tape it. I said, "Yes." The song she sang for the contest was one that belonged to Ferhat Tunç, a leftist Kurdish singer active in politics and against whom terrorist propaganda charges would be brought in 2018. The lyrics were in Turkish and went:

> For days under torture/those convicted for freedom/They num-
> ber thousands/Those convicted for freedom/Their hands are in
> cuffs/They have chains in their arms/Their tongues scream/Their
> chains clash/The area that was empty in the evening/became a dun-
> geon in the morning/Some of them are yet children/Those convicted
> for freedom/They are the ones who hold you/The end is nearing

them / There are millions after you / Those convicted for freedom / The
country has its masters and chiefs / The prisoners have a rebellious
temperament / They are workers, laborers and villagers / Those convicted for freedom.[69]

As the reader can guess by the phrase "those convicted for freedom," the song
refers to people who fight against power holders and the state and protest their
imprisonment and torture. I am not sure what Fatma or the producers and
the jury of the Popstar Contest thought during her performance, and I have
no intention of speculating on what happened when this song — situated in a
realm that is carefully excluded from televised popular culture — penetrated
the latter. I am also not sure why Fatma wanted to sing it in the context of my
interview with her mother. Did she want to lift the heavy atmosphere? Did
she want to bond with me in my mother tongue and greet me with a gesture
of inclusion? Did she simply want to sing, redefining her mother's lament also
as a song? My guess is that she wanted to separate herself from her mother and
her family tragedy in the space of the interview as she tried to do by entering
the Popstar eliminations, which at the time promised a speedy and clean path
to financial gain and cultural acceptance for many young people.[70]

I am also guessing that Fatma learned Ferhat Tunç's song from a cassette
circulating among family and friends who remember and commemorate
the death, torture, and imprisonment of their loved ones through music and
thereby contribute to the making of an oppositional culture and sensibility.
Despite her perfect Turkish and her desire to be included in the Turkish
public through her voice — by entering Popstar eliminations — Fatma failed to
do so exactly because of her voice, which she gained in a community where
songs often take the form of testimonies to injustice. Her song put her beyond
legibility and the law that was being formed during the Kurdish opening and
hinted at and embodied "aspirations that were wildly utopian," unwelcome
by the public as imagined by Popstar's definitions of audible enjoyment.[71] In
other words, irrespective of the language she spoke, Fatma's voice was already
shaped by Kurdishness and by the sonic "difference" of her people. Kurdishness and its oppositional history spoke through Fatma's body like a spirit
possessing her and made sure that the 1–0 deficit with which she began her
life stuck.

Addressing fantasies of identity, Joan Scott uses the term "fantasy echo,"
which for understanding the Kurdish case is quite useful. "Echoes," she says
"are delayed returns of sound; they are incomplete reproductions, usually
giving back only the final fragments of a phrase. An echo spans large gaps of
space (sound reverberates between distant points) and time (echoes are not

instantaneous), but it also creates gaps of meaning and intelligibility."[72] Scott's aim in evoking the term "echo" is to underline how fantasies of identity are transformed through inexact condensations "that nevertheless work to conceal or minimize difference through repetition."[73] I would like to use "fantasy echo" in yet another way. The ear of Turkish colonization listens carefully to Kurdish bodies to detect any echo that would link them to the "original," unleashing a constant and wild suspicion over accents, words, songs, and sounds. Meanwhile, the voice of Kurdishness changes while resisting, negotiating, or complying with the law and tunes and retunes itself, resonating new echoes. Fatma's voice is one such echo. That of stage actor Mîrza Metîn, whom I quoted previously, is another. The Turkish state fears these echoes: "Set loose from the signifiers" of the Turkish nation, these echoes are seductive, uncanny, and threatening.[74] The moment they appear, there is a danger that they will be transformed into unsettling demands to which the state must answer "no." The matricidal fantasies of the Turkish state are animated by the latter's desire to erase the origin of these echoes, which it regards to be the mother. The Kurdish movement, on the other hand, as I will explain in Chapter 2, entertains a different fantasy where the mother herself becomes an echo lacking fullness.

## Matricidal Fantasies: A Book, a Film, and a Prison

A generation of psychoanalysis-oriented feminists has problematized Freud's and Lacan's theories regarding the structural place of the maternal in the emergence of the infant into adulthood and entry into the symbolic (i.e., Baraitser, Irigaray, Jacobs, Kristeva). In Lacanian theory, "becoming a subject" involves a process whereby the infant takes a distance from the maternal and inserts itself into language through the law of the Father, who exercises the Oedipal ban against incest. Inspired by French psychoanalytic feminists, particularly by Irigaray and Kristeva, such operation of the Law is now called "matricide," where the mother becomes "the woman to be left behind, forcefully, violently if necessary, abjected in order that 'adult maturity' could be achieved."[75] In this scenario from infancy to adulthood the maternal figures only as something to be repressed, and the eruption of her "voice," as multiple as it is, in the psychic realm of the adult and against the unifying language of the paternal, would lead to psychosis.

Matricide, however, does not only refer to an erasure of the maternal as a meaning, language, and history producing force in the life of subjects. In Irigaray's words, the entire edifice of Western culture is erected on the silencing of the maternal body. While the maternal is relegated to the pre-symbolic and reduced to unknowability, mothers themselves, their bodies, and their experiences are muted and rendered beyond apprehension.[76] Motherhood is deadened twice: first in the sense of making it impossible to theorize its contribution to language and subjectivity, and second in the sense of banning it from forming a norm against which cultural, social, and intimate relations can be evaluated.

Jacqueline Rose points to a third way in which matricide functions. Mothers are excluded from the political space and can exist there only as objects onto which the unresolved tensions and conflicts of our cultures are projected.[77] Mothers are everywhere, but they are either demonized or idealized. Such demonization and idealization are ensured by keeping mothers constantly under surveillance, regulated and disciplined while simultaneously being the ground on which political projects are developed. Rose also argues that the demonization and idealization of mothers testify to the deeply rooted fears in the cultural unconscious about the infants' as much as the civilizations' vulnerability vis-a-vis mothers. Mothers can choose to kill or nurture their infants; they can refrain from bearing children and so doom humanity or contribute to the raising of "normalized citizens." This power must remain invisible, controlled, unaware of itself; it must remain depoliticized and hence the matricide that occurs at the public realm.

Feminist writers who have problematized "matricide" have invited us to rethink the maternal in theory and in everyday life in creative ways in order to contribute to imagining post-patriarchal futures. However, most of the time matricide in their writing is too abstract, read through metaphors, metonyms, and myths. I think one point that remains understudied in these feminist critiques is the context of violence and colonialism.[78] Rosalind Morris points to the regressive function of war that libidinizes all social fields.[79] Since contexts like war, colonialism, and violent conflict are imagined to remain outside of the reach of law, fantasy takes a violent form oriented toward what normatively should have remained at the limit of the symbolic and beyond the sphere of the doable. In such contexts rape, incest, and matricide, fluidities and excrements, sickness and misery are lifted to organizing principles, and the death drive enjoys supremacy over all other drives.

In the Turkish colonization of Kurdistan, matricide is an enduring fantasy. In times of turmoil such fantasies become literally enacted. From taking girls away from families to raise them as Turkified mothers to threatening Kurdish mothers that their misbehaving children will be taken away from them, matricide animates the Turkish state's discourse and practice.[80] In what follows, I discuss two examples in which fantasies of matricide become the resolving mechanism of national and familial problems raised by the Turkish nation state. The first of these is a book written when Kurdish insurgencies threatened the homogenizing project of nationalism during the early years of the Turkish republic. The second is a movie produced at the wake of the Kurdish opening when conflict with the PKK seemed to be the main obstacle to Turkey's membership in the European Union. Both examples sought to resolve national and familial conflicts by getting rid of the Kurdish father and mother, albeit in different ways.

In 1928, after the establishment of the Turkish Republic, Halide Edib Adıvar, one of the most famous female authors in early republican history, wrote a book called *Zeyno'nun Oğlu* (Zeyno's Son) as a sequel to the tragic love story *Kalp Ağrısı* (Heart Ache) she had written in 1924.[81] Halide Edib was educated in Western schools and was intimately familiar with the Western colonial missionary culture of philanthropy and pedagogy. In her adult life she was a friend, companion, and colleague to many of the founding figures of Turkish nationalism and played an important part in formulating educational policies. Her role during the Armenian Genocide remains controversial to this day. While some believe that she promoted the prosecution of those who committed the genocide and defended a process in which the truths of the genocide would be recovered, others argue that she actively participated in the Turkification of Armenian and Kurdish orphans and compare the policies she adopted in the schools she directed to the forced integration into white mainstream culture of Native Americans in schools in the U.S.[82]

*Kalp Ağrısı* depicts the heroine Zeyno, born in Istanbul and educated by her intellectual father. The narrative revolves around her love for a young officer named Hasan, a man who fought in the "eastern parts of Turkey" — that is, Kurdistan — and who is now engaged to Zeyno's sick cousin. The book ends with Zeyno sacrificing her love, despite Hasan loving her back passionately, so that her cousin could at least live in a fantasy of love until she died. This first book is an interesting and at times feminist attempt to resolve the tension between the passions, sexual attractions, and unpredictable intimacies women experience, on the one hand, and their socially defined and internalized sense of "dignity," on the other. The sequel to it, *Zeyno'nun Oğlu*, in contrast, explores those affects and acts that align subjects with reason, morality, and nationalism in modernity.

The second novel starts by narrating Zeyno's sensible marriage to a respectable army commander after her heartbreak and her travel to the "East" to accompany him while he is on duty. The officer is assigned the responsibility of suppressing the Kurdish insurgency, and Zeyno describes it as "chaotic," "irrational," and "meaningless." Soon after she moves to her new home, Zeyno finds her inferior double in a housemate with whom she shares her name

and her — now forgotten — illicit love. Kurdish Zeyno, who is stuck in an un-
wanted and unhappy marriage, fancies the same man, Hasan, with whom
Zeyno had initially fallen in love. However, the Kurdish Zeyno consummated
her love and now has a child from him named Haso. While the book contains
large sections where Kurdish men are described as promiscuous, obscene,
unreliable, and temperamental, it also shows contempt for the Turkish men
of the army and their "childish" enthusiasm for war. Kurdish Zeyno, on the
other hand, attracts the heroine's pity for the "miserable" life she lives, ruled
by lusts of the flesh, maternal instincts, and her fear of the men in her life.
In contrast to *Kalp Ağrısı, Zeyno'nun Oğlu* has a happy ending for the main
protagonist: the Turkish army kills the insurgents, including Kurdish Zeyno's
cruel husband. Turkish Zeyno, who is childless, is now in Istanbul, and we
learn that she and her husband have adopted the extremely smart Haso. As
his Kurdish birth mother is relegated to the background, he can now acquire
a place and a future in the newly created republic.

Almost eighty years after Halide Edip published *Zeyno'nun Oğlu*, the same
fantasy is evident in the film *Gönül Yarası* (Lovelorn), written and directed by
the critically acclaimed movie director and writer Yavuz Turgul. Screened in
2005 and acted by three of the most popular actors in Turkey, *Gönül Yarası*
narrates a love story between a retired Turkish primary schoolteacher, Nazım,
and a Kurdish bargirl he meets in Istanbul. Nazım spent his entire career in
"eastern Turkey" teaching writing and reading (in Turkish) to Kurdish children and is now back in Istanbul working as a taxi driver. This time it is
Nazım's daughter Piraye who is childless. We find out that her infertility was
caused by her father, who valued his Kurdish students over his own child and
who remained indifferent to the ovarian infections she got as a result of the
snowy weather in Kurdistan. Piraye blames him for her infertility and has a
very strained relationship with him.

One night, Dünya, the bargirl, who has a moving voice and speaks a broken
Turkish, rides home from work in Nazım's taxi. She is taken by the goodness
of him in the midst of wild and corrupt Istanbul. Later in the movie her
former husband, with whom she has a daughter, also comes to Istanbul and
terrorizes Dünya, because he wants her back and believes that their love has
not yet died. The movie ends with Dünya singing a song that confesses her
love for the teacher. As the husband witnesses the scene, he is overwhelmed
by jealousy, hopelessness, and anger and kills her and himself. Nazım brings
Dünya's now orphaned child to Piraye, who adopts her, and they all live hap-
pily after.

In both examples there are two problems that need to be resolved: the
childlessness of the Turkish female protagonists and the law of the Kurdish

fathers who come into conflict with the law of the state. While the second problem is resolved by killing the father, the first problem, which in my view also reflects the fear that one day the greater birth rate of the Kurds will somehow threaten the Turkish majority, is dealt with by getting rid of the mother.[83] This allows both the assimilation of the Kurdish child and the silencing of the mother's voice (which is literal in the second case). I contend that if the killing of the father reflects the political/ontological question that haunts the state (whose law will reign?), the killing of the mother has deep psychoanalytic roots whereby the voice of the mother is imagined to echo in the child, making her/him unable to be assimilated by Turkish law.

I want to finish this section with yet another example: that of a prison where matricide (in the sense of making individuals forget their mothers completely) became an explicit "desire" of the state[84] In the notorious Diyarbakır prison, which was built right after the military coup in 1980 and which held thousands of Kurdish prisoners between 1980 and 1984, the director of the prison Esat Oktay Yıldıran declared to the inmates that in this prison God was dead and the prophet was on vacation.[85] He informed them that they would shortly undergo torture to make them forget everything they knew, including their mothers. In Diyarbakır prison linguicide and the desire to replace the Kurdish voice with a form of Turkish that mirrors official discourse was reflected by the fact that first speaking in general and then speaking in Kurdish were banned, and the inmates were forced to sing Turkish national anthems for hours every day. In one often cited example, a mother who could not speak Turkish attended the prison every visiting day, and, each time, the only conversation that took place between her and her son was restricted to two sentences: "Kamber Ateş, how are you?" "I am good."[86]

Elsewhere, I have described the treatment of the inmates in the Diyarbakır prison in terms of a parthenogenetic fantasy that informed the state's actions. After citing various tortures, including hunger, thirst, beatings, walking on all fours, stripping, extreme cold and heat, rape, forced rape between prisoners, forced eating of urine, feces, mucus, and living rats, I concluded that

the Diyarbakır Prison, where state terror operated through the registers of the sexual and the linguistic, the anal and the oral of the prisoners can be read as the womb of the state. In this womb the prisoners were being undone and socially and symbolically erased as if they had never existed. They were stripped to a nothingness where no divine or human law existed, to be reborn to a new symbolic order without Kurdishness, all the while remembering the horror and trauma of their own painful birth.[87]

The Diyarbakır Prison is the staging of the Turkish state's most grotesque fantasy, which is that the state gives violent birth to its citizens as if they were born without mothers. It is the state that mothers/fathers them so that its laws will be fully and completely internalized. Whether in its most brutal (as in Diyarbakır prison) or compassionate form (as in the book and film that search for a resolution through adoption), in the fantasy of Turkish nationhood the Kurdish male is the enemy to be killed so that his law does not compete with the state, and the Kurdish female is the maternal that needs to be erased from the life of the Kurdish child to enable his entry into civilization and the discourse of Man (read: Turkishness). Once the maternal is dead/forgotten/erased, she will be prevented to speak Kurdish through her child and seduce it with the "Real" that her voice evokes. To go back to Meryem and Fatma, it is not enough that Fatma's father was killed. She must also be separated from her mother's voice by adopting Turkish as her main language and by internalizing the desire to leave her behind for a better life, a project, as I have shown, that is nevertheless bound to fail.

If for the Turkish state the mother and the mother tongue need to be erased as if they have never been, the Kurdish Freedom Movement responds to this fantasy with one of its own. In this fantasy what is foregrounded is what survives matricide and linguicide — that is, what remains despite history. Can the maternal that has imprinted itself in the Kurdish voice be resurrected as a norm with political force, and can mothers be subjects that are bound to a different law than the state's? In Chapter 2 I will provide an account of the Kurdish Freedom Movement's theorization of the maternal.

## 2

# Law(s) of the Maternal

*Kurdish Mothers in Public*

**The Law of the Mother**
You and your sisters ask your mother if it hurts on your wedding
    night when
your hymen is broken and she answers, it's a membrane and it doesn't
break, just gets nudged aside, and it doesn't hurt if you're gentle
    with each
other and take your time.
On hearing this, you are puzzled because everyone tells you the
    breaking
is the sign of a good woman but you grasp that she has told you the law
of the mother.
One day when you are five, a boy in the neighborhood says, let's play
Mummy and Daddy and when it hurts, he warns you not to say
    anything
to your parents.
And you tell your father
and the world fissures.
And who do you turn to then?
To shame, an internal script you learned
before the sin, and rehearse again and again.
Virgin. Fallen.
You are sentenced to your body,
your bitter body, your memory.
                    — GABEBA BADEROON, "THE LAW OF THE MOTHER"

I am mother. Mother I am. Mothers cannot be stopped.
— KURDISH MOTHER IN A PROTEST FOR THE HUNGER STRIKERS IN PRISON

I met Gönül in a district governor's office in Istanbul, where she was filing a form to prove her eligibility for the financial assistance that the government distributed every year to the poor. As I would find out later that day, Gönül, living in a family-owned house with both of her stepsons employed, was actually doing considerably better than her neighbors in terms of her financial situation and would by no means qualify as poor according to the criteria set by the government.[1] Nevertheless, she would explain, she still regarded herself as poverty-stricken, given that the money circulating in her household belonged to a paternal lineage over which she had no claim of blood. Like many women I knew, Gönül both identified herself with her husband and claimed individuality when it came to matters of money and kin, without necessarily experiencing the differences associated with being a wife and being an individual as contradictory. If the house and everything in it belonged to her husband and his sons (her stepsons), she told me, at least the monetary assistance she might receive could exclusively belong to her.

Gönül and her husband lived on the first floor of the family house with Gönül's bedridden mother, who could neither move nor speak. The stepsons and their families occupied the two floors above them, but since the doors of all the three apartments remained open, each family regarded the other's apartment as an extension of their own. As we were sipping our coffee in Gönül's living room, where she had invited me after a small chat in the district governor's office, she comfortably participated in the hide-and-seek game of her step-grandchildren — which had spilled over to the entirety of her apartment — by directing the smaller children to hiding places difficult to find and by giving false clues to the older ones. I was by then accustomed to the strong feelings of discontent that women accumulated over the years against their husbands and their kin and the gestures that accompanied such discontent. I therefore had already recognized Gönül's bitterness, despite the affectionate way in which she handled her step-grandchildren. However, when she started her life story, I was surprised to find out that her resentments were neither directed to her husband nor his larger kin but to her own bedridden mother.

Gönül was born in Wan, one of the bigger cities in Kurdistan. When she was still a child, her mother eloped with a man from Mardin, leaving Gönül's father behind and taking Gönül with her.[2] They moved to a small village at the border of Syria, since the man with whom Gönül's mother eloped was a smuggler moving goods and people across the border. Gönül didn't have many recollections from her childhood before or after this elopement except her daily chores, until one night, after which her life had changed forever. That night, her stepfather brought a guest to their house, a Turkish soldier, who facilitated the stepfather's smuggling by turning a blind eye to it. The house consisted of one room and a kitchen. After dinner, Gönül's mother made the beds, and, to Gönül's surprise, she put the soldier's bed next to Gönül's. Before going to sleep, she advised Gönül to keep silent whatever happened that night. A few hours later the soldier slipped into her bed and raped her in the presence of her mother and stepfather. Gönül accounted vividly the pain she experienced between her legs the next day and how she had to still perform her usual household chores without any complaint. Neither she nor her mother spoke about what happened. A few months later her mother announced to her that they were to travel together to Syria. However, in the middle of the journey, when they camped overnight, she left Gönül without a word in the care of a smuggler, who brought her to the Syrian side next morning. It was only then that Gönül learned that her stepfather had promised her as a second wife to an elderly man, whom he had come to know while conducting his smuggling business. It took Gönül ten years of struggle to come back to Turkey, and that at the expense of leaving her two birth children behind. When she came to Turkey, villagers she met on her escape route helped her to travel to Istanbul, where her father, whom she had not seen since her early childhood, was now living. In Istanbul Gönül met her current husband — a recent widower. One afternoon — soon after her wedding — the phone rang, and on the other side was her estranged mother. The man she had eloped with had died some months ago, and her health was deteriorating. She asked Gönül if she could come to Istanbul and live with her. Gönül accepted enthusiastically, looking forward to her newly found opportunity to torment her mother as she always dreamed she would.

Gönül's life was largely overdetermined by the colonial context in which she lived: smuggling between the borders of Syria and Turkey that divide the geography of Kurdistan, which is then reconnected through trade, kin making, and imagination; Turkish soldiers and other state officials watching over these borders, laying claims on young Kurdish girls through seduction, deceit, and rape; exchanging women, whose "value" had decreased in the marriage market, as second wives across borders. These are all recurring themes that constitute the everyday of Kurdish women and testify to the complicated ways in which colonial and patriarchal assemblages make and unmake them.[3] What was unique in Gönül's case was the way in which she told her story. Gönül actively demanded my cooperation with the terms in which she narrated her life — waiting for my nodding and approving words — which, accord-

ing to her, was completely determined by the actions of her mother. She
didn't care to hear about the dominating structures that shaped these actions.
Even when she talked about how she herself obeyed the patriarchal command
and left her children behind, where some "insight into her [sic] mother's life
under the law of the father" could emerge, she made sure that I saw this ep-
isode of her life as another effect of her mother's doings.[4] It was after all her
mother who had let her enter a marriage with an elderly man as a non-virgin,
with no kin around to support her. Gönül explained that her sexual "impurity"
and her loneliness put her in an unconventionally disadvantaged position in
her marriage and made her especially vulnerable to the gratuitous violence
that marriage entails for women.[5] It was this violence and not active "desire,"
as in the case of her mother, that eventually "forced" her to leave everything,
including her children, behind in Syria.

As rare as it is to meet someone like Gönül, who has remained so determined in denying her mother any forgiveness and understanding until such
a late age, it is not all that uncommon that women will trace back the origins
of their "destiny" to the figure of the mother and blame either her "present
absence" or "absent presence" for the ways in which their lives unfolded. In
their edited volume *Textual Mothers/Maternal Texts*, Elizabeth Podnieks and
Andrea O'Reilly show that the "absent mother," with her voice and subjectivity erased not only by society but also in the lives of her children, is almost
as common a literary trope as the "sacrificial mother" whose self-denial enables her children to have livable lives.[6] Indeed, several feminists have argued
that the tropes of the sacrificial (good) mother and the present-absent/absent-
present mother (bad mother) are two sides of the same coin and serve patriarchy both by producing unattainable norms for mothers and by submitting
motherhood to constant public surveillance and scrutiny.[7] In this chapter, I
would like to go in a different direction. This time, instead of trying to convince her otherwise, I want to take Gönül's narrative at face value as she meant
me to do. That is, I join Gönül in resisting an interpretation of her narrative
as a pre-feminist telling of her life shaped by patriarchy's tropes that could
be transformed by acquiring a feminist consciousness. I rather contend that
Gönül's unresolved resentment toward her mother reveals something fundamentally important about the maternal in patriarchy that escapes analysis
when her narrative is approached with a deconstructive feminist intent, just
like when it is appropriated by patriarchal discourses to capture motherhood
and discipline mothers.[8] Informed by the Kurdish Women's Freedom Movement's "feminist philosophy of history," which contributes to a "unique epistemic knowledge formation" about the intricate ways in which patriarchy,
colonialism, and capitalism dispossess women from their power, I will call

this something the law(s) of the mother.[9] Law(s) of the mother point to the processes by which the most wounding fantasies of patriarchy are prevented from realization. Gönül blames her mother because her expectations shaped by "the law(s) of the mother" failed to be fulfilled as a result of her mother following her desire, which left both women in a condition of eternal debt to patriarchy.[10]

One aim of this chapter is to show how these laws — latent as they are in cultural scripts — nevertheless inform cultural and political imaginations and agencies. Further, I argue that the concept of the law(s) of the mother sheds light on the various ways in which the Kurdish Freedom Movement — as a self-proclaimed women's movement — addresses the question of the maternal and tries to imagine a decolonial future where not only what has been destituted by Turkish colonialism but also what has been destituted by patriarchy (defined as the colonization of women and imagined to have a particular origin) are restituted.[11] In other words, my aim in this chapter is to think *with* the Kurdish Women's Freedom Movement and its theories about Gönül's life and the law(s) of the maternal that shape her yearnings.

In what follows, I will first discuss what I mean by the concept of the law(s) of the mother. While the law of the father is probably one of the most frequently invoked concepts of the psychoanalytical corpus, the law(s) of the mother is a rarely used term. As I mentioned in Chapter 1, this stems from the fact that the maternal is delegated to the sphere of the "Real" that the infant must leave as he or she enters the social world, obeys the demands of the Law of the Father, and becomes a subject. When the term law(s) of the mother is used in psychoanalytic thinking, it usually has a negative connotation and is a way of evoking how through unconscious processes we become condemned to repeat our mother's tragic destinies.[12] I will depart from this approach and follow Amber Jacobs's, Juliet Mitchell's, and Hortense Spiller's leads in my discussion of the law(s) of the mother, arguing that the concept is best employed for understanding the processes of subjectivization that operate as an-other to the law of the Father.[13]

In conceptualizing the term "law(s) of the mother," Amber Jacobs revisits the myths of Electra and of Athena's birth — a methodological choice suitable for criticizing certain assumptions of psychoanalysis that make it complicit with patriarchy and its fantasies. By a careful women-centered reading of these myths, Jacobs shows how the law(s) of the maternal operate counter to patriarchy's parthenogenetic fantasies. Her methodological choice also puts her in conversation with the Kurdish Women's Freedom Movement. This movement relies on mythological and archeological excavations in order to conjure up a deep archive of non-matricidal politics and processes of subjectivization. Following the movement's lead, I will engage with two Mesopotamian myths to theorize "the law(s) of the mother" and the fantasies it refuses to make the symbolic order inhabitable for women. It is by the unleashing and violent materialization of the most perverse fantasies of patriarchy that the world becomes uninhabitable in contexts of colonization and racialization. Here, black feminist thought, where black mothering "emerges as the harbinger of an insurgent horizon always in the making — an elsewhere and elsewhen,"[14] also inspires me. In North America and in Kurdistan — and I am sure elsewhere — "captive maternals" struggle to make the world re-inhabitable for themselves and their children by creating, sustaining, and performing maternal embodiments, lineages, and intimacies that transmit painful and pleasurable knowledges.[15]

The final section of this chapter will deal with what happens when mothers bring to bear the law(s) of the mother on political life and imagination. As Kurdish people became increasingly politicized and urbanized and as the reach of the movement extended, the voice associated with motherhood and the role of the *maternal* in the lives of the Kurdish *political* underwent mutations that were partially unforeseen. Kurdish mothers' increasing visibility, along with new theories about motherhood based on myths from Mesopotamia, redefined the identity of mothers and resignified motherhood. Today mothers are called on the political scene not only as caring ethical subjects for their children, but as revolutionary subjects to change the world. As they become orators, recruit new listeners, and challenge the voice of the Law, they create resonances mobilizing other mothers to vocalize their experiences, troubles, and stories in public. What comes to be known uncomfortably — uncannily almost — when mothers, who have been silenced and erased by narrative and disciplinary traditions, symbolically killed by patriarchal laws and orders and experienced as absent presences or present absences by their children, "make themselves public?"[16] How do the fantasies that bind subjects to the body and voice of the mother come into conflict with those that bind subjects to the Law of the paternal state? How do maternal intimacies (defined to be suffocating by psychoanalysis) and "the monstrous intimacies" of colonialism and patriarchy perform their encounter?[17] I contend that the struggle of Kurdish women to become public by producing matrifocal mythologies, creating positive maternal genealogies, and conducting matricentric protests, reveal that the mother's exclusion is a constitutive feature of our political present and mark that present's fragility. Meanwhile, in "the imaginary zone," which the figure of the excluded mother evokes, a new and alternative politics is remembered and performed.[18]

## Law of the Father / Law(s) of the Mother

The reason I opened this chapter with Gönül's story has to do with the strength of a particular feeling that it evokes and that I believe needs to be theoretically untangled. The feeling I am talking about pertains to the scandal that emerges when the figure of the mother does not deliver what it promises — namely, that the child will be protected from the perversities of patriarchy, kept "in the cultural space of ethics, relationality, and the sacred" and not be inserted into "the space of pure drive and unrestrained fantasy."[19] This space of pure drive is the space of the unconscious, traumatized by the realities of patriarchy, racism, and colonialism. It is where "others" become fully objectified, rendered undifferentiated and desire-less, and where the libidinal genocidal economy reigns.[20] It is where Gönül was raped, watched while being raped, and forced to dwell with and serve those who raped and watched her.

As should be clear by now, the maternal scandal I am talking about does not concern a Medeaesque situation. I am not interested in the injury a mother can cause to her child by intentionally denying her care or by deliberately inflicting harm on her.[21] I might even agree with the feminist strand of thought that recognizes some profound truth about maternal ambiguity in such acts, buried under the social turmoil they incite.[22] My interest is also not in the dyadic relationship of the mother and the child in isolation, which has recently emerged as a ground for ethical inspiration.[23] Here I am rather talking about situations where patriarchal power remains unchecked and children become unusually vulnerable to patriarchy's fantasies against which a "mother's law" should have been operating. I am curious about this law, different from and other to the law of the Father, which Gönül felt was lacking in her life.

In my inquiry, the emphasis is on the fact that the mother-child relationship unfolds in the context of patriarchy and under the law of the Father and is always already strained by the specific vulnerabilities that patriarchal power causes, accentuates, and utilizes.[24] This means that I take issue with the scenario that there is somehow first the mother and child and their all-consuming relationship, which is then interrupted by the law of the Father. Rather, I contend that the infant is always already interjected into a social field where there are different and non-harmonious laws and desires in operation that make themselves felt to the infant through the workings of the flesh and voice of the mother.[25] Patriarchal fantasies, as well as the processes that limit and ban them, the anxiety that they might be realized and the assurance by the law(s) of the mother that they will be diverted or at least consoled, mark all subjects with psychic, social, and political consequences. Gönül's mother was in bed and paralyzed. Her presence was limited to the space she took in the living room and the needs of her flesh that necessitated attending. The interruptions these caused to Gönül's everyday life, coupled with the importance Gönül attached to her in her narrative, rendered Gönül's mother a lingering ghost while subjecting Gönül to a haunted existence. Avery Gordon argues that making such haunted existences an object of analysis can be a basis for thinking about radical political change.[26] Radical political change, in her view,

> will come about only when new forms of subjectivity and sociality can be forged by thinking beyond the limits of what is already comprehensible. And that, Gordon suggests, will be possible only when a sense of what has been lost or of what we never had can be brought back from exile and articulated fully as a form of longing in this world.[27]

Talking about "the law(s) of the mother" in the context of Gönül's life is an attempt to do just that. By bringing "the law(s) of the mother" from exile, I want to think about Gönül's and other women's longings and the radical political possibilities these longings hint at.

One could call Gönül's and her mother's relationship, a reversed maternal relationship, if it weren't for their already lived history and lack of an anticipated future. Rather than living in the space of remembering where a mother and daughter are imagined to live in old age, they lived in the extended time of dead space. Such dead space does not come into being by itself but is created by patriarchy's operations, not unlike those of racism. Christina Sharpe calls such spaces that blacks live in the aftermath of slavery the "wake." To be in the wake in her treatment is "living the history and present of terror."[28] It is, however, more than that: "To be in the wake is also to recognize the ways that we are constituted through and by continued vulnerability to overwhelming force though not only known to ourselves and to each other by that force."[29] What is at stake for women is the capacity to know themselves and each other in ways other than the overwhelming force of patriarchy, which seems to have failed Gönül in relationship to her mother.

For such a knowledge to be produced, Christina Sharpe argues, a collectivized wake work is needed that will transform being and consciousness and enact an inhabiting that is both aware of its state of being occupied and its struggle for dwelling.[30] For analytical purposes I would like to differentiate these as the two different operations of law. One of these is the law of the Father; in the case of Gönül, this is the law of the state and patriarchy, which creates the deadened space in which she lives with her mother. The second pertains to the law(s) of the mother. I use the term "the law(s) of the mother" to name all the processes in which maternal lineages and heritages block or interrupt the reproduction of patriarchy and phallocentrism.[31] With the law(s) of the mother, I am interested in exploring how women build collective and political non-matricidal relations with their children and with each other, thereby opening up spaces for imagining post-patriarchal futures.

In the Kurdish movement, the relationship of the maternal, patriarchal law and colonial and anti-colonial politics is considered fundamentally important for imagining non-patriarchal futures. I think that the thought Kurdish women developed regarding these issues has relevance beyond the Kurdish context. Is it, after all, a coincidence that Antigone, one of the most celebrated tragic heroines of the Western literary canon, who has also become one of the most powerful tropes for feminist inquiry into the feminine and the political, suffers from a similarly absent present mother? Jacosta, Antigone's mother, is absent in all the plays where Antigone appears but is present nonetheless, since her "destructive desire" has shaped all that comes after her and haunts Antigone. Despite the ever-growing literature on Antigone, only a few scholars seem to have noticed that, and even then, they have mostly failed to dwell on how the maternal force shaped Antigone's actions.[32] With the concept of the law(s) of the mother, I am suggesting that a new reading of Antigone is necessary, one in which she is not treated as an individual, but as someone who has a mother and is linked to a particular feminine lineage. (I will return to this theme in Chapter 3.)

The Kurdish women's freedom movement points to three ways in which the maternal has a bearing on female relations: The first involves archeological and mythological excavations conjuring up the laws of the maternal, non-matricidal politics and processes of subjectivization. Here, the movement searches for ways to positively identify laws and norms that will shape desire and relationships so that women will be empowered and liberated against the law of the Father. Second are the modality of witnessing and the re-creation of a maternal lineage within female relationships. How, on the one hand, are maternal knowledges and memories transmitted so that witnessing matrilinearity survives as an echo against the dominant, repressive, and violent forms of patrilinearity and patriarchy? And, on the other hand, how by transmitting their knowledge to the next generation do women find themselves normalizing patriarchal cruelties? How is the interruption of this generational transmission possible? The third modality is how the law/love of the mother is pitted against the law of the state. How do Kurdish mothers lay a claim on political life by "making motherhood public," thereby making political actors accountable and so reconstituting the political field?[33]

## From Ninhursag to Tiamat: Mythological Excavations

Abdullah Öcalan, the leader of the Kurdish Freedom Movement, frequently encourages women to develop laws and norms (*ölçütler*) that are divorced (*sonsuz boşanma*) from the laws of the patriarchal state, thus enabling them to be liberated collective and individual selves (*xwebun*). He also recommends that women come up with a social contract (*toplumsal sözleşme*) to reflect the laws and norms according to which they want to conduct their lives. One source they can draw upon, he suggests, are the mythologies of Mesopotamia, which reveal how a matricentric society became transformed into a state-centered patriarchal society with the emergence of the Sumerian priestly states during the Neolithic Age. These mythologies provide scripts for Kurdish women to reinterpret the role of the feminine and maternal in social relations and in processes of subjectivization. On the one hand, these mythologies vividly illustrate the fantasies that support the emergent patriarchal and state-centered symbolic order. They can be read as dramatizations of the conflicts between women and men that reigned 5,000 years ago, testifying to the ways in which the means to define and name themselves, as well the means of self-defense and decision making, were stolen from women.[34] On the other hand, the myths illustrate the possibilities that were available for women then, even as they were progressively banned with the emergence of state and patriarchy.[35] By turning to myths and reading their latent meanings, Kurdish women can reanimate and conjure up such possibilities, thereby contributing to the decolonial struggle and opening up "coexisting temporalities" that will make sure that women are recognized "as always already present in history and participating in its production, but written out of it."[36] Myth, moreover, as Jackson says, is the only level at which "myths of history" that deem Kurdish motherhood both unrepresentable and dysfunctional (as I argued in Chapter 1) "can be countered." Rather than striving for ever-more-accurate representations in a world where each representation is appropriated by colonial and patriarchal discourse, the Kurdish women's movement invests in forming alternative epistemes and exchanges "recognition for myth."[37]

Three of the most quoted Sumerian myths that the Kurdish women's movement draws upon in order to search for hidden and latent law(s) of the Women/Mother in the Neolithic Age are the genesis myths "Enki and Ninhursag" and "Enuma Elish" and the epic poem "Gilgamesh." Interestingly enough, in all these myths the male deity Enki plays a defining role — first as the one who is integrated to culture by women, then as someone who steals from women their "laws," and finally as a patricide, who realizes parthenogenetic fantasies. Here, I will specifically dwell on the myths "Enki and Ninhursag" and "Enuma Elish," where the figure of the maternal plays a determining role.

The myth "Enki and Ninhursag," one of the earliest genesis myths in the Mesopotamian region, narrates the making of the city Dilmur by the deity Enki and links the origin of culture to the ban of incest, the initiation of exchange between genders, and the establishment of lineage, all enabled by women.[38] The myth starts with the complaint of the female deity Ninhursag (Earth Mother) to her husband, Enki, that no water exists where they live. Enki (God of Water) then makes water well up from the reservoirs over which he has control and thereby transforms Dilmun into a living space. Once the water that Enki provided turns Dilmun into an "urban emporium," the narrative quickly moves to the marsh. There, Enki lies together with Ninhursag, and the description of this sexual act not only sets the stage for the rest of the story but provides its repeated vocabulary.[39] After nine days Ninhursag gives birth to Ninsar, "smooth" and "painless," and the latter quickly grows into a beautiful woman who catches Enki's attention. Enki spies Ninsar, and, after consulting with his assistant Isimud and receiving his encouragement, he copulates with her. After nine days Ninsar gives an easy birth to Ninimma. The same act repeats itself a third time, and this time Ninimma, impregnated by Enki, gives birth to Uttu.

This time, however, the scenery has changed to a garden and a house. Ninhursag reappears in the myth to warn Uttu of Enki's intentions and tells her to demand fruits and vegetables from Enki. Enki, impersonating a gardener, brings apples, cucumbers, and grapes to Uttu and is welcomed to her home. After some flirtation they have intercourse. Either during intercourse or afterward, Uttu suffers extreme pain. On this point commentators disagree on whether Enki raped Uttu or the pain is a result of her pregnancy.[40] In either case Ninhursag comes to Uttu's rescue, removes Enki's semen from her, and plants it in the ground. Four plants emerge. Enki, as lustful and gluttonous as he is, spies the plants. Overwhelmed by appetite and consulting with Isimud, he eats the plants, thereby "knowing the heart and determining the destiny of each plant."[41] Furious, Ninhursag curses him, causing him to fall mortally ill. Other Gods, worried about Enki and his demise, call on Ninhursag with the help of a fox. When Ninhursag is finally convinced to rescue him, she rushes to the temple. The other gods strip her, and Enki is put in front of her vulva.

> Ninhursag asks Enki which part of his body hurts. As he answers,
> listing a series of eight parts — head, hair, nose, mouth, throat, arm,
> ribs, sides — she somehow facilitates the birth of a series of eight minor

deities. Each of the eight deities is named as it emerges. An element
in each deity's name puns with the name of a body part mentioned
by Enki. Enki (presumably) is healed. The narrative concludes with a
hymnic formula of praise for the god.[42]

Scholars have frequently interpreted the Ninhursag-Enki genesis myth as
a warning against incest. On the other hand, the Kurdish Women's Freedom
Movement interprets this myth, together with the epic poem "Gilgamesh,"
where a conflict between Enki and Ishtar is resolved in favor of Enki, who
seizes Ishtar's 104 laws. Both the myth and the poem allude to the capacity of
women to make laws for the social conflicts they engage in with men in order
for these laws to be followed. While we know little about the content of the
laws of Ishtar, in the myth "Enki and Ninhursag," Ninhursag puts limits on
Enki's actions, forces him to enter in an exchange with Uttu and later herself
(the naming scene where Ninhursag asks what the name the deities that are
born from her vulva should be and Enki answers), and prevents him from
further realizing his parthenogenetic and incestuous fantasies. Lineage in the
myth is defined maternally, and mothering, as we see in Ninhursag's relationship to Uttu, involves care, protection, and consultation. It is also important to
note that while "swallowing" enables Enki to know the heart of each plant, it
is only by letting the plants go free with the help of Ninhursag that the power
to name is acquired.

In opposition to the Oedipus myth, the myth of "Enki and Ninhursag"
problematizes adult male incestuous desire rather than the infant's incestuous
desire and formulates something like an Enki complex, which I think is crucial for the argument I am making. It is the law(s) of the maternal that inhibit
this desire and force it to be sublimated. Enki both witnesses the birth of the
deities, thereby gaining a paternal status, and names them together with Ninhursag, thus creating a form of intimacy that is beyond the incestuous. The
mothering function here emerges as a mediator between the children and the
father and transforms this relationship into one that needs to follow certain
norms and taboos.

Sumerian mythology is later taken over by Babylon civilization, and, according to the Kurdish Women's Freedom Movement, the Babylon genesis
myth of Enuma Elish best expresses the change in the status of women during
this period and how the capacity to make laws is confiscated by men through
matricide.[43] In the Babylon myth the female deity Tiamat, who represents
salty water, and the male deity Apsu, who represents sweet water, are conju-
gally bonded and conceive the other deities in their collective waters. Both-
ered by the noise and movement of these deities, Apsu suggests to Tiamat

that they get rid of them. Overhearing this conversation is Ea (Enki), who then kills his father. Marduk is conceived in the waters of Apsu by Ea and his wife and hence has two fathers. Described with overtly masculine traits, Marduk bullies the other deities. When they complain to their mother, Tiamat, who is already heartbroken and angered by the death of her husband at the hands of her own child, she unleashes terror on Marduk and other deities. In return, Marduk promises his siblings that he will kill Tiamat if the other deities promise a sword, a throne, and a crown to him. They do, and he kills Tiamat. Her mutilated body then is transformed into earth, and her blood gives life to humans.

Although conventionally interpreted as a war between chaos and order, according to the Kurdish Women's Movement's interpretation, the Babylon myth "Enuma Elish" should be read as a metaphor for the idea that matricide is what state power is based on and destroying maternal lineages and female political power is a precondition for the emergence of patriarchal imaginations of power and sovereignty.[44] The myth also gives clues to how femininity and the maternal have come to be equated with an objectified earth that gives life without having a subjectivity of her own. Still, Tiamat doesn't go without a fight, testifying to the power attributed to women and the fear that they will unleash dark powers when provoked.

I am not suggesting that these are the only possible interpretations of these myths. Rather, at the risk of repeating myself, I am following the path of the Kurdish Women's Freedom Movement's philosophy of history on the maternal and feminine. The interpretations they develop regarding these myths point to an original maternal law, which has then been appropriated by patriarchy. While before that, bans were exercised by women against adult men and produced social life, in patriarchy the child becomes the focus. S/he is imagined to have an incestuous desire that needs to be overcome through symbolic matricide in order to enter the social. Against misinterpretations, I should also note that in Kurdish women's thought real mothers and the maternal law are not the same. The emergence of the "state" within Sumerian civilization caused the "fall" of women, their "housewifization" and their colonization by men.[45] Once glorious and powerful goddesses, women have been violated by men and forced into an alliance with patriarchy, thereby losing their place in history. Nevertheless, the memory of their once powerful status lives in them unconsciously through certain traditions. For example, because she is excluded from state institutions and development machineries — also a result of patriarchy — the Kurdish mother remains the preserver of the Kurdish language and of those traditions, lullabies, laments, and fairy tales that embody the wisdom accumulated by the community as it defends itself against inequality and oppression. For this reason, the mother always has the potential of being redeemed.[46] Mothers are imperfect echoes of an original matrilineal culture and need to be elevated through their own politicization or by their daughters' interruption of the law of the Father as it is formed in colonial and patriarchal societies. In the next two sections I will discuss how these interruptions might occur.

## The Demand to Witness and the Intergenerational Interruption of the Corregidora Complex

During the peace process between the years 2013 and 2015, as a member of the Women for Peace Initiative, I went to visit the women guerrillas of the PKK in the mountains to discuss with them their expectations. As is often the case among women, the conversation quickly shifted to personal matters, and an unexpected intimacy developed, which we all tried to squeeze into the short time we had together. One of the guerrilla women — whom I will call Rojbin — told us a story that remains with me to this day. After Rojbin was born, her mother left her husband because of the domestic violence she was suffering. As is expected in Kurdish families, however, she had to leave Rojbin with him, since children belonged to the paternal lineage. Later, her father remarried and moved to the city with his new wife and Rojbin. When he and his new wife joined the Kurdish Freedom Movement and were arrested, Rojbin was given to child services until her paternal grandparents claimed her and took her to their village. At that point in her story, Rojbin took out a scarf and told us that it had belonged to her grandmother.

Rojbin didn't speak Kurdish when she came to the village and felt estranged from everyone, regarding them inferior to her educated urban self. This changed, however, when her grandmother called on her to share the secrets of a chest she was keeping in a dark room. In the chest she had hidden her bloodstained scarfs, remnants of the beatings she had to endure from her husband. For Rojbin this scarf gave flesh to the maternal lineage she had both with her paternal grandmother and her mother, since she believed that her mother must have had something similar to these scarfs, which were reminiscent of the violence she had endured from Rojbin's father. The scarves, Rojbin explained, enabled her to reconstruct the female kinship that was denied to her by the patriarchal structures of family and state.

Rojbin's case is an example of the conscious attempts of women to go against matricide by calling on their daughters or other young female kin to witness patriarchy's injustices, phallocentric logics, and parthenogenetic fantasies. I can multiply such examples wherein an inherited object, a lament, a repeated song, a story, or even a word can become a way for women related by kinship or friendship to render the space between them a scene of witnessing, negotiation, inquiry, and desire. Constituted by a longing for a different future and inassimilable by state or by patriarchal family, this space paves the way to a different heritage between older and younger generations and forms a legacy that interrupts the reproduction of the affective economies of patriarchy.

In her brilliant analysis of Gayl Jones's *Corregidora*, which is "the story about a family of Black women, linked by (post-)slavery kinship and the specter of the man that owned them (both in the real and symbolic sense)," Christina Shape talks about "something like a Corregidora complex" involving "the transgenerational racial hatred, sexual violence, and incestuous violation" constitutive of all relationships in the New World.[47] Tiffany Willoughby-Herard and M. Shadee Malaklou define how the black mother symptomizes the Corregidora Complex as follows:

> This m/other tends to the memory of racial slavery and engenders generations of witnesses who will testify to its horrors, even/especially as she continues to live them herself. "Corregidora," Sharpe explains, "allows us to explore how the family's demands on the subject to keep visible (but also keep repressed) horrific experiences of violence in slavery . . . become congruent with the law of the (slave) master." That is to say, Corregidora indexes "the 'proximity between antagonism and identification' in the demand" that black women "keep visible and . . . reproduce evidence of slavery's violence."[48]

A similar assertion can be made about Kurdish women in relation to patriarchy. Since mothers and maternal lineages are abjected by the phallocentric symbolic order, mothers have remained inassimilable to patriarchal law and therefore continue transmitting conscious and unconscious knowledges about patriarchy and its violence from one generation to the other. In other words, Kurdish mothering, like black m/othering, therefore, also "does not simply enter the symbolic world of the father and his laws" but is always shaped by other worlds carried as memory in women's flesh and voice.[49] Following Sharpe's lead, I should also say that "what becomes dangerous, however, is that, in the injunction to repeat/retell, the originary narrative of Black female sexuality (as captive) is reinstantiated as law."[50] That is, women find themselves normalizing patriarchal/slavery's cruelties, repeating norms and following laws in post-slavery conditions that shaped their mothers' lives. Being a guerrilla in the Kurdish case is one way that such law is interrupted.

In the story of *Corregidora*, the main character, Ursa, interrupts the law of the Father by her inability to reproduce. Since she is sterile, she is not going to repeat the destiny of her lineage. Rojbin also exercises an interruption; joining the guerrilla movement is a guarantee that she will have no children.[51] Instead, she engages in a search for law(s) of the mother buried in mythology that could be brought to life by collective thought and action, by "wake" work. For her, her grandmother is an echo of the originary law(s) of the mother that became appropriated by men. Her grandmother could not interrupt the patriarchal law. Nevertheless, the fact that she kept witnessing and telling of the violence of patriarchy is a proof that new norms informed by the law(s) of the mother can be politically resurrected to enable women to reshape their lives starting now.

While being a guerrilla and/or refusing to reproduce is the safest option, it is not the only one available to women for interrupting the law of the Father. Political organization is a way for mothers themselves to interrupt the operations of patriarchal law, find new positions in the affective economies of patriarchy, and invent new norms. In a workshop on motherhood published in the journal *Jineoloji*, Kurdish women discussed the difficulties and joys of mothering in a context of patriarchy and anti-colonial struggle. In the workshop, women problematized the equation of femininity with motherhood in the dominant culture, the traditional conceptions of motherhood, and the recent disciplining of motherhood through unattainable norms that keep causing them to feel guilt and shame. In other words, they ask the question, "How do we get from a conservative definition of mothering as a biological destiny to mothering as a liberating practice . . . ?"[52] Two of these women who have daughters say they were able to divorce their husbands only when they gave birth to daughters. Daughters strengthened them and endowed them with the necessary will to interrupt their lives. In both women's words, "Daughters became comrades to them."[53] They explain that now their priority is to create a social life for themselves, for their daughters, and other women against the individualizing and isolating laws of patriarchy and capitalist modernity.[54] Children have not caused them to become symptoms of the Corregidora complex, but instead pushed them to search for norms other than those according to which they had led their lives until now. Their struggle, as they define it, is not between individual desire and social norms, as Western psychoanalysis would dictate, but between upholding the collectively fashioned norms of an imagined matricentric culture and the everyday patriarchy in which they live. How to be capable of both sociability and individuality (*xwebun*) and raise daughters who are *xwebun* and not be seen as bad mothers in the spaces they move, specifically among their kin and their patriarchally inclined comrades?

In the next section I will further discuss the figure of the mother and the interruptions she is capable of enacting. But I will be more interested in the question of what happens when the laws of the mother and the law of the state come into direct conflict in public space, rather than what happens when intramural relations trouble women. What comes to the forefront when Kurdish mothers make motherhood public and interrupt the rhythms and spaces of the patriarchal state?

## Once Again: Law(s) of the Mother against the Law of the State

In the Kurdish Movement, mothers are crucial actors who almost always rise to the occasion when no one else can afford to do so. Mothers take to the streets under the most repressive and grim circumstances. For example, in public protests they take the place of their children, who are in prison on hunger strikes, and by going on hunger strikes themselves, they make the hunger strikes visible when no one is paying attention.[55] They dig up the bodies of people buried in mass graves that have been murdered by paramilitaries or died in combat with the Turkish army. They reach out to the mothers of those who seem to be on the other side when an urgent dialogue is needed. They turn themselves into human shields to stop armed encounters between the Turkish army and the Kurdistan Workers Party, the PKK. And, most recently, they stand guard at the graves of their so-called terrorist children in order to prevent these from being destroyed by Turkish F-16s. Using Rancière's theory of the political, Castro argues that politics "refers to the conflictual occupation of the unassigned place, by which . . . bodies interrupt the governing logic of that assignation, making visible what had no business in being seen and making heard a discourse where there was only place for noise.[56] The political visibility of Kurdish mothers in Turkey introduces a break in the stately order of things and in the temporality of events while making mothers' discourse be heard, replacing not only the noise the government condemns their children into by designating them as terrorists but the noise that is attached to the Kurdish maternal.

The figure of the mother who enters the public and makes demands on the state on behalf of her motherhood and in the name of her wronged children is a common political force that has emerged in various contexts of state violence in Argentina, China, Iran, Kenya, Russia, Turkey, and the U.S.[57] From its initial emergence, the figure of the mother in politics struck the public and feminists as an ambiguous figure to be both suspected and celebrated, as it challenged the boundaries that define the public and the private as well as the political and the personal. Whether "the mother" is acting "genuinely" out of pain and suffering or is a pawn used by radical movements to "creep back into" politics after they have been defeated by state violence has been an issue that has shaped its reception by rulers and dominant publics. Some feminists have perceived the figure of the mother as a problem for their own struggle, since in their collective action, mothers have valorized and essentialized the identity of *motherhood*. On the one hand, the fact that the private identity of motherhood has been utilized to make collective claims for justice during and in the aftermath of violence has been seen as an empowering maneuver for women victimized by violence.[58] These views also promote the idea that it is through such mothers' acts that hegemonic understandings of motherhood have been challenged. On the other hand, some feminists have also regarded the figure of the mother as limiting women's agency and contributing to an understanding whereby women can become visible and participate in public discussion only through extending their assigned roles in the family.[59] While these conflicting views have given rise to productive debates and ever-more-nuanced conceptualizations of motherhood, they nevertheless have often remained blind, both to the limits mothers occupy that are other than private or public and to the complicated transformations their agency undergoes when they remain true to the affirmative love of their children. They have rather remained locked in the question of whether mothers' mobilization and activism are beneficial for or detrimental to the women's movement. I want to sidestep this scholarly impasse by addressing head-on the maternal and motherhood otherwise — as scholars of psychoanalysis and Black feminism have done. I contend that only such an approach can help us appreciate what mothers' mobilization does to political fantasies about the state and what those fantasies reveal about operations of law. In other words, I am interested in how patriarchal fantasies of stateness are injured by mothers' political mobilization and how these injured fantasies are then reanimated or replaced. By the same token, what new political fantasies are conjured up once we center our analyses on mother's bodies and voices? I ask these questions because I think feminism and gender studies are much more than about the empowerment of women. They are most apt at remaking public and private fantasies, finding new joys and connections and making new worlds. Cast under this light, the mother's challenge, therefore, is to the very core of stateness, which is one of the most important structures that determines our gendered embodiments, political imaginations, and intimate encounters.

In Turkey, the first emergence of women as mothers in the public space was in 1995 with the foundation of the group Saturday Mothers, which was inspired by the Mothers of the Plaza de Mayo in Argentina.[60] Saturday Mothers are women whose children have been forcibly disappeared or extrajudicially killed — by paramilitary groups working with the state and the military — during the 1980–84 military regime and its aftermath during the Rule of

Emergency in Kurdish cities, which lasted until 2002. Saturday Mothers organize sit-ins while holding pictures of their children and demanding that their children be found dead or alive and be properly buried.[61] They share their stories, name those whom they think are responsible for their children's disappearance, and ask that the perpetrators be brought to justice.[62] They are also active in the trials where such persons are prosecuted.

In the initial years of their sit-ins the Turkish state reacted harshly to Saturday Mothers, arresting and beating them and their supporters. As a result, Saturday Mothers interrupted their regular gatherings in 1999, once again resuming them in 2009. Despite their marginalization by legal authorities, Saturday Mothers have managed to introduce a political discourse of "conscience" in Turkey. Such a discourse makes a call to people to mobilize on behalf of mothers' demands out of empathy for their suffering, captured in written and oral narratives and images that alternative human rights publics produce. Saturday Mothers' politics of "conscience" and its call for justice also index a new future, where those who are deemed abject under the current state of affairs will be able to find a dignified home.[63]

While many Kurdish women have participated in the sit-ins of Saturday Mothers, in 1996 they also created a distinctively Kurdish women's organization based on motherhood called Peace Mothers. Peace Mothers include women whose children have been killed while fighting against the Turkish state as members of the PKK. Different from Saturday Mothers, Peace Mothers prioritize the demand for peace rather than truth and struggle for transformative rather than retributive justice. Peace Mothers have encountered an even fiercer reaction from the state than Saturday Mothers and are often prevented from gathering or traveling, taken into custody and arrested, and made objects of police raids and harassment. The ruling governments and the dominant media question the legitimacy of their inclusion in the motherhood category altogether: since they raised "terrorist" children and propagate counter-propaganda under the guise of peace activism against Turkey's right to defend itself against such "terrorists," they should be legally and politically treated as supporters and harbingers of terrorism rather than as suffering mothers.

Despite all obstacles, Peace Mothers in Turkey have also succeeded in making an impact in both Turkish and Kurdish publics. By mobilizing their suffering to ask for peace between Turkey and the PKK, they have extended the politics of conscience to include empathy for the kind of suffering that emerges with deaths that aren't always perceived to be wrongful, illegal, or illegitimate. As Çetinkaya writes, "The presence and the 'visibility of 'Mothers' and their demand for peace serves not only as a way to speak of their children, but more importantly to speak of them alive, as lives that count despite the fact that their children are rendered dead by state discourse."[64] Moreover, instead of asking for a form of justice that holds accountable those who inflict pain, Peace Mothers make the whole public responsible and accountable for letting the suffering of war continue and for replaying itself repeatedly. They thereby engage in a "decolonial mourning" and "reconstruct an otherwise interdicted sociability."[65] Loudly voicing the tragedy of what befell them interpellates listeners of otherwise secluded communities and constitutes a public of Kurds and Turks whose coming together is normally carefully policed by the state.[66] Finally, mothers have also redefined "motherhood rights" as something more than the right to know, bury, and seek justice for one's children, transforming them into the right to promote one's children's ideals — if not actions — and to defend their memory. As with the rights Saturday Mothers articulate, such a right is not given, but pursued and exercised; it is a right that transforms and metamorphoses the "mother" as she endures repression and exclusion and speaks back to power. For example, while at first the activism of Peace Mothers was accepted as an extension of their private role in the patriarchal household and as agents who organize mourning, suffering, and remembering in the community, the fact that many men remained at home while women were taking to the streets (to protest state violence and participate in peace vigils) and being arrested soon transformed the public meaning of motherhood and fatherhood among Kurds.[67] Coupled with the undermining of their roles as breadwinners as a result of forced migration and neoliberal economic policies, men's passivity and melancholia in the face of loss became a sign of their weakness, at the same time that motherhood was becoming valorized as an active mode of engaging with public matters and being transformed from a mode of expressing suffering to a mode of public action with its own repertoire.[68]

The voice that Saturday Mothers and Peace Mothers produced in Turkey has proven to be contagious. The affects that inform their speech have circulated, and motherhood has become a ground from which other oppositional groups voice their own claims. Such groups include Mothers of Roboski, whose children were bombed to pieces by the Turkish army while smuggling goods packed on mules from Iraq to Turkey; Gezi mothers, whose protesting children during the Gezi events were insulted and threatened by then Prime Minister Erdoğan; and Gezi and Suruç families, whose children were killed by security forces and by bombings, respectively, and soldiers' mothers, whose sons in military school are prosecuted for planning and executing the attempted coup of 2016.[69] All have found a public space to speak and act and to show their state-inflicted injuries by appealing to the politics of conscience, whose primary architects remain Saturday Mothers and Peace Mothers.[70]

Elsewhere I have addressed how the figure of the mother is so uniquely suited to speak in defense of those whose singularity is erased by law and violence and what authorizes the words of mothers as truth and makes the politics of conscience they activate contagious.[71] I have argued that it is the fact that the mother oscillates between the two positions of descent into everyday life to do repair work and dramatic transgression that endows her with the capacity to speak truth and be listened to. This oscillation constitutes the mother as a limit figure who, on the one hand, because she dwells in the private of the everyday, "knows" truths inassimilable by law and, on the other, whose appeal, when she transgresses her assigned space and expresses such truths to larger publics, creates an exception that cannot be easily ignored.

The figure of the mother not only oscillates between the sphere of the private, where repair work occurs, and the public, which dramatic transgression addresses; she also destabilizes the private/public divide upon which the law and rule of the sovereign nation-state is predicated by using her "motherly right"—gained through the labor of giving birth and raising children—to speak in public. Or, put differently, while the power to define what is public and what is private, when, where, and for whom, is constitutive of the sovereign nation-state, the figure of the mother challenges this power by mobilizing the very affects, roles, legitimacies, and values that the nation-state endows her with in the private space in order to become a force in public. Her appearance in the public space as someone both within and outside of it, represented yet not presented, creates an exception: her love, which consoles, repairs, and nourishes (and on which the reproduction of the nation depends), is furnished and simultaneously forgotten when secular state law operates. It then erupts in the public space as a sovereign, affirmative, and enduring law of *another* register that momentarily wounds the nation-state's law.

A frequently circulating story in Kurdistan is that, traditionally, when a mother strips off and throws her white headscarf on the street, the gesture would stop any violent conflict. Although such is not the power of the Peace Mother, neither for the PKK nor certainly for the Turkish state, she is still surrounded by a reminiscent mythical aura, and her coming out of the house to protest is invested with an anticipation of apocalypse, after which the world as we know it will disappear. When she interferes in public, the mother embodies the "communal" of the community, its will to survive, and its decreasing capacity to be repaired, a truth superior to whatever reasoning informs the conflict and violence in question. The force she unleashes appeals to the divine in the sense used by Walter Benjamin in his seminal essay—a divine violence that will stop all kinds of earthly violence.[72] If the sorrow and tears of mothers in the face of loss erase any difference and address the sympathy and empathy of an undifferentiated public and its collective conscience, so does the anger of mothers — *anaların öfkesi* in Turkish and *hêrsa dayiken* in Kurdish — know no difference and bring ruin to power and civilization. Rosalind Morris argues that the expectation that the state will end all violence animates the fantasies of citizens and leads them to invest in its discursive and psychic reproduction.[73] The fact that mothers can evoke an equally powerful fantasy through their power derived from their everyday labor of care and love renders the state hollow and equates it with other patriarchal actors whose violence is seen to be tolerable only to a limit.

For the Kurdish movement, mothers' activism is a way in which the law(s) of the mother that have been confiscated by patriarchy are reanimated and put into conflict with laws of patriarchy and the state. I have explained how the spaces of patriarchy and state are troubled by the mother's making motherhood public and pitting the love/laws of the mother against state's law. It, however, also disrupts their temporality. By making public the time of motherhood that involves waiting, enduring, caring, and letting one's time unfold in relation to someone else, mothers are challenging the individualizing and progressive time of the state and capitalism.[74] In their actions they make visible the fact that they are now living in a temporality other than the one that shapes the public, in a time that is "no time" to which they invite others to live, as well. This is the temporality of those who wait for an impossible justice and in their waiting prevent others from forgetting the debt they owe to the deceased that fought for a better life and their death labor, which created new values in the Kurdish society.[75] This is also the "queer temporality" of civil disobedience where "the futurist temporality of desire" deemed proper by settler colonialism is challenged with the Antigonian pure desire that places its subject in a state of living death rather than obeying the rules of the Symbolic.[76] But it also refers to a mythical time when women had the capacity to name and ban; to establish norms and effect justice. In their collective presence in public, they cite this past and become harbingers of a future where children can actually be protected from the perversities of the patriarchal racist state. In that sense their action is also properly decolonial.

So now we are back to the beginning. Mother's activism and the Kurdish Women Movement's theorization of such activism change the matter of politics and enable the making of new political imaginations. Occupying the limits between everyday care and transgressive defiance, private and public, and the ordinary and the divine, mothers not only valorize the life of deceased children but politicize the mother and its laws. The progressive time of politics collapses and gives rise to a form of politics where the eternal time of waiting for an impossible justice, the deep time of myth, and the singular time

of pure desire meet. The "no space" where Gönül and her mother lived —
indebted to patriarchy and injured by each other, the "no time" of mothers
who lost their children, emerge as spatialities and temporalities in need of
political attending and caring. Living women of blood who are uncomfortable
with the sexed and social embodiments enforced on them enflesh politics
anew by connecting to each other, to their mothers, to their children, and to
Tiamat, Ninhursag, and Ishtar, creating otherwise interdicted sociabilities.
Words become forceful, tongues become passionately political. Every moment of everyday care and transgressive visibility is now a matter of gendered
death or survival, since it is no more one's own body one is responsible for, but
the whole maternal lineage from which one was forced into exile.

# PART II
*Politician*

# 3

# Antigone as Kurdish Politician

*Gendered Dwellings in the Limit between
Freedom and Peace*

One has to know how to be impudent. When life itself has taken a
strange state with all its hierarchy and affect, in sum, in all its aspects,
there are a few ways to breathe. One is to be valiant, the other one is to
be dignified and the last one is to be a bit impudent.

> — EVRIM ALATAŞ, QUOTED BY YILDIRIM TÜRKER, "EVRIM IS GONE"

There's no room for her if she's not a he. If she's a her-she, it's in order
to smash everything, to shatter the framework of institutions, to blow
up the law, to break up the "truth" with laughter.

> — HÉLÈNE CIXOUS, "THE LAUGH OF THE MEDUSA"

What if Antigone, along with those doomed to ontological suspension
on account of their unrecognizable and, in consequence, "unlivable
loves," declined intelligibility . . . ?

> — LEE EDELMAN, *NO FUTURE: QUEER THEORY AND DEATH DRIVE*

Actually claiming the monstrosity (of a female with the potential to
"name"), which her culture imposes in blindness, "Sapphire" might
rewrite after all a radically different text for a female empowerment.

> — HORTENSE SPILLERS, "MAMA'S BABY, PAPA'S MAYBE"

The monster always represents the disruption of categories, the
destruction of boundaries, and the presence of impurities and so

we need monsters and we need to recognize and celebrate our own
monstrosities.

— JACK HALBERSTAM, SKIN SHOWS

In December 2009, during a tense period in Turkey when the conflict between the state and the Kurds was once again accelerating after attempts at
peace and reconciliation, the then vice prime minister of Turkey, Bülent
Arınç, complained to journalists about the woman deputy, Emine Ayna. She
was a member of the Kurdish oppositional Democratic Society Party (DTP),
and he blamed her for sabotaging his government's initiative to solve the
"Kurdish problem." "There is a poor woman among them. I apologize to say
this among ladies, but she broke into laughter while saying that the initiative
is over. She is a very strange monstrous creature. God shall give her some logic
and sense."[1] As Lupton reminds us in her discussion of the figure of the creature, in theological imagination "creatureliness serves to localize a moment
of . . . an abjected, thing-like (non)being, a being of subjected becoming, that
precipitates out of the divine Logos as its material remnant."[2] By using the
expression "creature," Bülent Arınç evokes this theological imagination in
his speech in order to render Emine Ayna's laughter and disregard for his
government's initiative "abject," not only to his political world but also to
humankind and even to creation itself. His statement signals the stakes of
Kurdish women's political performance: their struggle takes place at the levels
of both ontology and cosmology.

In this chapter I focus on several moments in which Kurdish women politicians in Turkey made the news as monstrous figures who disregarded the
rules of conduct proper to peace politics and affective regimes of reconciliation and thereby pushed the limits "of what a given society finds it tolerable
to represent to itself."[3] I turn to (Western) feminists' discussions of Antigone
to highlight the injury that Kurdish women's defiant political performance is
said to inflict on the Turkish *polis*. But I also point out that the limits Kurdish
women occupy are different from the limit between life and death that Antigone occupies, and I discuss what feminist politics from these limits looks
like. I argue that even when Kurdish women's speech and deeds are "politically unintelligible" to sovereign power they are constitutive of new freedoms
and imaginative possibilities.[4]

## Antigone as Politician

The questions of whether and how the figure of Antigone bears on the political have been taken up by numerous feminist theorists in recent years.[5]

Partly moving away from and partly reworking Hegel's and Lacan's takes on Antigone, some of these feminists have interrogated the distinctions made by modern politics between kinship and politics, private and public, women's bodies and the political body. They point out that the latter terms are founded on the exclusion and subjection of the former. Antigone is a figure that questions these distinctions and so brings the political order to crisis.[6] By defying the rules of the state, she reinserts that which is excluded from politics and transforms its semiotics and aesthetics.[7] For many feminists Antigone is thus a political model in whose name woman's disruptive potential can be valorized.

Other feminists have been interested in the politics of subjectivity that Antigone embodies and how such subjectivity not only unmakes but also remakes the political world. Antigone is a figure who emerges from within the existing political order and uses its tools, but who nevertheless exercises an agency that anticipates another way of being and becoming in the world. In this vein Butler argues that Antigone's performance points to a universalism in which we can recognize our own vulnerabilities and mortality as well as how our connections and desires are rendered impossible by the existing order.[8] Critical of the "mortalist humanism," which she thinks is exemplified by Butler and Nicole Loraux, Bonnie Honig reads Antigone instead as an example of "agonistic humanism."[9] Julia Kristeva, in contrast, emphasizes that Antigone's importance lies not in the kind of humanity she evokes but rather in the freedom she exercises: Antigone is a figure of freedom because she makes her own rules and thereby gives birth to new political imaginaries.[10]

Discussions of Antigone also rework some of the more concrete tensions and dilemmas that contemporary feminist thought and politics face today. These include permanent war, bio-political racism, states of exception, the loss of truth, projects of assimilating difference and incommensurability within the market and social media, and the lack of accountability of states and non-state actors for the enormous devastation they have wrought. Across the world we see examples of women trying to hold on to the memories of their loved ones and remain loyal to their singularities, while these are systematically erased and rendered ungrievable. Unfortunately, international and national regimes of peace-making and reconciliation often fail these women, deadening their memories and turning their narratives into data for emerging auditing cultures.[11] How will feminism deal with the fact that for many women in the world the right to grief has become as much, if not more, of an urgent issue as their access to social goods and services, legal equality and political representation? How will feminism be on the side both of peace and of women's refusal to forget and forgive?

Revisiting Antigone opens up ways to rethink women's suffering and agency during and after civil war. Antigone is a figure of grief and mourning. She is implicated in the politics of burial, exile, and the body.[12] She produces truths about singularities and the irreplaceability of loss, which according to Copjec, are the cements of the social.[13] But Antigone also represents loyalty to a desire that defies the sovereignty of rulers and the moral exclusions on which the symbolic depends.[14] And yet, to what extent can we defend singularity and unsublimated desires in the polis without being the victims of the age of post-truth or without ruining the terms on which our collective life depends in the first place?[15] How can we reconcile the singular with the abstract category of the citizen?[16] And can we be fond of desire and the ethics of truth with which it is associated when we lack collectively accepted criteria that could make the necessary distinctions between the desires that bring freedom and those that bring devastation to the world?

There are yet other important questions: Antigone is explosive, full of anger and sadness, some would even say unproductively so. How can women's affects have a bearing on politics without being sentimental and melodramatic, as, for example, Lauren Berlant warns us?[17] To many of her fans' surprise, Antigone says that only a sibling is irreplaceable, whereas a husband or a child can be replaced. So, how is it possible to see suffering and pain as constituent of both subjectivity and community — the right to grief as part of humanity — without letting any one grief become a privileged site?[18] These are the questions that women living in zones of war and peace have to respond to every day. In this chapter I contend that the repetition of certain defiant performances by women produces new norms and truths that can be cited and reiterated.[19] Unearthing these new norms and truths can give us an understanding of emerging subjectivities and political imaginations in oppositional movements and provide us with the opportunity to trace the collective responses that women in different circumstances give to pressing questions of our times.

The women that I will talk about in this chapter seem alone at first sight, at least in the moment when they make their demands by shocking the limits of law. However, every one of them is part of a genealogy of Kurdish women's struggle and belongs to the wider Kurdish women's movement.[20] The desire that moves them toward the limit or the threshold — be it that of language, geography, or the legal — cannot be understood in the context of their individual trajectories as much as of the trajectory of their communities. This does not mean that their relations with these communities are without strain, nor that we can always assume a sorority from which they speak. In the long run, however, their desire and the truths they express become meaningful and "beautiful" only to the extent that they take up, mimic, cite, and parody the limits that constrain the wider community of Kurdish people. When Antigone travels to Turkey and to Turkey's Kurdistan specifically, she is working the intervals between the demands of the polis and those of community, between peace politics and the command not to forget and forgive, and between the affective registers of reconciliation and a desire to be free — not as a lone hero — but as an agent deeply embedded in solidarities, sororities, and communities.[21]

One more caution: We should not forget that while life might look a lot like "tragedy" in zones of war and peace-making, it still goes on.[22] In the play, as Antigone dies physically, so does Creon politically. In the contexts in which we must dwell, however, and despite our expectations shaped by the genres of the tragic and the melodramatic, the sovereign remakes himself, and evil survives. For this reason, in this chapter, I also address the question of what happens when Antigone must continue dwelling in the very space of loss when Creon does not face defeat.

In the temporality of politics — unlike that of the theater — camps regroup, adopt new strategies, deny lessons, and destroy possibilities. The women I take up in this chapter live in this temporality of the political; they are self-defined politicians. They hold public office as mayors in municipalities or as deputies in the Parliament. They are elected representatives of the Kurdish people, and hence they are always already more than themselves. Most importantly, they must defend Kurdish rights in an ongoing war and under conditions of colonization and do so in the negotiations for peace and reconciliation aimed at ending the conflict between the guerrilla organization, the Kurdistan's Workers Party (PKK), and the Turkish state. As we will see, these two tasks are not easy to combine. Working in the interval between the demand for peace and the experience of asymmetrical war challenges the relationship between representative and represented, the legal and the illegal. Often words fail these women as they seek "to communicate the incommunicable": the tension between wanting to be free and not being able to not want peace.[23] These women embody the Kurdish people in their defiance and use their office to bring *the polis* to crisis. They thereby both "profane" the political in Giorgio Agamben's sense and produce new visibilities.[24] By showing the impossible limits of the political and legal order that Kurdish people must occupy in their everyday existence, they bring to life new "imaginary universes."[25]

While the fact that the women I will discuss are politicians in the conventional sense might distinguish them from Antigone, who is mostly associated with the household, there are other characteristics that connect them to her. Two of these are important to mention. First, as Kurdish women and politicians, the women I discuss here are always already implicated in the politics of the burial of bodies that have been exiled from the *polis*, such as those of guerrillas, protestors, and victims of "honor killings."[26] As representatives of an oppositional community whose members die young and unnatural deaths that are ungrievable by the larger Turkish public, they are constantly in search of ways to make count the singularities of those who are lost.

Second, the oppositional politics they enact situate them in relations of (fictive) kinship that inform their desire and yet cannot be represented in politics proper. They have husbands, fathers (real and fictive), sisters, and brothers in the guerrilla movement and in prison. While these relations are not incestuous, they are still forbidden, unwelcome, and disruptive. The kinship burden women politicians carry both empowers and marks them.

In what follows, I focus on three moments of Kurdish women's political performances of defiance that express the limits these women confront as they work through the interval between the conflicting demands of community and citizenship, freedom and peace, legality and illegality. Each of these performances is interrupted, and even if they weren't, as Lacan says, it would be impossible to bear remaining in them, since they unmake the symbolic that secures intelligibility. However, when the performances are repeated, cited, and mimicked they create the contours of a new political imagination that endows women with a new grammar to make sense of their experience, desires, and truths. In the last section of this chapter, I will come back to the feminist interpretations of Antigone to discuss how the experience of Kurdish women might force us to rethink the political as a space whose boundaries, law, and grammar are radically transformed through defiant performances from within the zone of occupation and dispossession.

## Leyla Zana: A Betrayal in Kurdish

The figure of the Kurdish female politician erupted on the Turkish political stage at the very moment of her entry in the early 1990s. This eruption involved both a transgression of the law of the state and a betrayal of the political opposition to which she belonged. Despite the many transformations that Kurdish female politicians subsequently underwent in terms of their power, ideology, and practice, this formative first transgression haunted them and kept them apart from their male counterparts. The transgression involved a sentence uttered and a hairband worn within the walls of the Parliament. The sentence and the hairband, as minimal as they were, brought Leyla Zana the tragedy of being imprisoned for a decade. The wound they caused to the law of the nation-state, however, remains open and bleeds still.

The first Kurdish legal political party in Turkey was created in 1990 when several members were expelled from the leftist Social Democratic Pro-

People's Party (SHP) for having participated in a conference in Paris with the title "Kurdish National Identity and Human Rights." (The Kurdish issue was at that moment taking increasingly more lives because of the ongoing guerrilla war.) The expulsion was followed by the resignations of those who protested the decision; the expelled and the resigned together created the People's Labor Party (HEP), a coalition of Kurdish and Turkish left-wing politicians. In Turkey, there is a 10 percent voter threshold for political parties to be represented in the Parliament, according to a law passed by the 1980–83 Military Junta. Before the 1991 national election it seemed unlikely that the newly formed HEP would receive 10 percent of the vote. However, since a majority of its members were Kurds and known human rights activists, it would likely get a majority in the cities populated by Kurds. In order both to increase its votes and to secure the representation of some oppositional Kurds, SHP made a pre-election agreement with HEP and ran several HEP members as SHP's candidates. As a result, twenty-one members of HEP were elected to the Parliament, and, for the first time in Turkey's parliamentary history, several Kurdish-identified activists became deputies. One of these, and the only woman among them, was Leyla Zana.

Leyla Zana came from a poor rural background. She was born in 1961 in the city of Silvan, where oppositional Kurdish politics was influential. Still, rather than her natal family and place of origin, it was her marriage that determined her life course in politics. When she was sixteen years old, her father married her to thirty-five-year-old Mehdi Zana, who would become the independent socialist mayor of Diyarbakır in 1978. After the military coup in 1980, Mehdi Zana was arrested and put in the notorious Diyarbakır Prison; he remained incarcerated for sixteen years, there and in a number of other prisons. When Leyla Zana won her seat in the Parliament in 1991, she had already accumulated many unaccountable losses specific to women living in zones of war and repression. She had received no formal education, since her father had banned her from school after one and a half years; she had then become a child-bride and child-mother. Her life changed drastically after her husband's arrest. She followed him from city to city with her two children as he was moved from prison to prison. During these years she received first elementary and then high school diplomas and became active in the Kurdish human rights movement as the wife of a tortured prisoner.

Leyla Zana's candidacy from Diyarbakır, where once her husband held municipal office, was no surprise to anyone, since until then, especially in the legal arena, it was the wives and mothers of deceased and imprisoned male human rights activists and politicians who were mobilized in the Kurdish Movement. Leyla Zana's marriage and her activism after her husband's arrest endowed her with enough symbolic and cultural capital for her to be accepted by the larger Kurdish public. She soon became the beloved "sister" Leyla of the Kurdish people, dressed in simple clothes at meetings. She spoke fluent Kurdish and a broken Turkish, both marks of authenticity. She also received considerable attention from international audiences as the first Kurdish-identified female deputy in the Turkish Parliament. Leyla Zana was already an object of curiosity and passion when she entered the Parliament on her first day as deputy.

On November 6, 1991, Leyla Zana was invited to the floor by the head of the Parliament to be sworn in, a ritual of official recognition for all new members. The ten-year ban on speaking the Kurdish language, which had become a symbol of Turkey's denial of the existence of Kurds, had been lifted only months ago. Speaking Kurdish in official spaces was, however, still illegal. Leyla Zana was wearing a hairband in yellow, red, and green, the colors of Kurdistan, and for this there were protests from the entire room as she walked toward the stage. After swearing the parliamentary oath, Leyla Zana switched to Kurdish, adding, "I take this oath for the brotherhood between the Turkish people and the Kurdish people."[27] The head of the Parliament was Ali Rıza Septioğlu, a Kurd himself, from the majority Right Path Party (DYP). After Zana finished her words, he first called her back informally with the words "my daughter" and "girl."[28] Then he commanded her in an official manner to repeat her oath without changing it. Echoing the words of the law, which has numerous times represented the Kurdish language in official documents with the sentence "the defendant spoke in unintelligible language unknown to the court," Septioğlu — ironically himself speaking in a broken Turkish — addressed the audience and said, "I didn't understand what she said either." Zana complied with his orders when she was called a third time to the microphone; she repeated the parliamentary oath in Turkish, this time without adding anything to it.

Kurds say, "The Turkish state never forgets." In 1993, HEP was closed down by the Constitutional Court, and soon afterward Zana was stripped of her immunity. In December 1994, along with four other Kurdish MPs, she was arrested and charged with treason for membership in the armed Kurdistan Worker's Party (PKK). While the treason charges were never brought to the court and she denied membership in the PKK, she still ended up being sentenced to fifteen years in prison. With Turkey applying to become a member of the European Union, the EU repeatedly called for her release on human rights grounds. In June 2004, after a prosecutor requested quashing the prior verdict on a technicality, Zana and her friends were released. I will now turn to Leyla Zana's narrative of the night of the oath:[29]

On November 6, 1991, we were in the parliament for the oath ceremony. The president of HEP, Fehmi Işıklar, came, and told some
of our friends that nobody should give any message during the oath
ceremony. . . . Hatip and I made our decisions. We were going to give
our message, he in Turkish and I in Kurdish. Before the ceremony
I braided in my hair my hairband in yellow, red, and green.[30] I had
never taken those colors out during my electoral campaign. In 1989
these colors were banned. Shepherds, only because they wore these
colors, were arrested and tortured. . . . Truck drivers were banned
from traffic for carrying these colors. The most interesting was what I
had witnessed in a wedding during my electoral campaign. We were
in a village of Bismil. There was music, and everybody was having
fun. After I finished my speech I went to a room to thank the hosts of
the wedding. I asked where the groom was and his mother told me
that he was gone. One of the guests told me that he was taken by the
special teams. I was shocked. I didn't know what to say. The mother of
the groom braided a scarf with these three colors in my hair and told
me: "You will promise me something. You will go to the parliament
that banned these colors like this." I promised that mother. "Even if
it means giving up my life I will fulfill your wish." The groom was
arrested only because he wore those colors. The reproach of this
woman, her broken heart and her sorrowful look had affected me to
the extent that no power could make me break my promise. It was
the Diyarbakır deputies' turn to give their oath. Hatip went to the
stage and when he said: "My friends and I are reading this oath under
constitutional repression," chaos erupted. They were attacking the
stage and it was as if they were going to tear Hatip into pieces. Kurdish
MPs were fearful. They were coming one by one to me warning me
not to say anything. Then, a parliamentary official came and told me
that Mehdi was calling me. Mehdi asked me "why did you call me?"
I told him "I didn't call you. They told me you did." Meanwhile, a
friend, who apparently had called us both, said to Mehdi "tell Leyla
not to give any Kurdish messages." Knowing me well, Mehdi told him
"Leyla makes her own decisions. I cannot tell her what to do." Then it
was my turn. I walked towards the stage, my heart pounding. Deputies
from the governing party kept screaming "down with the flag on your
head." I read the oath. After I finished I said [in Kurdish], "I read this
oath for the brotherhood of Kurdish and Turkish people." It was as if
I had put dynamite on the walls of the Parliament. All the deputies
were pounding on their desks. They were trying to come to the floor

to attack me. They called me again. I read the oath once again. And I repeated the same words. They objected again. They insisted that we take back our words. I didn't want to take the floor a third time. Hatip came to convince me. He said, "We have made two steps. There is a saying. Two steps forward one back." I objected again and said, "no." He went to the stage and took back his words. The message had found its place. So, I did the same.

Leyla Zana's memoir reveals her stubborn insistence to carry the colors of Kurdistan and disfigure the oath in order "to give a message," despite her friends' multiple attempts to convince her not to. Her friends even called her husband (recently released from prison) to accomplish what they couldn't by evoking his marital authority over her. Leyla Zana — despite all the attempts to remind her of her dependence on men in different capacities (party discipline, male comrades, husband, the head of the Parliament using kinship terminology) — exercised an autonomy reserved only to men and remained indifferent, even deaf, to their demands. It is, moreover, not enough for her to defy the state once. She does it three times by wearing the hairband first and then by speaking twice in Kurdish.

Leyla Zana is well aware of the violence unleashed by her performance, as her words testify: "It was as if I had put dynamite on the walls of the Parliament." Where does her desire come from, and what feeds it so that she ends up not only betraying the nation-state but also the very people who welcomed her into their party? The similarities with Antigone are striking. By disregarding Ismene's advice and by disrespecting and defying Creon, her father-in-law-to-be, who gave her shelter and food, Antigone is not only transgressing the limits of state law, but also the limits of the laws of hospitality

Figure 3. Leyla Zana in the Oath Ceremony (Özgür Politika Archives)

and generosity. By associating Creon with the law of the state, I think many feminists are missing the point that Antigone commits treason in the realm of the household, as well. I am wondering whether this points to an enduring feminist attachment to the distinction between the public and the private, kinship relations and civic relations. Even Butler, who discusses the mutual constitution of kinship and the polis at length, seems to disregard the fact that it is not only Antigone's desire (for her brother) but also her act (betraying his uncle and her father-in-law to be) that is transgressive of kinship relations. She is, in other words, not only anticipating a different kinship but already exercising it, as Kurdish women politicians do by foregrounding their loyalty to women at the expense of their political comrades.

As Antigone explains her deed by reference to the promise she made to her brother in the play *Oedipus in Colossus*, Leyla Zana explains her decision to do what she did by the promise she made to the woman whose son was taken by the police for carrying the three colors of Kurdistan. Antigone must keep her promise because her brother is irreplaceable and singular. Why can Leyla Zana not break her promise to a stranger when all her comrades are trying to convince her to do otherwise? Whether Leyla Zana uses the story strategically to give meaning to her behavior in her biography, written years after the event took place, is beside the point. The fact remains that she is juxtaposing the oath and the promise exactly as Antigone does in regard to her promise as the ground for her refusal of the command of the law. Zana's promise places her outside of the parliamentary walls and transforms the Parliament into a threshold between the legal and the illegal, the demands for peace and compromise, and the demands for not forgetting and forgiving. With this promise she herself becomes a limit figure between the represented and their representatives, and her performance is a way to *show* the reproach, heartbreak, and sorrow of women living in the zones of war and peace and under the impossible conditions of colonization. Her appendix to the oath in Kurdish and her hairband are the ways in which she works through the interval between inclusion and exclusion, the illegality that Kurds are condemned to and the legality of the Parliament that is supposed to represent the people. There is more to it, however.

As a Kurdish woman who spent her life waiting in front of prison walls together with other women whose sons and husbands were also in prison, Leyla Zana must have felt an intimacy toward them bordering on sororal kinship. Arguably, the promise she refers to is informed by that kinship, which is unaccounted for in higher politics. The content of that kinship, as I know from other studies I have done, is shaped by anger not only toward the state but also toward those who, even as they provide shelter and food for such women, are offering gifts with strings attached. Since the life cycles of these women are interrupted by the loss of their husbands, they are unable to experience or enjoy the normalcies of the everyday: they must be constantly in control and grateful and remain dependent on the whim of others.[31] They must ask their male relatives for money, get permission from their mothers-in-law to leave the house, take over the burden of housework, and prove their loyalty to their husbands, despite the many advances they might receive from other men. Leyla Zana's betrayal of her party (the SHP), then, can also be read as an expression of a gendered dwelling in zones where intimacy and alienation, protection and patronization, hospitality and hostility cannot be differentiated. It can be interpreted as an embrace of being in exile in the home of those who welcome her. As far as normal life is concerned, Leyla Zana never lived one, just as Antigone never did, as the exiled daughter of an incestuous marriage. Zana's parliamentary oath might be read as the crafting of visibility for those who suffer different forms of slow death imposed on them by patriarchy, colonization, and occupation.[32] Like Antigone's speech before she disappears into her tomb, Zana's performance transforms her presence in the Parliament into an *Ate*, an unforgettable act of defiance. That this defiance would occur through an oath delivered to the nation-state, in Kurdish and by the colors of Kurdistan, is over-determined by the law's bans, their very edifice.

Leyla Zana ended up being punished by law and put in prison for a decade. Contrary to Creon in the play *Antigone*, no tragic ending befell the sovereign power after her imprisonment. To this day, moreover, people with different worldviews comment that Leyla Zana harmed the Kurdish cause, since it took almost twenty years to repair the damage done by the oath crisis and to re-create a working electoral alliance with the democratic left. Despite being the first Kurdish-identified woman in the Parliament, a symbol of authenticity, and someone who sacrificed years of her youth to the struggle for freedom, Zana remains an ambiguous figure in the landscape of Turkish and Kurdish politics. She is someone who is always a little too independent, making decisions such as visiting President Erdoğan to talk about peace and using Kurdish in an oath ceremony in 2015. Her defiance, however, and the political imagination she evoked, lives on in other Kurdish women politicians. Like hers, their performances continue to challenge the *polis* and its symbolic and ethical rules.

## Emine Ayna: A Laughter That Gives Away

While Leyla Zana's defiance became an important cornerstone in the making of Kurdish women's public visibility, Kurdish women politicians now rarely claim her as their inspiration. This has many reasons, including the different political affiliations and inclinations of Leyla Zana, which make her more of a traditional figure as opposed to the radical and revolutionary politics her sisters now embrace. Also, Leyla Zana has a singular and lonely image not necessarily acclaimed by the Kurdish Women's Movement, which values solidarity and sorority. Solidarity and sorority are enabling, and yet they also discipline and circumscribe individual agency and initiative. In contrast, the Turkish public sees the new generation of female politicians, who are referred to as "falcons"—as aggressive, conspiratorial, and self-interested—unlike Zana, who has more authenticity. For example, when talking about Aysel Tuğluk, one of the leading female Kurdish figures, a lawyer who entered the political stage as a deputy in 2007, a Turkish journalist predicts that she will break the law repeatedly just to become famous: "Since she is not a nice-looking woman as Leyla Zana was once, she will make up for her lack of femininity by being frequently incarcerated and becoming legendary. In short, we are encountering not a political but a 'womanly psychiatric case.'"[33]

The journalist's comments are important not because of their shockingly open sexism, but because they reflect how women after Zana are suspected of disingenuousness and insincerity. According to this view, their actions stem from their wish to become popular rather than being a result of an authentic claim for freedom. Despite their many differences, several of the woman politicians of the new generation share certain characteristics that indeed make them "less than authentic." For example, Aysel Tuğluk, Emine Ayna, Gültan Kışanak, and Sabahat Tuncel, all of whom have taken leadership positions in Kurdish political parties, do not speak Kurdish. They come from secular backgrounds and are often from the minority Alevi religion. All three, except Gültan Kışanak, are single. They dress in Western clothing, and they come from the urban middle class. Almost all of them belong to the Kurdish women's movement, which flourished after 2000, and it was women who brought them to power. Before taking their posts, they were mostly unknown to the wider Kurdish public, and few had relations with political groups not connected to the women's movement. As if these are not enough to mark them as inauthentic, the conditions of politics have changed as well, providing deputies and mayors with new opportunities. They eat well, dress well, and have drivers and advisers that set them apart from the people. In the case of women, a privileged life is specifically charged with meaning and is regarded as an additional reason for their constituency to dislike them. In that sense what the Turkish journalist writes about Tuğluk also partially reflects how Kurds feel about their women representatives. None of the women politicians enjoy the same love and sympathy that male politicians receive, and when they don't like their actions, people speak of them as undeserving, having acquired their positions because of women's quotas. Neither endowed with the authority and sanctity of motherhood nor promising sacrifice as a guerrilla fighter who is ready to die for her people, the woman politician is therefore open to many forms of resentment. She is continuously attacked and interrogated for everything, including her clothing, her link to the guerrilla movement, her "terrorism," and her failure to meet the standards of femininity.

Nevertheless, women politicians' labor-intensive activities and their travels to participate in meetings and rallies have changed the understanding of how politics is done. They attend burials of guerrillas condemned by the state and honor-killing victims who are not mourned by their kin. They become human shields — along with other people, including the Peace Mothers — whenever the possibility arises for combat between the armed forces of the Turkish state and the PKK in Kurdistan. In Kurdish people's rallies, protests, and meetings, the police often use gas canisters and pressurized water to disperse crowds. Interestingly, women politicians are always targeted first. After every gathering, numerous images displaying the injured bodies of women politicians circulate on the Internet. A wounded leg, a face full of tears, wet hair, a broken arm attached to an aching female deputy or mayor are as much a symbol of Turkey's oppressive regime and its dismissal of Kurdish politicians as they are testimonies to the gendered operations of power. Through such aggression, women politicians are reduced to criminal gendered bodies composed of vulnerable organs.

Emine Ayna is a pioneer among the new generation of women politicians. She has twice become a deputy and has also served as the vice president of the DTP and co-president of the DBP before her resignation from politics.[34] I want to turn my attention to her problematic laughter and her statement announcing that the Kurdish initiative was over, which made the vice president of the government call her a "strange monstrous creature."[35] Similar to Zana's, her transgression takes the form of speech, and yet, unlike Zana's (and Antigone's), this transgression seems less voluntary and more coincidental. Emine Ayna's controversial words were uttered in a press conference she held with the Democratic Society Party (DTP)'s leader Ahmet Türk to respond to terrorism allegations that the Supreme Court's attorney general had brought against the party in November 2009. The Constitutional Court was expected to make its decision soon, and indeed, a few days later, its members unanimously voted to disband the DTP. Kurds believed the decision to be political rather than legal, since the allegations and the decision were triggered by recent events.

Two months earlier, thirty-four members of the guerrilla organization the Kurdistan's Worker's Party (PKK) had entered Turkey from Iraq in response

Figure 4. Pervin Buldan, MP at the time when these shots of gas canister injuries were taken. (Özgür Politika Archives)

to the PKK's leader, Abdullah Öcalan's, call to embrace the government's Kurdish initiative.[36] The government had ordered several district attorneys to meet them at the border and had released the arrivals without opening any investigation. Allegedly this was also a political decision aimed at showing the determination of the dominant party in the government (Justice and Development, or AKP) to bring an end to the war against the PKK and to pardon PKK members. Everything was going according to plan until fifty thousand Kurdish people gathered to welcome the guerrillas, thus hijacking the event from government control and transforming it into a celebration of their fighters coming home alive and victorious. As a result, the government received intense criticism from the nationalist public. It soon found itself in a difficult position, since it had failed to pass any regulations to handle the returning guerrillas or to establish an official framework for its Kurdish initiative prior to these events. It therefore hastily denounced the celebrations, rushed the decision of the Constitutional Court regarding the DTP, and blamed Kurdish politicians for being indifferent to Turkish sensitivities. Despite its promises for a solution to "the Kurdish problem" that has haunted Turkey since its foundation, the government was now suddenly both defending the dissolution of the DTP and rejecting Kurdish politicians' insistence on an investigation of the conditions of Abdullah Öcalan, who had been in solitary confinement in a Turkish island prison since 1999. Among Kurds it was rumored anxiously that his health was deteriorating.

In the press statement given by the DTP prior to the Constitutional Court's decision, a journalist asked about what Ayna and Türk thought would happen to the Kurdish initiative if the party that represented oppositional Kurds were to be closed down. To this question, Emine Ayna responded with a laugh and said that the initiative was over. But why and how did she become, as a result of that statement and laugh, a "strange monstrous creature" without logic and sense and a name not to be uttered in the company of "ladies"? In her analyses of the creature Caliban in Shakespeare's *The Tempest*, Lupton argues that "in modern usage, *creature* borders on the monstrous and unnatural, increasingly applied to those created things that warp the proper canons of creation."[37] By using the word "creature," then, the vice prime minister was implying that Emine Ayna was unnatural, reminding one once again of Antigone. Butler argues that one of the crimes Antigone commits against the state is the fact that she, as a woman, is assuming sovereignty and manhood in her speech act.[38] Stating that the Kurdish initiative was over before the government had declared any such thing, Emine Ayna also claimed a sovereignty and thereby a certain masculinity that was denied to Kurds in general, let alone to Kurdish women in Turkey.

The Kurdish Movement has been arguing since 1993 that it has been willing to peacefully solve the Kurdish issue within Turkey's national borders through democratization.[39] They also argue that the government has been unwilling to accept their proposals, deceived them numerous times, and restarted the war by attacking their base in the mountains of Qandil. Given international regimes of law and peace-making that reinforce the asymmetry between state and non-state organizations, employing such a discourse is mandatory for the PKK to become recognized as a legitimate actor and to acquire intelligibility in various publics. However, such a discourse also establishes the state as the only sovereign agent able to make decisions of war and peace. Kurds, in contrast, must commit speech acts that explain their commitment to peace and democracy, and they do so over and over again. Emine Ayna's declaration that "the Kurdish initiative is over" goes against the grain as an attempt "to speak in the political sphere in the language of sovereignty that is the instrument of political power."[40]

Emine Ayna is also making a claim for the responsibility of the state to stick to a bargain it made to negotiate peace. By pushing the Constitutional Court for a decision against the PKK, the state effectively interrupted the peace process. While it remained unsaid, both the Kurdish and Turkish publics believed that the arrival of PKK members was part of a deal between Kurdish and Turkish political actors. Emine Ayna's speech act is both a testimony to that and an implicit call for accountability, but it cannot be heard as such. Butler's analysis of Antigone's speech is relevant here:

> Her language is not that of a survivable political agency. Her words, understood as deeds, are chiasmically related to the erring and defying imperatives at the same time, inhabiting the language of sovereignty at the very moment in which she opposes sovereign power and is excluded from its terms. What this suggests is that she cannot make her claim outside the language of the state, but neither can the claim she wants to make be fully assimilated by the state.[41]

This double bind of speaking in the language of the state and not being intelligible to it is what both Antigone and Emine Ayna suffer. Emine Ayna's speech act is not only strange but also uncanny, since it gives away the secrecy on which all asymmetric negotiations depend. It injects a kind of equality in a space of structured inequality and is therefore doomed to remain unassimilated.

While her interruption of the political process in the form of an "improper" speech act and with the "wrong" affect (laughter) made Ayna a "monstrous creature" in the eyes of the government, neither was she appreciated by the Kurdish public. And in that sense, Ayna was different than the "monstrously beautiful" Antigone. Rather, her laugh was like the tic of Claudel's Sygene de Coufontaine, which Lacan analyzes in juxtaposition with Antigone:

> When mortally wounded after receiving the bullet meant for her despicable and hated husband, [Sygene] refuses to confer any deeper sacrificial meaning on her suicidal interposition, there is no tragic beauty in this refusal — her "NO" is signaled by a mere repellent grimace, a compulsive tic of her face. There is no tragic beauty because her utter sacrifice deprived her of all inner beauty and ethical grandeur — they all went into it, so that she remains a disgusting excremental stain of humanity, a living shell deprived of life. There is no love here either; all her love went into her previous renunciations.[42]

I contend that Ayna's laughter, criticized openly by the Turkish state and not well received by the Kurdish political opposition either, expressed the tragic sacrifice that Kurdish women live through when they face a forced choice between freedom and death. It testified to the fact that by dwelling in the place of loss and demanding peace from the state in the legal realm, Kurdish women politicians are at the same time sacrificing their very reason to live: their freedom and their desire neither to forget nor to forgive.[43]

Since the beginning of the peace process the government, the public, and the Kurdish Movement agreed upon one thing: The tears of mothers should be stopped. In this they operated in a shared humanist framework, which Honig rightly describes as "mortalist." This humanism finds communality in death, lamentation, and mourning. As both Kurdish and Turkish politicians have many times repeated, tears and suffering know no nation or ethnicity; Turkish and Kurdish mothers of the soldiers and guerrillas who fight against each other are united in their suffering. According to the rules of the economy of mortalist humanism as it unfolds in the Turkish *polis*, women are distributed tears, and these tears are metaphorically the ink that enables the exchange between the Kurdish Movement and the government. As a woman, laughter, then, was the wrong emotion for Emine Ayna; she should have been sad if the initiative were over, since it would mean more deaths — this was tragic, not comic. Therefore, unlike Antigone, she was purely monstrous without being beautiful in this economy that she implicitly rejected. Her words singlehandedly interrupted the exchange, but more importantly, her laugh unmade the ink with which the exchange was being crafted. Therefore, something in the cosmos was injured by Emine Ayna's speech act.

According to Zupančič, who reinterprets Lacan's analysis of her, Sygene faces the modern tragedy between life and freedom.[44] By marrying Turelure, whom she hates, Sygene chooses life and dwells in the space of loss of freedom. Peace with the government and accepting its sovereignty are a similar sacrifice for Kurds and might have some tragic beauty. At the same time, however, watching peace be sacrificed by the government in the name of its sovereignty is where that beauty ends and gives way to a repellent grimace, a compulsive tic. The laugh, similar to Sygene's compulsive tic, made Emine Ayna into a creature with "too much body and too much soul," revealing her gendered ambiguity, her ethnic autonomy, and her mourning for a sacrifice that — after all — had no consequence.[45] The declaration that "the Kurdish initiative is over" was therefore a gesture of defiance (against the command of speaking the language of peace), of "Up yours!," as Žižek would have it, directed at the norms of intelligibility underlying the peace negotiations.[46]

Eventually Emine Ayna could not be assimilated. Deemed as radical and rigid, the Kurdish political movement first limited her appearances at public events and then reassigned her to a regional role. In 2016 she resigned from politics altogether when in the city of Cizre government forces burned dead, wounded, and living insurgents, killing them all. Her last public statement was, "I do not believe that one can develop a political solution with a partner who tortures dead and living bodies, destroys homes and burial sites, something that no human can accept."[47]

## Gültan Kışanak: Representing the Spine of Kurds

On December 28, 2011, at 9:37 P.M., Turkish air forces bombed a group of forty Kurdish villagers as they were moving from Iraq toward the Turkish border. The group was returning to their village, Roboski, located within Turkish territory. They were smuggling cigarettes, tea, and diesel oil into Turkey, packed on mules. United States Intelligence Services had supplied the Turkish Armed Forces with information based on drone surveillance that a group was on the move at the border, suspected of being Kurdistan Worker's Party (PKK) guerrillas. The Turkish Army took immediate action, and two Turkish F-16s hit "the target" without any further investigation. The next morning relatives found thirty-four dead bodies. In the following days a few survivors and the villagers stated repeatedly that the smuggling of small goods to meet their financial needs in an area of poverty was common and well known to the security forces.

Turkish media only reluctantly reported the deaths, and it was only after Kurdish and other alternative media established the fact that those killed were civilians that the Turkish media admitted that the dead were probably not terrorists. In the coming weeks, however, the government accused the victims of lawlessness and criminality, and in a news interview, the minister of interior declared them to be "extras" in terrorism, suggesting that their smuggling activity aided terrorists. The president and the government also declared that such collateral damage was inevitable in the fight against terrorism, which would end only when they succeeded in eradicating all terrorists from the area.

Twenty-eight of the thirty-four dead belonged to the Encü family. Having lost most of their sons, the Encü family was taken to be suffering a literal and metaphorical genocide, and their lot soon became an allegory for the Kurdish nation, a nation without a state, dispersed among the four nation-states of Iran, Iraq, Turkey, and Syria, and facing repression and violence in each. The villagers of Roboski were killed while crossing the nation-state borders illegally, and yet the blood they shed bore witness to another nation that haunted

Figure 5. The
funeral in Ro-
boski: The Spine
of Kurds (photo
by Mahmut
Bozarslan, (VOA
Turkish)

from within and across these borders — that of Kurdishness. Their funeral was attended by thousands, and the image of thirty-four caskets carried on the shoulders of villagers lined up in a slight curve, imprinted in the Kurdish consciousness as the "the spine of Kurds."

Many people, including leaders of civil rights and feminist organizations, visited Roboski during and after the funeral. Kurdish deputies remained in the area for a longer time and listened to the stories of mothers, fathers, sisters, and brothers. They came to Roboski not only to share the pain of the families, but also to challenge "the frame" within which the killings and the funerals were interpreted.[48] The government had refused to recognize the atrocity of the event, denying dignity and citizenship to the dead by prohibiting a national mourning and by blaming the dead for their own deaths — they were, after all, smugglers and enablers of terrorism. The image "the spine of Kurds" disrupted this frame by bearing witness to the fact of a stateless nation bleeding through the borders of existing nation-states and forming itself in flashes of intensely affective scenes. Nevertheless, words still failed the witnesses, their experience captured by conventional rhetoric.

On the surface there were the questions of Kurdish citizenship. To what extent would this be an important event for all of Turkey? Would it become visible in the national public space or remain a local event interesting only to Kurds? Did these boys, who were denied equal citizenship in their lives, die "into and for a citizenship" that could not include them except in their death?[49] Could mourning their death as a national tragedy stabilize "the norms upon which citizenship is based?"[50] Or would their deaths, as their lives, remain unaccounted for in the national-legal order of Turkey?

Both Kurdish politicians and Turkish civil, human, and women's rights organizations answered these questions from the perspective of mortalist and moralist humanism: Roboski villagers were poor, and they were smuggling because of their poverty. Most of those who died were children, so how could they be guilty?[51] Several of them were going to the university and high school, and they were going to buy books and make their earnings into pocket money. Finally, how would any human being not show empathy to the tears of the Roboski mothers? Screenshots of the dead boys' Facebook accounts were circulated, inciting people to identify with their concerns, sufferings, pleasures, and desires. In other words, despite the government's attempt to create a rift between those annihilated by the military and the proper citizens of Turkey, activists were trying to reframe the events by foregrounding shared vulnerabilities, compassion for the poor and children, and (middle-class-based) human commonality (going to the university, being Facebook users, etc.) in order to create a larger community of conscience that could participate in the mourning and tears of mothers. Despite their good intentions, these initiatives barely escaped a reductive utilitarianism in which tragic death becomes translated into a sacrifice that provides those who remain alive with the opportunity to create an improved polis. Kurds and Turkish activists who identified with them wished these deaths to be "useful," become a "lesson," a bridge between Turks and Kurds, thereby opening a new page in Turkey's political history.[52]

Two months later, in the beginning of March, Prime Minister Recep Tayyip Erdoğan's wife, Emine Erdoğan, visited the Roboski mothers. Meanwhile, Erdoğan himself continued to voice his anger toward those "who sat down and stood up saying Roboski," and he scorned politicians and journalists alike for not letting the event be forgotten.[53] Eventually, he promised monetary compensation to the relatives of the victims. The relatives had a history of having worked as village guards, financed and armed by the government to assist the military in its fight against the PKK, and hence were no strangers to cooperating with the state and engaging in an exchange relationship with the government. Still, they rejected the compensation and asked instead for those responsible to be made accountable.

The Roboski case was a turning point for Kurds in Turkey because it showed the limits of their citizenship and testified to the failure of the state to mourn "innocent" Kurdish deaths. On the contrary, now, these deaths were turned into "a cypher" for the "serially unachieved and constitutionally unachievable citizenship" of Kurds.[54] It also once again made clear that, despite the government's statements to the contrary, little had changed in Turkey in terms of accountability, since nobody was charged with the killings. At the same time, however, the Kurds' discontent about both the failure of the state's accountability and its inability to transform the mourning for Kurdish deaths into a national sentiment could find a language only in the rational public register of demands and thereby also partook "in the ghoulish, vampiric consumption of" the Roboski boys' bodies:[55] Kurds wanted more democracy, empathy, and recognition to forgive what had happened. Erdoğan wanted to give them monetary compensation. I am not denying the difference between these two, but what I want to underline is that all of the public actors sought to move the protestors from the sphere of lamentation, "which is inconsolable, into an economy of commensuration in which consolation or at least compensation is possible." "This logocentric economy of reasoning and exchange" made invisible another affective and political register for Kurds.[56] To illuminate that register I want to revisit the image of the spine of Kurds, which eventually found its verbal expression in the speech of the Kurdish female deputy Gültan Kışanak.

The image of the spine of Kurds reveals three forms of excess that critically address citizenship claims based on the mortalist humanism found in the opposition's discourse. First, the funeral is haunted by the fact that within the caskets there are no whole bodies, just melted flesh, incomplete organs, and burnt cloth. The Roboski group was bombed to pieces. Hence, when the villagers went to recover the bodies, they found only fingers and arms, intermingled bodies, and bits of clothing stuck on bones. The Muslim ritual of burial includes washing the whole body, putting it in a casket, and finally placing it wrapped in a white shroud into the burial site so that it embraces the earth without mediation and so that the body lent for this earth is given back to its real owner, to God. None of this could be properly performed, since there was no "body" to start with. In that sense, the Roboski boys, rather than dying into citizenship, had died into an abyss. Any wish, desire, or hope for a public initiation into citizenship and for equality was denied by this very curse/gift. They could not be represented; they could only become an allegory.[57]

The second excess was the geography that bled from within and without the national borders. How could the two laws that materialized in the event, one of the nation-state and the other of the nation without a state, be negotiated, worked through, represented, and commensurated? It wasn't that one of the geographies in question was fake. The Turkish geography where citizenship demands were made was real, materially and affectively, as was that of Kurdistan, with no state but with ties that were produced and reproduced by activities of neighboring, kinship, smuggling, and trade. Marriage bonds transgressed ethnic borders to the West and nation-state borders on the East. Exchange relations connected Roboski to Turkish cities through seasonal work and to the Kurdish territories in Iraq, Iran, and Syria through smuggling and trade. Social policy located Kurds within Turkish national space. They were, however, simultaneously situated in a larger Kurdistan by national imaginaries and by guerrilla warfare. How could the interval between Turkey and its Kurds be worked through?

The final excess put not only the discourses of citizenship and of mortalist humanism in question, but also existing discourses of Kurdishness itself. The Roboski event was a family tragedy that could not completely be assimilated into the melodrama of innocent Kurds versus the evil Turkish state. Most of the deaths belonged to one family and all the deaths to one village. This family and their village had already suffered through war in the 1990s, disappearances, the village guard system, forced displacement, deruralization, and poverty. Their destiny, unspoken as it was, reflected the internal inequalities among Kurds across class and regional lines, revealing that Kurdishness as such might be experienced as an imposition (a curse and a gift) by some, hiding the fact that the price of war and resistance is differentially distributed.

On January 3, 2012, only a week after the Roboski event, Gültan Kışanak, a Kurdish deputy and the co-president of the Peace and Democracy Party (BDP), made a much-acclaimed speech in the Parliament that lasted only ten minutes. At the time, she was one of the very few women politicians who had escaped being called a "falcon." Having spent her youth in the notorious Diyarbakır prison during the 1980–84 military rule (which the AKP government also condemned as it pitted itself against the previous more secular governments under the influence of the army), Kışanak was partially seen as a sacrificial figure with whom reconciliation might be possible.[58] The following are some excerpts from what she said:

> I want to address the people, who have a conscience. What happened
> in that village? No lie will be enough to cover this truth. When the
> warplanes bombed the thirteen, fourteen, and fifteen-year-old chil-
> dren, those children hid under the bellies of mules. They thought
> they could protect themselves from the bombs. But their torn bodies
> and their blood mixed with the torn bodies and blood of the mules.
> I suspect the humanity of those who don't get goose bumps when
> confronted with this picture. . . . When we took their bodies out from
> under the rocks, the child of a village guard and another were hold-
> ing each other's hands. Maybe, they thought, if they held hands, they
> would cheat death. . . . I suspect the humanity of those who do not
> apologize before this picture. One child was found with his index fin-
> ger pointing to the sky, confessing his belief in God. I suspect the reli-
> giosity, the humanity of those who don't question what has happened

there. Everybody knows what happened there. What smuggling? Can bringing one pack of cigarettes be called smuggling? The homes of those villagers are in Turkey; the land they cultivate is within Iraqi borders. Those villagers smuggle and transgress borders — in your words — every day in order to cultivate their land. For years, they have been doing this activity in the daylight and in the knowledge of the state and all the authorities. How can you now say, we didn't know, we didn't see, we thought they were terrorists, it is collateral damage? In a situation where thirty-four people died, nineteen of them children, a human being wouldn't say, "what can we do, it's an accident." . . . First, one questions their conscience, one becomes embarrassed, feels sadness and shame. . . . What terror? Is there anything you didn't excuse in the last ninety years, by saying that you are fighting against insurgents, against bandits, against terrorists? For ninety years you have been massacring a people: the Kurdish people. Who are those terrorists? Whose children are they? Did you once ask yourselves? There are a people there: A people with rights and with an identity. There is the Kurdish issue, there is no issue of terrorism. And there is the issue of lacking humanity and the issue of lacking conscience. . . . We will live here equally and free and dignified. Even if you do [a] thousand more massacres, we will not live undignified lives. . . . Some tell us that they will not let us take root. What root? What taking root? We have been here for thousands of years. Our roots are already in rocks, in stones, in the mountains of Gabar, Agiri and Cudi, in the rivers of Dicle and Munzur. We are here. What roots are you talking about? Our ancestors are here, our language is here, and our graves are here. . . . I see my anger as legitimate as a woman, as a human being, as a mother. I have gone there, I listened to them, and I hugged them. . . . We will never let this be forgotten.[59]

Much is lost when this emotional speech is put in writing, since what makes it unique are the intonations and the voice of the speaker. Moreover, there are constant interruptions from the floor, some protests and clapping, which give it the character of a dialogue with a chorus, rather than a monologue. I see this speech as dwelling in the limits between the work of citizenship and humanism that activists have done in relation to Roboski and the excess of Roboski that could not be represented in that work. Its power comes from the way Kışanak positions herself on the threshold of legality and illegality, private and public, communal and universal, the demands of peace and not forgiving or forgetting, between representation and allegory. The metaphor of being rooted in nature as Kurds evoke the flesh of the boys and their limbs and blood that became enmeshed with those of the mules and dirt. The Kurdish people cannot be uprooted; they cannot become the kinds of citizens the state wants; nor can the boys be separated from the mules and the rocks and be given a proper burial. They cannot be individualized and represented. They can only be performed momentarily and insurgently at the ruins of history, escaping the rules that govern speech and body. The ending of the speech, where she interrupts herself by saying, "I see my anger as legitimate" and brings closure to her words by reminding herself and others that she is a mother, a woman, and a human being, is the moment when her attempt to work the intervals, the thresholds, and the limits that she and the Kurdish people are occupying is most revealing. Desires that cannot be fulfilled in the given symbolic and political order, the anger that rejects reconciliation and the abyss of lamentation, must give way to intelligibility. That intelligibility, which Gülten Kışanak seems to need more than her parliamentary audience for whom her voice still remains a noise, can only be secured by recourse to the laws of the mother and of womanhood, on the one hand, and on an alternative humanity based on conscience (that takes account of the unintelligible), on the other. Gültan Kışanak became the first women mayor of Diyarbakır in 2014; she was arrested and has been in prison since December 2016.

## Conclusion

Antigone is a figure that continues to capture feminist imagination and spur debate. Especially so now, when bio-politics and sovereignty intersect to create impossible conditions of living and mourning in zones of colonialism, occupation, asymmetrical war, and conflict. Maybe, too, Antigone keeps inspiring feminists because she belongs to art and literature. The tragedy that befalls her (and everyone else in the play) can be addressed from within the safety of theoretical language without necessarily taking into account what really happens when women break the rule of the sovereign and exercise subjectivities that are injurious to law and order, to peace and reconciliation. The forces unleashed by Antigone's act bring doom and death to her and to those who are unjust to her; the play brings an end to all violence by means of the "tragic," which finally appeals to divine destiny and biological finitude. Living in Turkey and witnessing the struggles of Kurdish women under colonization and occupation, where violence does not come to an end, I am interested in what happens when Creon does not die, when Heamon marries another, and when Antigone is reiterated by other women and is thereby transformed into a historical force.

My analysis of Antigone, as I have emphasized throughout this chapter, is greatly indebted to her feminist interpreters. Butler's take on Antigone is crucial to my analysis, since it stresses the possible forms of kinship revealed by Antigone's desire, as well as how this desire undoes both the mutually constitutive realms of the political and the familial. Still, I think that this analysis must be complicated further because Antigone's loyalty to her brother, unintelligible to the sovereign, also involves a rejection and a betrayal of her other immediate kin. In my discussion of Kurdish women politicians, Leyla Zana betrays her comrades and her party for the sake of lamenting women, and Emine Ayna betrays the tears of mothers and unties the connection that is assumed to exist between her and other victimized and lamenting Kurdish women. In contrast, Gültan Kışanak, who made herself a name as a rational, agreeable, and accommodating woman politician, injures her own image and her own public work to become a Kurdish citizen of Turkey by evoking the existence of the bleeding geography beyond and within Turkish borders through the figure of the Roboski boys.

Honig's take on Antigone is situated in opposition to Butler's and promotes an agonistic humanism instead of a mortalist one. Whereas in Butler's take, the power of the figure of Antigone derives from lamentation and her performance and speech point to the communing and commensurating potentials of death, suffering, and vulnerability, Honig underlines how Antigone plans, strategizes, and conspires to become a political actor. I agree that mortalist humanism is an inadequate discourse to address oppositional politics. It neglects the fact that in lamentation and mourning there is always an excess that moves and compels people to speak and to act. This excess is the *Ate* of the community, its desire and its spirit, its singularity, "its maternal materiality," its Real, which is difficult, if not impossible, to look at and dwell in.[60]

In Honig's analysis Antigone's defiance is put in a sociological context, and she is associated with the lamenting practices of the aristocracy. Her acts are looked at from a utilitarian perspective in the sense of always already contributing to the making of agonistic politics. But, I argue, this might not be always so. Sometimes defiant acts might be useless, harmful, and destructive. Yet the women I have discussed here feel compelled to act as they do because a historical force works through them. This historical force cannot be sociologically grounded, nor can it be categorized as affirmative. On the contrary, directed more by the death drive (or maybe freedom drive) than anything else — like Ayna's uncanny laughter — their actions, gestures, and words emerge, despite their best intentions, revealing the impossibility of having a narratable past, present, and future as colonized subjects.

Indeed, in this chapter, I have shown that the impossibility of living in colonial conditions situates Kurdish women on the threshold between the demands of peace and the demands of not forgiving and not forgetting, between the represented and those who represent, between representation and allegory, and between the legal and the illegal. It is not (as Honig suggests) one law (the aristocratic) and the other (the democratic) that come into conflict in the play of Antigone. Like the women I talk about, Antigone has a cursed memory of incest, exile, and betrayal. I contend that it is the memory of being perpetually stuck in between the legal and the illegal that comes into conflict with "law" that produces Antigone and the women I discuss. Their acts are not entirely mimicking the sovereign state as Butler would have it, nor does their claim to sovereignty reside entirely in their willingness to achieve their ends, as Honig has it. Their acts are sovereign nevertheless, because they embrace the fact that they dwell in the zone between legality and illegality and put their bodies and speech to use as pure means without a foreseeable end.

# 4

# Kurdish Women Politicians at the Border between Body and Flesh

Occupation is both a legal and an affective category, at once a regime of power and a structure of feeling that shapes the logics of rule while transforming space, place, nations, and communities.

— MONA BHAN AND HALEY DUSCHINSKY, "OCCUPATIONS IN CONTEXT"

The colonial subject is a man penned in; apartheid is but one method of compartmentalizing the colonial world. The first thing the colonial subject learns is to remain in his place and not overstep its limits.

— FRANTZ FANON, *THE WRETCHED OF THE EARTH*

One's life, one's land, sovereignty, emptied out, in order for other things to pass through.

— AUDRA SIMPSON, "THE STATE IS A MAN"

Women's energy does not lend itself to a particular form or formalism. Instead her energy retains its fluidity.

— ABDULLAH ÖCALAN, *DEMOKRATIK UYGARLIK MANIFESTOSU III*

I first met Ayşe Gökkan twenty years ago in a two-day workshop that the Association for the Support of Women Candidates in Ankara was offering to women politicians. Ayşe was one of the two Kurdish women who were attending the seminar I was teaching on gender and power. At the time, she was working in the Bağlar district municipality in Diyarbakır for one of the first and few woman mayors in the region and in Turkey. Soon after we met, she started a project in the municipality on "honor killings," which was then the term used to describe femicide in Kurdistan to explain away the gendered effects of war and colonization.[1] In this project Professor Nükhet Sirman and Ayşe worked together. Through interviews and by collecting court, medical, and police documents, they tried to reconstruct murdered woman's stories. In order to do that, they traced how women interjected themselves into the worlds and words of their neighbors and relatives and into state documents that did not account for their lives and injury. Their meticulous work unraveled the multiple levels in which state and kin, official and everyday language conspired in the committing of femicide.

I have never forgotten two stories that Ayşe told me, and this is how I recounted them in an essay I wrote in 2012:

> One of these stories was about a woman, who was newly wed and had an elastic virginal membrane. When there appeared no blood after her first marital intercourse, her husband and his family blamed her for not being a virgin and threatened to send her back to her natal home for punishment. When in the following weeks they regularly tortured her in the bathroom of their house, she kept silent — even when she visited her family and they asked her how she was doing — out of fear for being publicly marked as dishonorable. Eventually, her husband and in-laws killed her. Her dead body was full of cigarette burns, shackle prints and bruises. Where did this family learn to torture and to put out cigarettes on another person's body? To kill slowly? When did the state normalize such refined engraving of death and violence on bodies in Kurdistan? In another case Ayşe cited, a woman reported to her neighbors, family, her husband's kin and the police that her husband was beating her and threatening to kill her. A message from her, starting with the words "I am afraid," still lingered in the voicemail of a woman's organization when Ayşe did her research. This woman had imprinted herself everywhere and yet, her story ended up with her death.[2]

When Ayşe told me these stories, they reminded me of Mahasweta Devi's *Douloti, the Bountiful* about which Gayatri Spivak wrote in a 1992 essay.[3] The main character in the story was Douloti, an Indian woman whose life was shaped by the ongoing legacy of the British colonial empire, the indifference of the Indian nation state's law to singularity, the bodily pains she suffered from the exploitation of her labor and sexuality, and last but not least, the violence of men in her life. She was depicted as bountiful because everyone took a piece of her body, utilized her, and claimed sovereignty and right over her. Douloti responded with generosity and shared her body, milk, and blood with them. At the end of a day when she was once again the target of different forms of violence, she died. It was midnight, the first seconds of the twentieth anniversary of India's liberation from colonial rule. She gave her last breath on the map that a teacher had drawn for his students to explain nationalism and left to dry in the schoolyard. Her blood from her torn body spilled onto the map. Devi wrote, "Filling the entire Indian peninsula from the oceans to the Himalayas, here lies bonded-labor, spread-eagled, kamiya-whore Douloti Nagesia's tormented corpse, putrified with venereal disease, having vomited up all the blood in her desiccated lungs."[4]

The stories of the women Ayşe collected in Kurdistan resembled Devi's story, since the various and multilayered forms of violence they were subjected to had everything to do with Kurdistan's colonial and patriarchal history. From the indifference of the police, to the ways in which desire gained a communicative value only through violence, to the torture that had become possible to imagine to inflict on a body, the life of the women victimized by femicide were structured by the conditions the colonial state had created. It felt like the violently drawn map of Turkey's Kurdistan was scraped on the deceased women's flesh as they tried to make a home in it. When I listened to those stories, I had little known that Ayşe would turn herself into the map of Kurdistan, albeit in a different manner.

In the 2009 local elections, Ayşe became the mayor of Nusaybin, a district of Mardin, Turkey, located right across from the city of Qamislo, which is within the borders of Syria. Before the borders between Syria and Turkey were drawn, Qamislo and Nusaybin — as many other cities on the two sides of those borders — made up one larger district. It was only after the mining of the borders in 1954 that the everyday activities of those cities became disconnected and the trade between them was made illegal. Still, the border remained porous, and transactions of brides, goods, people, and political ideas in both directions continued securing a sense of "popular sovereignty" among the inhabitants.[5] After the Syrian Revolution and the Rojava Revolution that followed, these transactions become intensified as increasing numbers of young men and women from (Turkey's) northern Kurdistan, lured by the idea of having an autonomous government and fighting a globally acclaimed war against ISIS, joined the Kurdish fighters in (Syria's) western Kurdistan.[6]

Meanwhile, Ayşe and the Kurdish Women's Movement declared Nusaybin a woman's municipality. During her time in office, Ayşe held meetings with women residents, convened conferences, and invited Kurdistan's and Turkey's feminists to the city. She prioritized women's employment and services for women, created a gender-equal budget, and passed decrees that prevented men who were domestically violent from receiving jobs in the municipality.

"Haunted" by all the femicide that occurred in the region, Ayşe and her co-workers made sure that no woman would face a similar destiny in the city she governed.[7] As revolutionary as these policies were for a public office, however, this was not how Ayşe became a public figure in Turkey.

When the Turkish government decided to build a wall between Syria and Turkey to securitize and stabilize its border with Rojava and the rest of Syria, protests were unleashed around Kurdistan. Although the government promoted the wall by arguing that it would stop the entry and exit of "jihadi" fighters in Syria, which by then had grown into an international problem, Kurds believed that the policy was specifically tailored against them, since there was some convincing evidence that the government was in reality providing weaponry, health care, and leadership for certain factions of Islamist fighters.[8] The wall, Kurds in Turkey believed, was aimed at preventing them from giving logistical support to the armed forces and people of Kurdish Rojava in the form of goods, fighters, and spectatorship.[9] As importantly, the wall had symbolic meaning. Now, because of the Rojava Revolution and the autonomous regional government of Kurds in Syria, Kurds in Syria and Turkey felt closer to each other than ever. They both adhered to Abdullah Öcalan's ideas of democratic confederalism and regional autonomy and followed the leadership of the Kurdish Freedom Movement. The wall targeted their affective proximity and intimacy and would force separation. It would declare Turkey's sovereignty over its Kurdish territories exactly at a time when it had become most fragile because of the permeability of its borders.

In her capacity as mayor, Ayşe wrote a letter to the military commander in Nusaybin, to the governors of both Nusaybin and Mardin, and, finally, to the minister of interior to inquire about the wall. Who had authorized it, and what was its legal framework? Under whose jurisdiction was the wall, and why was it being built? She also demanded an audience to explain her objections. Having been denied a response to her requests, on November 1, 2013, Ayşe crossed the border by tearing apart the barbed wire separating Nusyabin and Qamishi. She sat down in the minefield between the two cities and began a hunger strike. When a government spokesperson declared that she was just performing "a show," she turned her hunger strike into a death fast.[10]

Ayşe's hunger strike — and later death fast — evoked different temporalities.[11] First, there was the history of Turkish nationalization and the building of its national borders, which artificially separated Kurds from each other. People had died or been injured crossing these borders while being pursued by the border patrol for "illegally" trading goods or people through the mined landscape. Second, there was the temporality of the war and revolution in Syria. When ISIS attacked the border town of Kobane a few kilometers west of Qamishli, people had gathered in Suruç and watched the explosions and battles from afar when their kin and — at times — their own children fought. People from Nusaybin had also gathered on the border to give support to their neighbors. Some of them even had managed to cross the border and join the fighters on the other side, despite the attempts of the border patrol to stop them.

In order to talk about "an animated state in which a repressed or unresolved social violence is making itself known," Avery Gordon uses the concept "haunting."[12] It seems that when Ayşe tore the barbed wire apart, she was haunted by the different temporalities of the pierced, walled, and wounded geography of Kurdistan alongside the flesh of the victims of femicide. She felt there was something to be done and moved with great urgency.[13] After having tried all the official channels to stop the building of the wall, the time for "refusal" had come for her.[14] She simply could not allow another part of the "geography" she belonged to, and with it another piece of dignity of the Kurdish people, to be stolen. The following is another excerpt from the same article I wrote, four days after she crossed the border:

> Right now, Ayşe is sitting in the middle of the mines. The people of Nusaybin, who are supporting her with their children, are being tear gassed day and night. On the other side of the border, the people of Qamisli are saluting her with drums and pipes. . . . Ayşe is on the border of hunger, on the border between life and death, on the border of a country and in the middle of another one. She is on the border between femininity and masculinity, the representative and the represented, the state and truth. A wall is rising up at the border. Between us and Ayşe. In the middle of Ayşe's body. I once again think of Devi's story. Men's offices remain indifferent to Ayşe, her requests and responsibilities. Another femicide is occurring in front of us. . . . There is a need to end the carving of borders on women's and people's bodies, the carving of bodies on maps and the carving of maps on lives.

Following Castro, who writes that "by occupying the place that has no place in the Symbolic order, politics . . . refers to the conflict that force the social to confront its deficit, the uncounted, those who cannot be recognized within its Symbolic order, those whose needs and interests are never counted as 'real' needs and interests," I argue in this chapter that acts like Ayşe's are deeply political.[15] Ayşe's protest against the wall and for unity with the other side of the border brought political representation to crisis and "showed" that which lies beyond it. Ayşe forced an encounter with the unrecognized needs and interests of Kurdish people and their desire for forms of togetherness forbidden by the Turkish state. Further, by occupying the border/the no place between Turkey and Syria with her flesh, Ayşe transformed it into a "demonic ground," paving way to new ways of imagining it, as a place that is inhabited rather than an emptied-out vessel of colonization.[16] This chapter explores the ways in which women politicians like Ayşe challenge national borders with their bodies/flesh. It discusses how their longing, anger, love, and desperation appear as "symptoms" of the existing order and bring the symbolic into crises.[17] I also contend that with their urgent acts, women politicians use their skin to make metaphors literal. Like Douloti dying on the map of India, Ayşe sits and starves herself between borders that divide Kurdistan. As Douloti unmakes the map with her blood and vomit and literalizes abjection, so does Ayşe achieve the same effect by putting her starving flesh in the no-place between borders.

On the one hand, Ayşe's bodily defiance, her occupation of the mined border, and her claim of it for the Kurdish people, and on the other, starving herself, inflicting pain on her own body, and risking her life, made visible the impossibility of Kurdish lives under occupation. Her body stood against territorialization and shrinkage. Her supporters on both sides of the border testified to the connected geography of Kurdish everyday life and imagination. Eventually, after Ayşe's situation became the topic of many newspaper columns, the government promised that it would stop building the wall. It was then that Ayşe ended her hunger strike. When the state started building the wall again in 2016, Ayşe was no longer the mayor of Nusaybin but still active in the Kurdish Women Freedom Movement. As I write these words, she is in prison charged with terrorism and terrorist propaganda, begetting once again the question I raised in Chapter 3: "What happens when Creon survives Antigone's act and remains in power?"[18]

In Chapter 3 I discussed the ways in which women politicians push the limits of the political and thereby enact an alternative feminine political imagination. I argued that occupying these limits exposes the incongruence between the law and Kurdishness and the impossibility of living under colonial conditions. I also explained how women politicians use speech as pure means without a foreseeable end and how, by making difficult (conscious or unconscious) decisions about what to say and what not to say, they develop a Kurdish feminine form of life that can be cited and reiterated. This chapter looks at how woman politicians use their "flesh" to *show Kurdishness* and its troubles. While the women I discussed in Chapter 3 use the floor of Parliament or statements to the press to address a broader audience, the women I will talk about in this chapter transform the limit between flesh and body into a means of addressing others, refusing the state and claiming autonomy for women and Kurds. Once again in this chapter, I show, it is through Kurdish

Figure 6. Ayşe Gökkan in hunger
strike (Özgür Politika Archives).

women politicians that the *Ate* of the Kurdish community becomes a matter of
politics. Despite the fact that Kurdish women politicians eventually "step back
into the symbolic order," this *Ate* lingers, haunts, and survives.[19]

Another theme in this chapter will be how the state seeks to reduce Kurds
to either flesh or the body; that is, to the raw material of violence or to individualized criminal bodies. Women politicians respond by occupying the
limit between flesh and body — which I will denote by the expression "flesh/
body" — and by realizing an impossible togetherness. In the images of Ayşe that
circulated, she is shown as a lonely body. However, in her loneliness, she is not
individualized. On the contrary, revolutionary acts that reveal "the failure of
the symbolic" necessitate the annihilation of subjectivity and the unmaking
of the body's borders.[20] Sitting in the middle of the mines that go through the
landscape of Kurdistan, Ayşe ceases to be a mayor. She "enfleshes" occupied
and divided Kurdistan by making herself absolutely vulnerable.[21] I would also
argue that in her act Ayşe mobilizes that part of herself that escapes a liberalism that commands "live" rather than "live a form of life."[22] Her image in that
sense is an invitation not for recognition or for "empathy," but for rebellion
and refusal.[23] This chapter relies on such images of the flesh/body that claim
autonomy and perform "resistance in vulnerability."[24]

## Images

Various scholars have shown the crucial role that images play in the constitution of political imaginations.[25] Images enable people to envision the political communities they belong to and the borders of those communities. They
produce the means through which people give meaning to political turmoil.[26]
They also help imagine new ways of being, becoming, and relating.[27] In an
article titled "Pornographic State and Erotic Resistance," I argued that in Turkey, images play a crucial role in organizing the fascination with and desire
for Kurds into a national sentiment.[28] Images of tortured, killed, gassed, and

beaten Kurds render them available for collective violence, discrimination, and possession. I also explained the different technological, affective, and aesthetic modalities by which such rendering is made possible and how such modalities feed into an obsession with Kurds and Kurdishness. The Turkish state imposes poses on Kurdish bodies and produces "frames" within which Kurdish bodies will be experienced and interpreted.[29] Kurds, in contrast, produce their own images in order to transgress the frames imposed by the state. They corrupt the state's frames and inject new bodies into the picture. These new bodies, such as those of dancing guerrillas, stone-throwing youth, or politicians walking toward a police barricade arm in arm, make new ways of sensing possible and produce new understandings of beauty and fascination. As the women politicians that I discuss in this chapter challenge national borders and the borders between flesh and body, their images destabilize the borders between what is seen and unseen, what can and cannot be represented, giving rise to new imagos and new political imaginaries.

Aside from Ayşe Gökkan's image, I will dwell on three more images in this chapter. Two of these images are taken in protests. One shows MP Sebahat Tuncel as she tries to slap the face of a police chief during the Newroz celebrations in Silopi in 2012. Another depicts MP Feleknaz Uca as she tries to protect a woman from police aggression in a protest that took place in 2016 in Diyarbakır. Both images testify to togetherness beyond the borders of state institutes. By juxtaposing Sebahat Tuncel's and Feleknaz Uca's images I also develop a reading of the changing meanings of bodies and flesh, reconfigured spatialities and distances, and symptomatic affects as they occur in a given moment. Specifically, I trace both how the Turkish occupation was transformed and the stakes for Kurds have changed during the peace process and after the Rojava revolution. The strangulation of space and bodies has become a crucial modality of Turkish colonization as Kurds have shifted from a politics of recognition and negotiation to one of refusal and autonomy.

The last image I will take up is a photo of MP Gültan Kışanak embracing a guerrilla in the border city of Şemdinli in 2012. This photo enables me to further comment on the capacities of flesh and the impossible togetherness that woman politicians achieve through occupying body/flesh. By embracing the guerrilla and attaching her flesh to his, Gültan Kışanak invites him into the frame opened to her as an MP and incites the public to talk about what has been excluded from the sensible. Dwelling on this photo also paves the way to my next section, where I discuss guerrillas and their struggle to perform alternative ways of being human.

The images I examine in this chapter have not been produced out of nowhere but follow certain visual lineages that developed at the margins of the mediated public in Turkey, specifically during the first half of the 2010s. First, as I have discussed in Chapter 3, with the increase of Kurdish women politicians in the Parliament and in municipalities, the fight of the state against them became more violent. Each time they participated in a protest, they were singled out, tear-gassed, shot with rubber bullets and gas canisters, and soaked with pressurized water cannons. This resulted in images of women politicians reduced to their body parts and "ungendered" flesh while testifying to the fact that "when the (master) signifier faces the subjectivity of the slave [and the colonized], the result is a wounding of the flesh, a somatic branding of the body."[30] The images I dwell on in this chapter come from that lineage. Specifically, as Feleknas Uca transforms herself into a shield to protect other women and Ayşe Gökkan starves herself for her people, they embrace the violence exercised on them in order to reverse the effects of that violence. Their acts restore the vitality and "sentience" of women whose injured limbs were isolated by cameras.[31]

A second lineage follows images that depict Kurdish people and politicians at the borders, in mountains — that is, at the limit spaces of Kurdistan. One tactic that Kurdish people adopted to prevent the outbreak of armed conflict in areas where the PKK and the Turkish army approach each other is occupying zones of war and combat as "human shields."[32] Pictures of long convoys on destroyed roads, crowds walking toward the zero degree of the border, and politicians addressing people in the middle of mountains during "human shield actions" give a different sense of Kurdistan as an opening, rather than an occupied land. This opening is located beyond the mountains and borders, where on the one hand, the guerrilla is, and on the other hand, the Turkish state is imagined to cease to exist.[33] These are spaces where the occupation becomes most visible — because of soldiers stopping the crowd from going further — and yet most fragile. All the images I dwell on in this chapter relate to this lineage because they represent moments when the body/flesh of an MP signifies an otherwise, a beyond the existing borders and a beyond the fragile sovereignty of the Turkish state. Hence, they are images of longing that transform "imagined spatialities."[34] In that sense they not only reflect but constitute new political imaginaries and introduce new mappings to the symbolic.

Images of politicians walking with people toward the police also circulate when the politicians join villagers who are protesting the building of dams or large military posts, which not only destroys the environment and prevents access to mountain routes, but also securitizes and territorializes Kurdistan as part of the Turkish nation state. Dams and military posts divide and shrink the Kurdish geography that the guerrilla movement connects and enlarges.[35] Women politicians' bodies, as they travel from conflict zones to protest sites,

contribute to imagining a connected and enlarged Kurdistan that goes against
the shrinkage the occupation enforces. Their presence also lends legality to
people's protests and human shield actions while destabilizing their own parliamentary identity.[36] They defy the state while putting themselves at risk, all
the while reducing the risk that people would face if the MPs weren't there
in the first place. The images I take up in this chapter follow this lineage,
where MPs use their "bodies" to prevent the rendering of their constituencies
into "flesh."

The images depict performances both for the gaze of the state and its marginalized Kurdish citizens. However, they are also for the wider civil society
to the extent that they incite a "non-governmental viewing."[37] Azoulay defines
"non-governmental viewing" as "a viewing that will turn the traces of constituent violence that became the law . . . into traces of disaster and that will show
the expanded field of disaster."[38] Women politicians' presence at these different events produces a continuity, which is otherwise erased when each event
appears as singular. This continuity has the potential of making people recognize the disasters that the sovereign law of the Turkish state enacts on Kurds.

Finally, as Kurdish women politicians make themselves present and available during these disasters, become objects of violence, or make their bodies
available for the use of people, they occupy a threshold between flesh and
body. They are not anymore the subjects of formal politics as MPs, nor are
they completely reduced to their flesh. This threshold is a particularly effective space for addressing the impossibilities of living under colonial conditions. Occupying this space invites people to witness both what is targeted by
the state and what survives the disasters that ensue.

## Flesh / Body

I owe the distinction between flesh and body to Hortense Spillers, who argues,
". . . before the 'body' there is 'flesh,' that zero degree of social conceptualization that does not escape concealment under the brush of discourse or the
reflexes of iconography."[39] Flesh is not a given but is produced by social processes that wound. As Weheliye reminds us, flesh, "while representing both
a temporal and conceptual antecedent to the body, is not a biological occurrence seeing that its creation requires an elaborate apparatus consisting of 'the
calculated work of iron, whips, chains, knives, the canine patrol, the bullet'
([Spillers,] "Mama's Baby," 207), among many other factors, including courts
of law."[40] Spiller's intention in conceptualizing "flesh" is to invent an analytic
of blackness that can account for the lives and afterlives of slavery. However,
I am encouraged by Weheylie — who proposes that "flesh" is a better way of

conceptualizing devalued lives in modernity than, say, bare life — to take it out of the context within which it was produced and use it for an analytics of Kurdish women's life under patriarchy, colonization, and occupation.

In my understanding, the concept of the body denotes how biopolitics produces the individual and the bounded subject and how the legal framework produces possessive personhood. Flesh, on the other hand, "interdicts the biopolitical inscription" and "indexes the body's libidinal energies and an erotic potential that remains unseen."[41] Flesh indicates an unmaking of subjectivity through the operation of law and a stripping from social identity. At the same time, it denotes what remains after bodily devastation and cruelty and what escapes ideological interpellation. Therefore, I think it is a useful term to express cruelty and oppression, the theft of desire and motive and joy, resilience and reversal simultaneously without letting the latter be overwhelmed by the former.[42]

Kurdish women's bodies under patriarchy are open to men's gratuitous violence. This violence and the "slow death" imposed on them reduce them to flesh, as we have seen with the victims whose lives Ayşe reconstructed.[43] Parallel to this, there is also the genealogy of massacre and torture that have turned Kurds into flesh. Kurdish women politicians' performances are always already haunted by these two lineages. When writing about black life, Weheyliye argues that "the hieroglyphics of the flesh do not vanish once affixed to proper personhood (the body); rather they endure as a pesky potential vital to the maneuverings of "cultural seeing by skin color" ("Mama's Baby," 207)."[44] What I understand from this in this particular context is that the ways in which bodies have been rendered flesh have longevity beyond the events to which they are attached, which is particularly influential for how we view things. Hence the viewing of the scenes I will talk about are informed/haunted by femicide and massacre. A reading of images and the relations that images reveal through the category of flesh and enfleshment enables the tracing of these structures "that render the colonial state a Man."[45] It is also crucial for appreciating both the force and the significance of the images I pick up in this chapter in the life of the Kurdish feminine political imaginaries.

Both Wilcox and Terrefe relate flesh to the concept of the "abject" as theorized by Kristeva.[46] According to Kristeva, the abject refers to a part of the self that must be rejected in order to acquire a self: "Abjection works symbolically to expose the psychic, social and political work necessary to preserve the illusion of whole bodies with unbroken surfaces, bodies that are made to appear whole on the basis of expelling the abject."[47] Bodies become flesh when that which is abject resurfaces and the body cannot appear as an unbroken surface. While causing enormous pain, this situation also challenges and destabilizes the symbolic order by making visible that which is excluded, endowing it with agency. In Ayşe's case, for example, and as far as the national body is concerned, what she makes visible is the abjected mined area between borders, that no man's land that separates neighboring cities. Meanwhile, her flesh, as that which hungers, urinates, and freezes, threatens to reveal the Real of her body and becomes a force that moves people and endows them with a "nongovernmental viewing" that sees the wall that is being built as a disaster in continuity with the mining of the border. Ayşe is never absolutely reducible to flesh, however, because of the title she holds as the mayor of a city. She rather occupies the site flesh/body as the other characters I take up in this chapter.

Finally, as Wilcox argues, "Power molds and constitutes the border of the body and state simultaneously."[48] Flesh, therefore, when embraced, challenges not only the symbolic but also state law. The MPs that I talk about in this chapter, by embracing flesh and its monstrosity and vulnerability, transgress the borders of the individual body while simultaneously transgressing the border that the state sets to isolate Turkey's Kurdistan from the rest of Turkey and other parts of Kurdistan. In that way both the feminine skin and Kurdistan's skin leak and show through the cracks of the mask of the MP persona of Kurdish women politicians granted to them by state law.[49]

## Sebahat Tuncel and Feleknas Uca: Performing Autonomy through Flesh

If the Turkish nation state performs itself through its borders and uses its eastern and southern borders to deny the existence of a country called Kurdistan (as Ayşe's case shows), ironically, invisible internal borders that separate Kurdistan from the rest of the country remap Kurdistan every day anew. One way this is done is through the geographical division of the country into seven separate regions. While these regions are supposedly divided according to their different climates, culture, and folklore, they also correspond to different ethnicities and political orientations. Kurds populate the so-called southeastern and eastern regions of Turkey, having enjoyed considerable ethnic diversity and autonomy before the Armenian genocide and the founding of the republic.[50] Today, although the division of different regions in Turkey has no governmental function, regions are still hermeneutical tools for the public to read the country, since they are used as units to conduct statistical comparisons. Numerical indicators of development usually set southeastern and eastern regions apart from the rest of the country as the "least developed," and, as a result of counterterrorism acts and securitization politics against the PKK, measures of emergency rule are normalized in these spaces, which further mark them as "different." Hence, epistemologically these regions (correspond-ing to Kurdistan) are publicly "known" to have distinctive characteristics from the rest of Turkey, all with negative connotations.

Internal borders between Kurdistan and the rest of the country also be-come materialized when Kurdish bodies travel in Turkey. When a Kurdish body leaves Kurdistan, that body must make itself invisible as a Kurd, since otherwise it is seen as a security threat or an object of hatred in other parts of the country. Lynching attempts, beatings, and killing of Kurds who speak Kurdish in public are increasingly regular events in certain parts of Turkey, which are designated to be dangerous for Kurdish bodies.[51] These hate crimes serve to purify Turkish areas from Kurds and the Kurdish language while giv-ing a sense of popular sovereignty to people in a country that is becoming in-creasingly authoritarian.[52] In bigger cities, where diversity is the norm, Kurds tend to live together in the same neighborhoods and work in the same places, producing their own habitat within the geography of Turkey.[53]

Ideas about how Kurdish women's and men's bodies are situated in relation to each other in Kurdistan are another way in which the imagined borders be-tween Turkey and Kurdistan are drawn. While popular culture depicts Kurd-ish men as more patriarchal, violent, and oppressive than their Turkish coun-terparts, Kurdish women are believed to be docile and obedient. That Kurdish fathers do not send their daughters to school or that they marry them against their will are stereotypes sustained through discourses of the state, media, and NGOs. Cultural texts that disseminate such beliefs have deep resonances among many people. In my fieldwork in different parts of Turkey, I have often heard that a marriage between a man from the "eastern" regions and a woman from the rest of the country would never succeed, since they have different "expectations" when it comes to gender relations. In that sense men's and women's bodies, how they dress, walk, behave, and speak, enact the invisible boundaries between Kurdistan and Turkey. These boundaries are reproduced ideologically despite the official state discourse that denies the difference of Kurds and promises equality to all. However, since they constitute Turkishness as superior to Kurdishness, they add further to the delegitimization of Kurdish demands instead of destabilizing state discourse against Kurdish autonomy.

My interest in this section is in two images where women MPs' bodies became the signs of other forms of boundaries between Turkey and Kurdistan and incited new ways of thinking about and imagining gender, borders, and Kurdishness. In these images women MPs used their body/flesh to limit state violence and claim autonomy for their people. One of these images was taken during Newroz celebrations in 2011 and is of the MP Sebahat Tuncel trying to slap the face of a police chief while soaked by pressurized water. The other one displays the MP Feleknaz Uca as she tries to protect different women from police violence during protests in 2016.

## A Slap in the Face of the State

The year 2011 was a particularly difficult one for the Kurdish MPs of the pro-Kurdish Peace and Democracy Party (BDP). The state had increased its pressure against them as a result of the collapse of the secret peace talks between PKK leaders and state officers in Oslo in 2009.[54] It had forbidden yearly Newroz celebrations in most places in Kurdistan.[55] House raids and mass arrests targeting activists in Kurdish cities aimed at outlawing the Kurdish Freedom Movement. Every day clashes took place between the forces of order and crowds protesting mass arrests and the prevention of gatherings. Every day, images of angry Kurdish MPs soaked by water cannons debating with the police were posted on the Internet.[56] The escalation of police violence toward BDP MPs came to such a point that the Human Rights Association felt the need to issue a report that condemned the police for intentionally provoking and targeting BDP MPs and for failing to investigate the death of two and the injury of 178 people during the protests. It was under these tense conditions that an image of Sebahat Tuncel trying to slap the face of a police officer appeared in newspapers and circulated in social media.

Sebahat Tuncel was elected to the Parliament in 2007 when she was in prison for alleged membership in the PKK. After winning a seat in Istanbul with 93,000 votes, she was released from prison and joined her party in the Parliament. In 2011 she was reelected. During this time Sebahat Tuncel was especially active in creating alliances between the Kurdish movement and feminist and leftist movements in Turkey. She was considered to be one of the most active woman MPs in the Parliament. Here is an account from one of the journalists on the scene on how the situation in Silopi escalated:

> On the morning of March 21st more than seventy thousand people celebrated the Newroz. 70 percent of the crowd was composed of women. Around 3 pm, the crowd started walking towards the Democratic Solution and Peace tent [created to promote a democratic solution for the Kurdish issue and peace between PKK and the state]. The police had put barricades to stop the crowd. Sebahat Tuncel and the police chief had a short talk where Sebahat Tuncel promised the chief that there would be no provocation coming from the crowd. The police did not allow the walk saying that it would disturb the traffic. Meanwhile the crowd started a sit-in to protest this. As Tuncel was

walking towards the crowd, the children threw two or three stones at the police and that is when the police started soaking the BDP mayors and MPs with pressurized water and then threw gas canisters at the crowd and gassed them.[57]

The journalist added that, since the alley where the crowd was sitting was very narrow, people could not escape the gas, and children and women were injured. Many lost consciousness. Also, gas canisters were thrown into the tent where the Peace Mothers sat. Soaked in water and watching all the women and children running around, Tuncel got very angry and tried to slap the police officer. The next day several people from the government issued statements condemning Tuncel, and columnists expressed their contempt, asking the government to "break the hands that targeted the police."[58]

Sympathetic journalists read the slap of Sebahat Tuncel differently: as the slap of the people. Equating the body of the policeman with that of the state, they attributed the reaction it evoked to the wounded pride of the state. For example, Ertuğrul Kürkçü wrote that Turkish people were used to seeing male MPs from the governing party or their relatives scorning or slapping the police. However, that a woman MP from an oppositional party would dare to oppose the police had shocked everyone who identified with "the phallic position" of the state.[59] Hakan Karakoca, while condemning the slap as violence, advised the public to recognize that the police action in the region had been of a much greater violence.[60] Both Kürkçü and Karakoca invited their readers to a "non-governmental viewing" of the situation. This would entail witnessing the continuously shrinking rights of Kurds and the disaster that the state condemned them to.

Writing about black women's anger, Judd invites us to ask why instead of remaining silent, women choose to show their anger despite knowing its risks: What do they think is at stake?[61] Sebahat Tuncel's face, which showed through the cracks of her parliamentarian's mask, displayed a pained anger rather than a proud one. Her slap was an "enough is enough" slap missing its target. It signified Tuncel's frustration and emerged as a symptom of the social order that did not care about Kurdish suffering and did not recognize the Kurds' dignity. As a representative of the people, she acted in the name of all those that were reduced to flesh by gas canisters and pressurized water. Bradley argues "that the agency of the flesh has to do with its generativity, its capacity to persist as a site for staging a retrieval, a recovery and a reclamation of a certain worth and dignity that has been lost."[62] Sebahat Tuncel's slap performed a border, a limit on what might be done to Kurdish flesh — Kurdish women's flesh specifically — and what transgressed acceptable violation. While her promises to the police before the gas canisters fell was to discipline the crowd into the liberal conceptions of what is "doable" (do not provoke the police) in line with the politics of negotiation and recognition that dominated the first decade of the 2000s, once the canisters hit the women and children, she acted on what was "necessary" for Kurds, their seemingly impossible dream of autonomy, and anticipated what was soon to come.[63] Moreover, she claimed autonomy for the Kurdish people not through an act of self-determination but through a gesture that pointed to the right to make the decision when an act of violence is too much. Autonomy in this context, then, appeared not as a matter of bodily persona and possessive rights but was instead closely linked to flesh and its generative capacity to retrieve worth and dignity. Sebahat Tuncel's slap makes one recognize that in the Kurdish case, as in any case of occupation, autonomy and the dignity of the flesh are the same. Autonomy is not a claim to individual sovereignty, but to saying "enough" as flesh. It is not an individual choice but a collective need. It is the self-defense of the community.

It is also worth noting that Sebahat Tuncel as a woman is saying "enough" not only to an abstract state, but to a patriarchal state. She places herself in the lineage of women struggling against gendered violence. If the crowd weren't "predominantly" composed of women and if the police had not targeted Peace Mothers in the tent with gas canisters, maybe the degree of police violence would still be acceptable to her. While gas canisters and pressurized water ungenders, Sebahat Tuncel's "no" is a gendered "no," targeting male power and defending a crowd that consists "predominantly" of women. In that sense the slap performs a gendered border between Kurdistan and Turkey. This gendered border is not the one imposed on Kurds by popular culture (which contrasts emancipated Turkish women and obedient Kurdish women) because it differentiates the Turkish patriarchal state from Kurdish women. Therefore, its instantiation produces new images for identification and inserts new imaginaries.

Sebahat Tuncel's slap denotes one way in which Kurdish woman politicians occupy the threshold between body and flesh and transform their bodies to pure means to perform autonomy and to enact an impossible togetherness with other women in time and space. While after the slap Sebahat Tuncel continued her political career, once the peace process collapsed, she was arrested. She has been in prison since October 2016, charged with terrorism and terrorist propaganda. The case that was opened against her because of the slap was heard in May 2016, and she was sentenced to one year in prison and a fine. Nevertheless, the political community of Kurdish women that she evoked with her slap and the desire for autonomy and for limiting suffering that her slap signified continue to shape the ways in which other women MPs act as flesh/body.

## Flesh That Does Not Let Go

After the peace process collapsed, in 2016, a new wave of mass arrests targeted mayors and MPs elected from the pro-Kurdish People's Democracy Party (HDP).[64] When the police arrested the co-mayors of Diyarbakır, Gültan Kışanak and Fırat Anlı, on October 25, 2016, protests broke out in the city of Diyarbakır, which was already under siege. One of the several MPs present at the protests was Feleknaz Uca.[65] Below are two images of her protecting protesting women with her own body/flesh to prevent the police from taking them into custody.

In the first image, she is standing in front of a woman to defend her against a civilian police officer; in the second image she is lying on top of another woman so that the police cannot pull the latter, isolate her, and take her into custody. While nationalist newspapers printed the second image with condescending titles and depicted it as the fall of an MP from dignity, the first image was circulated in the Kurdish press as a sign of pride.[66] The second picture also circulated in Germany where Uca was born. Sharing with the Turkish state the same gaze but differing in their interpretations, German politicians communicated their disappointment to the Turkish government for having put an MP in such a situation.

Feleknaz Uca's images resemble Sebahat Tuncel's in the sense that both are trying to limit police aggression. There are other aspects, however, in which they differ. First is the expression on Uca's face: rather than being sad and in pain as Sebahat Tuncel was, Uca's face challenges the civil police with its determined and proud expression. Mouth closed, she refuses the communication that Sebahat Tuncel's open mouth suggested. Secondly, whereas Sebahat Tuncel's slap performed a border between the police and the entire crowd,

Figure 8. Feleknaz Uca protecting a woman from the civil police (Özgür Politika Archives)

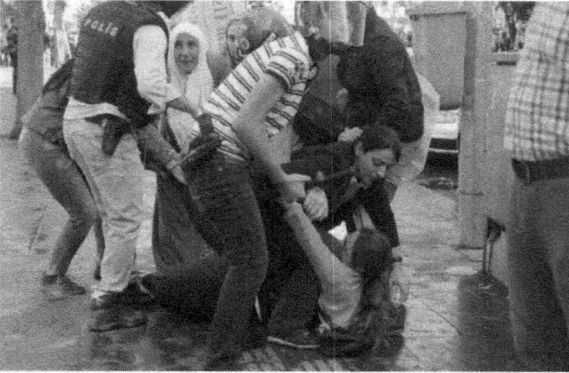

Figure 9. Feleknaz Uca preventing a woman from being taken into custody. (Özgür Politika Archives)

Feleknaz Uca protects each woman separately, occupying the in-between of the policeman's body and women's flesh. Finally, while Sebahat Tuncel is reacting to the gas canisters and pressurized water that ungenders Kurdish flesh, Uca is struggling against individualization and the will of the law to give a name and body to people participating in the protests by arresting them.

Feleknaz Uca's performance cites performances where Kurdish women MPs try to protect protesting Kurdish people with their presence on the scene. However, while before, this protection occurred more or less abstractly — that is, their presence gave some legality to the action and a negotiating power to the crowd — now, Feleknaz Uca's protection has become literal. Each and every woman must be defended flesh by flesh in a war zone that targets and constitutes individuals. One question, then, is how the scenery of the struggle changed; why did the abstract become literal? Or, to put it differently, how did the space around the MPs shrink? Related to that is another question: "What is at stake in Feleknaz Uca's anger?" Or, better yet, "How have the stakes changed in the five years between Tuncel's and Uca's actions?"

During the peace process and partially independent of it, a shift from ne-gotiation to refusal took place on the part of the Kurdish women's movement that is reflected in the difference between the images of Sebahat Tuncel and Feleknaz Uca. From the mid 2000s onward, the Turkish state controlled the psychology of Kurds through the hope and promise that the Kurdish issue would be solved through democratic means. A mode of negotiation charac-terized Kurdish spaces and psyche that disavowed violence and blame. Espe-cially in the political/legal realm, a shift from a "life of resistance" to a "life of negotiation" took place.[67] This involved NGO-ization, the proliferation of human rights discourses, and the neoliberalization of the economy, which "signaled a shift from reorganizing the self toward struggling against the col-onizing other to reforming the [Kurdish] self now bound to state law and institutions."[68] Sebahat Tuncel's slap is the result of the period of negotiation, where the slogan *edi bese*, enough is enough, mobilized people to pressure the state for peace.

During the 2010s the Kurdish position transformed in a number of ways. First, Abdullah Öcalan's ideas of democratic autonomy, women's revolution, and ecological life became popular among Kurds, delinking them from the liberal democratic utopia of capitalist modernity. Women left NGOs and be-came part of the Democratic Free Women's Movement as activists and mem-bers of the Freedom Movement. The ideas of democratic autonomy and free-dom also brought them together with different oppositional groups, giving them a leadership status and remaking their psychology. The Turkish "other" ceased to be constitutive of the Kurdish psyche, especially Kurdish women's psyche, as Kurds felt themselves elevated to universal subjecthood. The war against ISIS further helped, as it designated Kurds and, again, primarily Kurd-ish women, as the defenders of universal human values.

As far as the Turkish occupation is concerned, a shift from crowd man-agement to strangulation occurred. Writing about Palestine, Sheeshi states that strangulation involves "how the built environment melds and reengineers natural space and topography to reorganize the spatial syntax of the Occu-pied Territories in order to 'shrink and expand' space around Palestinians."[69] A similar process was enacted in the space around Kurds through dams, mil-itary posts, and housing projects while targeting their bodies through house raids and mass arrests. The overtaking of municipalities by the AKP through governmental decrees and the arrest of mayors that led to the protests where Feleknaz Uca's images were taken are also part of this process and designate the new mode of occupation that the Turkish state engages in Kurdistan. In this form of occupation what is at stake is the capacity to produce the social and the spatial. As Sheeshi further elaborates, the soldier, the police officer, and the appointed mayor, "whom the State inserts into [Kurdish] space," not only disrupt life "but constantly remind the [Kurd] of the State's invasive presence" and aim at breaking down Kurdish psychological coherence and social cohesion.[70] Feleknaz Uca's body/flesh then struggles for a togetherness the state makes impossible and for regaining the capacity to produce the social. If, in other words, autonomy meant in Sebahat Tuncel's case the ability to limit violence, now it has become the capacity to remain a collectivity. If it meant being seen as "humans" that suffer in the case of Sebahat Tuncel, it became retaining the generative capacity of collective flesh against the breaking down of the collective psyche in that of Feleknaz Uca.

In this new form of colonization, the Turkish state engages in two different endeavors at the same time. On the one hand, it reduces Kurds — including the MPs — to flesh by killing, beating, and mass arresting them. On the other hand, it individualizes and endows them with bodies that can be counted, numbered, accused, interrogated, and punished. Hence, while gratuitous violence marks Kurds as the ontological enemy of Turks, their elevation to bodies through the system of prosecution separates them from the collectivity. Meanwhile, as increasing numbers of MPs are arrested, lose their immunity, and are prosecuted, they also lose their capacity to make sites of protests safe for the people. MPs are absolutely profaned, with no remaining aura. Feleknaz Uca's attaching of her flesh to other women should therefore be read as an attempt to enlarge the space around them with her own flesh. Now that the aura, the abstract space around MPs, has been denied, skin has become the only gift she can give to other women as an immune surface that protects them from the touch of the state. In short, as the mode in which colonization and occupation changes, so does the defense against it, and each photo that circulates emerges as a singular allegory that collapses state's projections on bodies and produces knowledge about "ruination" in Kurdistan.[71]

Writing about the deaths of black women at the hands of the police, Patrice Douglass states that "when . . . women of color are victimized, the problem is cast as something other than a case of gender violence."[72] She argues that the core of Black feminist concerns is how to "account for the gravity of gender violence that lacks a proper name."[73] Sebahat Tuncel's and Feleknaz Uca's use of their body/flesh to protect other women from police aggression is also an attempt to name this violence, which remains unregistered in the symbolic order (including in feminist discourse) as gender violence. By putting themselves on the line as MPs with bodies that embrace flesh, Tuncel and Uca viscerally signal gender violence for what it is and link the scenes in which they find themselves with those that Ayşe collected and embodied in her own defiance. They make themselves part of a heritage of women struggling against male violence in Kurdistan and remap Kurdistan as a space where women resist rather than obey patriarchy.

Next, I will look at another scene that took place in 2012 and discuss a case where it is a man for whom the women politicians put themselves at risk and what happens when Gültan Kışanak introduces the supreme abjected subject in the Turkish state's order, the guerrilla, into the frame.

## Gültan Kışanak's Embrace

On August 17, 2012, a group of Peace and Democracy Party (BDP) members were touring the district of Şemdinli located at the border between Iraq and Turkey. Şemdinli is a familiar name in Turkey, since it is one of the places where the PKK has control over the surrounding mountains. PKK guerrillas and Turkish soldiers, who are located near the city, often come in conflict in this area. Recently, clashes had intensified, destroying nearby villages. It was common knowledge that the guerrillas were now controlling parts of the roads that went through the district. Therefore, and as expected, in the middle of the tour, the BDP convoy was stopped by a guerrilla squad that was conducting identity checks in the area — as a performance of acquired sovereignty. The convoy included the MPs Gültan Kışanak and Aysel Tuğluk, among others. The next day news broke that after the guerrillas gave a propaganda speech to the people in the convoy, Kışanak hugged them as they were departing. Images of her and a male guerrilla in an embrace while Aysel Tuğluk watched with a smile on her face were distributed widely in the hopes of inciting shock and awe. A few days later, newspapers reported that the guerrillas were identified, and the commander whom Gültan Kışanak embraced was suspected of having some time ago participated in an attack on a gendarme station that had resulted in the death of eight soldiers and thirty-two PKK members.[74] Soon, the attorney general prepared accusations against the MPs in the convoy and requested that their parliamentary immunity be revoked so that they could be prosecuted.

Figure 10. Aysel Tuğluk and Gültan Kışanak saying their farewells to the guerrillas (Özgür Politika Archives)

Meanwhile, Gültan Kışanak defended her embrace in a press statement with the following words:

> We knew that they had a checkpoint there. But we didn't know that they would let themselves be seen. Actually because the media was there, we thought they wouldn't. . . . We have hundreds of times passed checkpoints put there by soldiers. Each time we see some soldiers who are ready to embrace us. Yesterday, it was not different. If it weren't for this enforced hostility, we would embrace the soldiers as well. There are some soldiers who do not smile at us out of fear but salute us by winking their eyes. . . . Mothers who lost their children want us to curse those who are the architects of the politics of war. But I tell the mothers to pray so that God will give those people reason, conscience and a sense of justice. . . . The young people on the mountains are the children of the Kurdish people, our relatives, acquaintances, friends, kin; they are our children. Nobody can force us to treat them as terrorists.[75]

In her explanation of why she embraced the guerrillas, Gültan Kışanak makes two rhetorical maneuvers. First, through the concept of "war," she equates the two sides of the conflict: She could have embraced the soldiers on checkpoints just like she did the guerrilla. She is taking neither the guerrilla's nor the soldier's side, since it is not they who are the architects of war. Second, she introduces real or imagined kinship and "cultural intimacy" as a factor of how people are positioned in relation to what the state calls terrorism.[76] People are not going to call their relatives terrorists because the state wants them to. On the contrary, they experience this demand as a violation of their values derived from the kinship system in which they live.[77] Hence Gültan Kışanak uses both objectivity (two sides of a war are equals) and subjectivity (they are our relatives, children, friends, etc.) to explain her position.

These two positions correspond to two different ethical paradigms. On the one hand, Gülten Kışanak's stance toward the guerrilla is grounded in intimacy, relationality, and hence particularity; on the other hand, it is universal: War is bad, and it is those who are the real architects of war that should be cursed. Gültan Kışanak continues:

> I am also a mother. When I saw those guerrillas I experienced an intensity of feelings. Nobody would take a gun and go to death if not for a greater cause. Those young people will maybe lose their lives in a few hours by an air bombardment. How can conscience accept that?

Nobody forces them to go to the mountains. Nobody should think that we would fear them as threats. These are very complicated feelings. To run into people who have taken up guns for a freedom struggle has caused us to experience very complicated and difficult feelings. Have we adopted a discourse of hostility against Turkey? They are trying to prosecute us because we had a smile on our face. . . . Especially, as a mother realizing the imminent death they are facing has overwhelmed me with emotion. Only a few kilometers away from them there are soldiers equipped with world's most technologically advanced weapons. On top of this there are all those warplanes. These are people who can smile under those circumstances. One has to comprehend that.[78]

Several times, Gültan Kışanak evokes her complicated emotions. These are symptomatic of a symbolic order where the rights and interests of Kurds as they are cannot be represented. Most importantly, the love and sorrow they feel for the guerrilla must be continuously abjected and repressed. However, the image caught those abject feelings, and this brought the law of the state to crisis. Apart from love and sorrow, Kışanak also experiences guilt and wonder. On the one hand are the MPs endowed with parliamentary rights and immunity; on the other are the guerrillas who are at total risk. The guerrillas can be murdered easily, without any accountability. In that sense this is an encounter between Gültan Kışanak's body and the flesh of the guerrilla. Gültan Kışanak wonders and celebrates the fact that this flesh does not surrender and still has joy. Throughout her speech she is searching for words and experimenting with different rhetorical strategies to make people comprehend what kind of "truth" effect this experience had on her in terms of the power of flesh. And once again as she did before (see Chapter 3) she is making recourse to the laws of the mother and conscience.

While her words are powerful, I think what Gültan Kışanak performed somatically and aesthetically in the image of embrace is as interesting as what her words tried to accomplish emotionally, ethically, and epistemologically. By embracing the guerrilla, Gültan Kışanak in a sense becomes two. On the one hand, she is embracing her own monstrosity: what the Turkish state suspected all along is true. The Kurdish MPs have — to say the least — sympathy for the guerrilla. On the other hand, she embraces the abject of the Turkish nation with the very body and persona that have been granted to her by the law of the state. The embrace attaches her legal body and her persona grounded in her being an MP to the flesh of the guerrilla, which is open to harm, injury, and death. The Turkish publics' visual access to the guerrilla is normally always mediated by the gratuitous violence the Turkish state directs to them.

Hence, a guerrilla-seen is always already a corpse made invisible by the noise in which the discourse of terrorism envelops it. By attaching her body to the flesh of the guerrilla, Gültan Kışanak brings him into the stately frame as a living, breathing being who cannot be unseen. She thereby gestures to a different form of sensibility and legibility and opens up a different political possibility.[79] With her very body/flesh, she lifts up the guerrilla and introduces him into humanity while risking her own excommunication.

The Turkish newspapers fought against Gültan Kışanak's gesture by individualizing the guerrilla and giving him an identity and body. He is a known person, legible by the state, an attacker of a gendarme station. In order to explain what is at stake in this individualization, let me make a detour and discuss a scene in a recent movie titled *The End Will Be Spectacular*. Produced by the Rojava Film Commune, *The End Will Be Spectacular* revolves around the urban war between the youth of Kurdistan and the Turkish state at the end of the peace process. One of the main characters, a guerrilla commander, who joins the war at the request of the youth, is named Çiyager. Toward the end of the movie a military chief calls Çiyager by radio and tells him, "Çiyager, I know you. I know your name. I know where you come from and the actions you carried out." Çiyager answers back, "You might know my name. You might know one or two things about me. But you don't know who the Apoists are."[80] Çiyager refuses to be a subject of his life story. As the police chief individualizes him and tries to give him a body and subjectivity that can be convicted, deceived, or destroyed, Çiyager resists that: He is Apoist, nothing more, nothing less. Apoists are unknowable and illegible to the state; they are a collective entity. They enflesh Kurdistan and escape the state's ideological interpellation. Kurdistan, wounded, bombed, occupied also escapes the state in the last instance since it continues producing Apoists and remains "in excess of the discourse[s] that seek . . . to locate it, to know it, to translate its 'noncommunicability'."[81]

By attaching herself to the body of an Apoist and by occupying the threshold between flesh and body, Gültan Kışanak as a parliamentarian makes visible what the political system of Turkey refuses to account for. I would contend that this threshold between body and flesh traces a different way of being human. Putting Hortense Spillers in conversation with Sylvia Wynter's search for a new genre of the human, Weheylie writes, "In other words, the flesh is not an abject zone of exclusion that culminates in death but an alternate instantiation of humanity that does not rest on the mirage of western Man as the mirror image of human life as such."[82] When Gültan Kışanak asks for conscience and comprehension, she is asking for the recognition of a human who can have joy in the very instance of his death; who can find pride in his disappearance and erasure as the subject of his own life history. She is, in a sense, gifting her body, loaning it to the guerrilla so that he can become visible and imaginable without being a possessive individual himself.

## Conclusion

Despite the fact that three of the four woman politicians whose images I discussed in this chapter are in prison, what survives them is the tradition of flesh and its feminine capacity to name the unnamable by transforming skin into a gift. I started this chapter with Douloti the Bountiful. Let me conclude with the bountifulness of woman politicians who use their flesh to remap Kurdistan in ways that open it to forms of togetherness that the state interdicts and thereby perform different modes of autonomy. Ayşe Gökkan occupies the no-place in the mined field between Syria and Turkey to enflesh Kurdistan and to signify the desire to remain connected across borders. Sebahat Tuncel remaps the border between Turkey and Kurdistan as one between Kurdish women and the Turkish state and occupies the limit between body and flesh to say a gendered "enough" to the state. Feleknaz Uca uses her flesh to name police violence as gendered violence against Kurdish woman, all the while fighting for the right to remain a collectivity under occupation. Finally, Gültan Kışanak's flesh gives an aesthetic and ethical life to the guerrilla in public imagination. If the women in Chapter 3 performed the distance between Kurdish life and the law of the Turkish state and the impossibility of living under colonial law, the tradition of flesh that the women I discussed in this chapter built instantiates a new humanity where it is not state law but the law of the flesh and its openness and its pull to other flesh that shape being. In Chapter 5, I will further elaborate on these new ways of being when I discuss the figure of the woman guerrilla.

# PART III
*Guerrilla*

# 5

# Who Are We and How Must We Live?

Being a Friend in the Guerrilla Movement

. . . the question is not whether we engage in violence or not but an insistence that the time of violence is already here.

— ERIC A. STANLEY, *ATMOSPHERES OF VIOLENCE*

We must strive, in the face of the here and now's totalizing rendering of reality, to think and feel a *then and there*.

— JOSÉ ESTEBAN MUÑOZ, *CRUISING UTOPIA*

Tomorrow the cops could come back, or the bank, bringing the violence of speciation, against which there is just this constant and general economy of friendship — not the improvement that will have been given in one-to-one relation but the militant preservation of what you (understood as we) got, in common dispossession, which is the only possible form of possession, of having in excess of anyone who has.

— STEFANO HARNEY AND FRED MOTEN, *ALL INCOMPLETE*

The war has carried you to me, me to you and to many others. It has brought us to so many people we met, made us love them, and connected us to them and to some invisible things. And then it took us apart, sent us to other worlds, other mountains, other plains, other lands, other cities. . . .

— SELMA DOĞAN (C.N. ZINARIN), *ZINARIN'IN GÜNCESI*

When I did fieldwork in Turkey's Kurdistan, my friends in the Kurdish Women's Freedom Movement often told me that they hoped that one day I would be able to meet the women guerrillas of Kurdistan. As confident as they were in their own struggle against the repressions of the Turkish state, they felt that there was a reality of the Kurdish women's movement that lurked underneath the façade of everyday politics that could only become accessible by interacting with guerrilla women. I also knew from other friends doing fieldwork or NGO work in the region that villagers, young people, and women frequently insisted on bringing them to places near the mountains so that they could converse with the guerrilla forces. People thought that one should talk to these fighters if one wanted to understand the Kurdish resistance. Slowly but surely, such events engrained in many of us the idea that we would re-main deprived of the "truth" of Kurdistan and banished from what we were seeing, hearing, touching, and smelling there in a fundamental and yet in-communicable way, as long as we failed to encounter the Kurdish guerrillas of the mountains.[1] The guerrillas seemed to have a quality of "realness" oth-ers lacked, and, despite the fact that people attributed this "realness" to the discursive and ideological competence of the guerrillas, one quickly grasped that it rather stemmed from the place the guerrilla movement occupied in the Kurdish political imagination.

The guerrilla as a figure is "Real" because it is beyond everyday matters and outside of the colonized space of Kurdistan. It can only be integrated there as a trace: a picture in a house, a casket at a funeral, a reference in a song, or a name given to a newborn. Ghostly in the 1990s, when it first made its impact on people's everyday life, and mythological in the 2000s, when it retreated, this was the case even in the 2010s, when the guerrillas had become much more accessible to people visually, spatially, and ideologically.[2] Layers of linguistic and gestural veiling hid the guerrilla from the gaze of the state and the stranger, while the very same act of veiling made her omnipresent in Kurdistan's life. To the extent that the capacity to recognize the veil that sig-nals the absent presence of the guerrilla defined the landscape of Kurdishness, it remained both open and exclusive.

The guerrilla's designation as "Real" points to yet other qualities of the Kurdish political imagination. Occupying the threshold between nature and culture, life and death, present and future, the figure of the guerrilla is always already endowed with trauma, sublimity, and incomprehensibility — other characteristics of the "Real." The guerrilla is the one who dies for her people, walks the mountains, risks her name, and who replaces the intimacy with the family with that of friendship and the intimacy with the state with that of revolt. It thereby unleashes violence, destruction, sadness, and worry, longing, awe, pride, and love all at once. As a space of jouissance beyond pleasure and pain and as a manifestation of a death drive escaping narration and resisting representation, the guerrilla is she who disrupts the structures of intelligibility imposed by the state order and blows life into "Kurdish endurance."[3] The figure of the guerrilla also represents an immense effort and willpower to be "ethically otherwise."[4] Lightly armed, walking in small groups, dependent on nature for shelter and food and on the loyalty of people for survival, she is, on the one hand, immensely vulnerable. On the other hand, however, her body manifests both freedom and volition, and her words emanating from this body and validated by action carry a "truth" and "realness" beyond everyday conversation.

This chapter is an attempt to witness the women guerrilla's incarnation of the "Real" as she figures into the Kurdish political imagination. By using the questions of "Who am I?" and "How should I live?" that orient guerrilla life as entry points, I want to understand how the death drive of the guerrilla is animated and what form of life and humanness are produced in the mountains. My argument is that the guerrilla performs a human-as-friend genre in her struggle to decolonize truth, freedom, and being. In the mountains, which in the Kurdish imagination stand "for the order of things that we have left behind, the anticipatory mood that accompanies all claims of coming after something, and the unknown future that, for now at least, still beckons from the horizon," and under the constant threat of turning into a corpse, she remakes relationships, loyalites, bodies, and life and searches for laws and norms that are other to the colonial, capitalist modernity.[5] As she enfleshes the "not yet" and "the already passed," which is the time of revolution and "inscribes the flesh of" Kurdistan with her acts and speech, she becomes a figure whose constitutive exclusion and illegibility must be reckoned with by Kurdish people.[6] That means that Kurdish people must find ways to symbolize and signify her and in that endeavor change their social and symbolic world. But first, let me start by explaining why the figure of the woman guerrilla is a constitutive feature of the Kurdish Freedom Movement's political imagination and why it is primarily she who initiates this communication.

## The PKK as a Women's Movement

The PKK defines itself as a women's movement as much as a national liberation movement.[7] It puts great emphasis on women's participation in the guerrilla forces and leadership and believes that decolonization can only occur through the liberation of women and the norms they will perform and the laws they will animate through their collective organization.[8] According to the Kurdish Freedom Movement's interpretation of history, exploitative power emerged in human history with the dispossession of women from the means of production, self-defense, and knowledge, the devaluation of their reproductive labor and care work, and their consequent enslavement, which lasts to this day. This puts Kurdish men and women in different positions in the social order and the guerrilla struggle. Whereas "the structural violence" of colonialism "makes life unlivable" both for Kurdish men and women, the fact that women are in addition "subject to the hellish condition of fungibility" under conditions of patriarchy and its institutions condemns them to social death.[9] Becoming a guerrilla for Kurdish men entails a sacrifice, a giving up of a promised position and autonomy in the social order (gained in return for cooperating with patriarchy). In the organizations they create, therefore, men tend to replicate patriarchal agencies and relations to regain what they have given up. For women, on the other hand, there is no such position promised that they long for: they are "structurally" rather than "contingently dispossessed."[10] This makes them particularly suitable subjects for coming up with new laws for their desires, unsupported by the existing order, although this could not be accomplished by individual transgressions alone. Through their exile to the mountains and the organization, they can collectively find forms to their "way of not giving way to [their] desire" and become radical actors in politics.[11] In other words, since women are historically the first colony and enslaved on whose objectification the social order rests, it is only through women's liberation and an understanding of humanness and sociality based on the struggle for their liberation that society can be freed and delinked from the laws of family-ism, colonialism, capitalism, nationalism, religion-ism, industrialism, and science-ism — that create hierarchy and exploit people as well as nature. Women's performances crafted in communities that search for new ways of being and becoming can initiate imaginations according to which the world can be reshaped symbolically and materially.

Today women comprise more than one-third of the Kurdish guerrilla force. Together with its ideological commitment to women's freedom, women guerrillas explain why the PKK supported women's participation in the freedom movement by citing several other reasons. First, the party was in danger of turning into gangster squads in the early 1990s, when the war in Kurdistan was most intense. Patriarchal guerrilla leaders who monopolized authority, arms, trade routes, information, and relations with villagers threatened the leftist path to liberation. Against this, Abdullah Öcalan, the leader of the PKK, supported the women's struggle as they challenged the patrimonial structures of the organization, and this kept the risks under some control. In 1993, again with the support of Abdullah Öcalan, women formed autonomous armed units that disrupted channels of secrecy, transformed relations with locals, and monitored and limited abuses of power.

Second, Öcalan saw the great potential that women had for organizing society and social relations. Specifically, he encouraged women to play central roles in the insurgencies that erupted against the Turkish state in Kurdish cities. The channels of communication among women, their care and pedagogical work, and the fact that it was through women that the liberation ideology and practice could penetrate families made them crucial for revolutionary practice.

Third, the PKK also sees participation in the guerrilla forces as the most important way in which women can affect society. Women's participation in guerrilla forces enables them to develop their material, ideological, and organizational capacities and endows them with military and political skills to collectively regenerate and claim the means that have been stolen from them. Being a guerrilla, entering combat as women's units, and organizing autonomously gives women social and political recognition and transforms them into a constitutive power in the struggle.

Finally, women's participation in the guerrilla movement is crucial, because the Kurdish Liberation Movement, despite the fact that it relies greatly on family relations for support and recruitment, defines itself against the family institution ideologically. Family is where nationalism, capitalism, and patriarchy anchor themselves, enslave women, and shape individuals through intimately exercised power. It thereby forecloses rebellious and disorderly affiliations and futures. Separating oneself from the family is therefore a necessary condition for women to attain freedom, and this separation is best achieved by becoming a guerrilla. As I argued in Chapter 2, this also interrupts women's suffering in the household transmitted from generation to generation and enables the making of a new women's history and memory.

Women's presence in the guerrilla movement is a further reason that the PKK is seen as the "Real" among people and is endowed with a sublime force. The PKK argues that sexual relations between men and women under conditions of patriarchy, nationalism, and capitalism are the primary means by which women are subordinated by men and enslaved. Therefore, a voluntary critical asexuality exists among members of the PKK.[12] The guerrillas say that instead of heterosexual eroticism, a diffuse and intense eroticism is lived in the mountains as people passionately orient themselves toward nature, friendship, politics, and combat, all of which enable them to strongly sense the animating force of life.[13] Women guerrillas' refusal to reproduce through marriage and sexuality both endows their bodies with an auratic quality and transforms them into a collectivity inassimilable to the laws of the institutions of family, tribe, and kinship. Their non-heterosexual bodies are similar to that of the figure of the queer in the sense that both are negating a future secured by reproduction.[14] The body politics of the woman guerrilla is concerned with the generous use of bodies to transform the present, all the while being dangerous and lethal. Women guerrillas live in the limit between the past and future: they are already past, destined to die, un-reproductive, and anti-generational. Yet by living the freedom denied to Kurdish women by the state, patriarchy, and capitalism, they are bringing a foreclosed future into the present. Their presence in Kurdistan, Turkey, and the broader Middle East presents potentialities: the potentiality of recovering forgotten genealogies of defiant asexualities and the imagining of alternative and decolonial futurities.

## Meeting the Guerrilla

It was only when the peace process between the Turkish state and the PKK started in 2013 that I met women guerrillas for the first time. After the declaration of a ceasefire and the retreat of Kurdish armed forces from Turkey, we, members of the Women for Peace Initiative, struggling for peace between the state and the PKK, visited the women guerrillas in the PKK headquarters in the Qandil Mountains of southern Kurdistan. Our goal was to establish a women's side in the peace process, and as an initial step toward that goal, we were trying to produce a written report that included the perspectives of the women guerrillas along with the demands of women's organizations and women MPs.[15]

During the period between 2013 and 2015, when we visited Qandil, the mountain was unusually busy. It was frequented by relatives hoping to see their surviving sons and daughters they had not heard from in years and families trying to catch a glimpse of their children who were newly recruited. Journalists, national and international committees, official and non-official organizations, oppositional groups, and individuals populated the mountain. Guerrillas retreating from Turkey after the ceasefire and guerrillas leaving for Rojava to fight the ISIS contributed to the density, making Qandil a special spot in the world where time and bodies intensified. From a space that had been abjected by the global order, these mountains were transformed into a site of familial, journalistic, and political exchange. The guerrillas became so used to visitors that they even established a fixed program for them. Each guest was first taken to a memorial for an Iraqi Kurdish family killed in an attack by Turkish planes and to a graveyard where hundreds of guerrillas lay. These visits ensured that the guests witnessed the cost of the fight for liberation and created a common affective state between them and their hosts. The guests were then taken to a guesthouse, where they waited until their appointments and trips to different parts of the mountains could be arranged.

When we arrived, the guerrillas were expecting us and had prepared for the meeting by inviting women representatives from different mountains and from different women's organizations within the PKK. When our minibus stopped in the area from which we would take a short walk to our meeting place, we ran into two women guerrillas who welcomed us with an embrace and scorn: Why had we come so late, after so much suffering and violence? This question addressed us as women rather than as Turks and included us in a common universe of responsibility and obligation. The embrace gave us a specific status as much-sought and already beloved friends, while the scorn reminded us that we had nevertheless failed in terms of our capacity to change the world. As forceful and as flattering (since we never thought of ourselves as world-changing actors) as their gesture to include us in a common world of responsibility and obligation was, it also pointed to the different meanings attributed to the meeting. While for us, meeting the guerrilla women was an affective and political event in itself, for them it was an occasion where women's collective path to liberation could be coordinated. For those of us from Turkey, this meeting was formative for our life-story and identity, whereas for the women guerrillas it was strategic for a women's revolution's trajectory. I visited the women guerrillas a few more times in the Qandil mountains, where we shared ideas, laughter, memories, and analyses, until 2015, when the peace talks collapsed. Through it all there remained a radical — one could even say an ontological — difference between us. This chapter is also an attempt to give meaning to some of these differences while letting some other differences remain unexplored.

First of all, the symbolic and real power emanating from the bodies of the guerrilla women were difficult to bear for those of us who belonged to the spaces of capital, nation, and family, despite our best intentions to be otherwise. A Kalashnikov was constantly attached to the body of the guerrilla like a prosthesis. They never took off their uniforms, and around their waists they carried an "eight inch high waistband of patterned material which, in a striking way, draws the body in, a body ready for action every inch."[16] They were no fathers and no mothers, no citizens and no consumers; they didn't have belongings beyond a gun and maybe some photos and a diary. They moved swiftly through a few tents and shelters, making one think that these were built for us rather than them. They also always talked passionately and forcefully with an energy that they attributed to being revolutionaries and that to us seemed otherworldly. Their speech, formed under the sign of a guerrilla movement that brought together Kurds from Iran, Iraq, Turkey, Syria, and Europe, addressed a global audience and utilized a vocabulary of immense volition and willfulness. I agree with Michael Taussig, who describes the power of the Kurdish guerrilla, specifically the woman guerrilla, as "magical" in an essay he wrote in 2015 on his visit to Kobani.[17] To Taussig the magical power of the guerrillas, as actors of a history as exception, stems from the bodies they constituted, bodies that are also exceptional in the sense of being celibate, awake, threatening, and, I would add, always on the move, appearing and disappearing constantly.

While it was our appearance, speech, and capacity of movement that differentiated us at first sight, as we became more familiar, it became obvious to me that the questions that gave our lives meaning and our responses to these questions were more important in making us humans that belonged to different genres. I borrow the term "genre of the human" from Sylvia Wynter and would like to take a moment to explain it. While I am sure that they never read each other, and despite their different interpretations of history, Sylvia Wynter's thought on the human and the coloniality of being, truth, and freedom and Abdullah Öcalan's thought on the metaphysics of being, truth, and freedom resemble each other in profound ways.[18] First, both thinkers want to overcome the genre of the Man, which is hegemonic in our contemporary world and is the source of all -isms.[19] Instead they theorize how the creation of a new human could be "delinked" from capitalism, colonialism, and patriarchy.[20] Second, for both thinkers, human beings are hybrid in the sense of being "both biological/organic and symbolic/myth-making."[21] In other words, humans create their genres of the human and produce different kinds of humanisms by asking the question, "Who are we?" The response to this question involves storytelling. Specifically, it involves how we tell ourselves the story of our origins and give meaning to our past, present, and future. For Wynter, since the sixteenth century, the response to this question has been that "we are biological creatures caught in a natural struggle for resources and only confirm our relative success through the accumulation of wealth."[22] Öcalan doesn't specifically comment on how this question is answered in the contemporary world in the ways Wynter does. However, he states that patriarchy, capitalism, colonialism, state-ism, religion-ism, science-ism, nationalism, and industrialism orient how we act in the contemporary world. Instead, he encourages people to autonomously and collectively provide their own answers to the question of "who we are" in order to "restitute" what has been "destituted" by these ideologies.[23] Both authors also make use of natural sciences to make their argument and to show the ways in which our stories become sensed as nature. While Wynter makes use of neurosciences, Öcalan draws on quantum physics and DNA studies to show the ways in which the socially produced world became second nature and how freedom is nevertheless a necessity that cannot be repressed.

Both Öcalan and Wynter also point to where and how to find a "a different, nonreductive, ecumenically human" answer to the question of "who are we."[24] Wynter believes that when one looks at the world from the position of liminal subjects who exist inside the system "through their constitutive exclusion," one can see a potential "for a radical outside."[25] For Öcalan, too, people who have been excluded from the system can become a basis for imagining other ways of being human. Kurds, for example, who haven't been assimilated into the project of capitalist civilization, still retain aspects of life that haven't been totally colonized. For Wynter as for Öcalan, "human" is not a noun but a praxis that is not who someone is but what someone practices. In that sense for Öcalan specifically, the failure of assimilation is not a guarantee but a potential for practicing humanness. Such humanness can only become a sustainable praxis through the creation of new sociabilities in institutions that promote the kind of relations, stories, and values that follow the principles of democratic autonomy, a women's freedom-based orientation, and ecological life (products of a democratic modernity that is in a dialectical relationship with capitalist modernity).

Öcalan and Wynter differ in one fundamental aspect. While Wynter agrees that gender is a "foundational archetype" and sees "gender as the emergence of genre as such because it introduces a fundamentally human cleaving, locally producing corporeal meaning while generally creating the conditions of possibility for other codes to produce differentiation," she nevertheless argues "that the 'founding,' or what she has elsewhere called the 'master' code of our current iteration of Man — Man2, or biocentric homo economicus — is race"; and thus, according to her, "all other code words for genre (class and gender, but also sexual orientation and religion) become ultimately legible through the master code. Race, in other words, provides the 'genre d'cohérence' or the axis along which all other demarcations of difference rotate."[26] Öcalan, in contrast, believes that even today gender is the master code and the axis around which all demarcations rotate. If for Wynter it is the pieza framework — which created the standard measurement of value for human chattel that could render enslaved persons fungible — that is foundational in making race the master code of our current iteration of Man, for Öcalan, marriage under conditions of patriarchy — where women are enslaved through the violent control of their sexuality, labor, and subjectivity — is how women became and continue to be fungible. Therefore, for Öcalan, it is of utmost importance that women respond to the questions of "who are we?" and "how should we live?" autonomously as a class of their own, independent of family and sexual relations, and it is only through their revolutionary praxis that being, freedom, and truth can be decolonized. Finally, whereas for Wynter we should turn to Africa, where humans first emerged, in order to look for new genres of the human, Öcalan sees Mesopotamia, where the first Neolithic revolution occurred as the space where a new genre of the human can be developed. Indeed, one can say that his whole endeavor has been directed to the creation of this new human among the guerrillas. The decolonization of being, truth, and freedom through the praxis of friendship in the mountains and through occupying different temporalities harmonized by revolution, which I will discuss later, is constitutive of this new human.

## Who Are We and How Should We Live?

In one of my trips to the mountains, I met a woman guerrilla whose codename in English means, "Who am I?" She had all the personal reasons to take that name, since she was raised by adoptive parents, far away from her birthplace, and had never met her kin and siblings. She did not think she lived a life that mattered before participating in the Kurdish Freedom Movement, and the movement alone was what gave her an ontological and ethical compass. She explained to me that finding out her capacities and limits and giving meaning to her existence was so important for her that she wanted to be called by a name that stood for her quest. I would later find out that while her personal story before joining the movement, which she could not signify beyond a void and could barely narrate in more than a few sentences, is quite unique, the quest that she carries as her name marks all women guerrillas, irrespective of how they are named.[27]

Elaborating on the thought of their leader, Abdullah Öcalan, women guerrillas think that the answer to the question of who they are must be first and foremost sought in history and mythology. Mythology and history are two different genres in which the past is told with varying ideological repercussions, as well as potentialities, and for the Kurdish guerrillas they are both sources for understanding present conditions and resources for transforming them. Indeed, one of the aspects that make the guerrilla a different kind of human is the different temporalities in which she dwells. On the one hand, she sees herself as a historical and universal subject emerging from the ruins of history and moving the world toward equality and freedom. On the other hand, the woman guerrilla also sees herself as occupying a mythological and a cosmological time. Meanwhile, the life of the guerrilla is structured both by the fast time of war and the slow time of everyday labor.

"Women's history," in which the woman guerrilla sees herself to be a main actor, refers both to Kurdish women's involvement in the guerrilla warfare since the end of the 1970s and the wider global history of women as the colonized and oppressed sex. This temporality connects her to the world and to other struggling actors in the Middle East. Mythology in general, and Sumerian mythology in particular, enables the guerrilla to understand and explain how men have succeeded in dominating women. By attributing the beginning of women's colonization to a specific date — that is, the emergence of the Sumerian priest states — they also are able to believe that this colonization will come to an end. Moreover, mythology inspires women to contemplate the laws they can give to themselves if they follow their collectively articulated desires and remake the future.

Yet another temporality is cosmological. Based on a reading of physics, specifically the current experiments on light and energy, the guerrillas believe that their work takes different forms but never disappears; their labor toward freedom and equality becomes part of the cosmos and the second nature that humans are producing materially, ideologically, and spiritually. Therefore, their lives as much as their deaths (what I call death labor) that are inscribed in the flesh of the world initiate communication and produce values that circulate and on which other people can then act.[28] Finally, guerrillas also live the fast life of war and air attacks and the mundane temporality of the everyday, which ensures the sustainability of guerrilla organizations.[29] All these different temporalities in turn are harmonized by revolutionary time, the organizing principle that gives meaning to their lives.

Revolutionary time allows guerrilla women to approach women's past holistically (a term I use to denote interdependency rather than coherence), and they craft their perspective on the universality of women's struggle against patriarchal power by weaving into a singular narrative different women's movements, women's mobility in socialist and nationalist revolutions, woman figures such as "goddess," "priestess," and "witch," personalities such as Rosa Luxemburg or Emma Goldman, and their own woman "martyrs."[30] Revolutionary time is also crucial in animating their political imaginaries. Borrowing from Karen Barad's exploration of electrical energy and its repercussions to rethink the social, I would say that these imaginaries informed by quantum physics are "attuned to the condensations of past and future condensed into each moment; imaginaries that entail superpositions of many beings and times; multiple im/possibilities that coexist and are iteratively intra-actively reconfigured; imaginaries that are material explorations of the mutual indeterminacies of being and time."[31] Women guerrillas see women's everyday tactics, cultural forms, and memory as the ground to discover these condensed moments where multiple beings and times are superimposed and thereby animate im/possible futures. They also believe that such an understanding of revolutionary time and holistic history is continuously and intentionally attacked and fragmented by patriarchal power embodied in the state, science, and the family.

Fighting not only against the Turkish state but also "the state form" in general, they have little interest in investing in a women's rights discourse. Rather, they want freedom for themselves and their sex, which they believe can only be achieved by the foundation of organizational forms where women can define themselves and shape their acts autonomously. Spaces that the Kurdish Freedom Movement creates in the mountains or within the party are where they try to realize this autonomy, leading a fierce and very painful struggle against men and masculinity. One answer they would give to the question of "who are we" would be, then, that they are seekers of freedom and truth, that they are the products of women's labor and the heirs of women's struggle in different periods, while also putting their lives on the line as they fight against the specific oppressions of Kurdish people.

For the Kurdish women guerrillas, the question of who they are is also closely linked to the question of "how they should live." The past sheds light on how they should live as mythology becomes a source for finding women's/mother's laws, as the ethical choices of individual women (animated by the death drive) become norm-forming and exemplary, and as ideological and strategic failures of women's movements become critical lessons. Organizational structures, which they create and frequently renew, calibrate their thought and action, orient them, and endow them with relations where they can practice "being infused and informed and deformed and reformed" against capitalist modernity.[32] The question of how to live must, however, also be answered individually, as it is in friendships, in relation to other women, and in war and death, that each individual will put her singular name on the line and determine her place in the world. In other words, the Kurdish guerrilla woman becomes who she is by the simultaneous work of collectivization and individuation.[33] This work involves the making and remaking of genres and styles, ethics and aesthetics as it involves the processes of meaning making and organizational participation. The lives the Kurdish women guerrillas live, the vocabulary they use to explain their choices, and the framework within which they narrate their stories in turn become a major component of the emerging genre of human in the political imagination of the Kurdish movement. This human is "a friend" to the world, someone who has cultivated a self whose thought and deed are the same and who is capable of finding solutions to problems. She is in a constant struggle to free herself from the residues of colonialism, capitalism, and patriarchy in her personality and, in her care of self and others, produces an alternative ethics and aesthetics. Finally, she is to be a leader whose success is measured by the "queer communications" and unexpected "flirtations" she can initiate.[34] From Arin Mirkan, who committed a suicide bombing against ISIS to motivate her friends to stand their ground in an almost completely invaded Kobane in 2014 to the founding member of the PKK, Sakine Cansız, who is famous for initiating impossible dialogues with women who distance themselves from the Freedom Movement, to Berivan Cizire, who single-handedly mobilized people and ignited an insurgency in Cizre in 1992, women leaders of the Kurdish Movement are expected to deploy "seductive overtures" that lead to "powerful discharges."[35]

Keeping an archive, writing journals, debating their past, revisiting their painful struggles, and giving meaning to the death labor of individual woman fighters are extremely important practices through which women guerrillas constitute themselves. Despite the fact that they continuously express their inadequacy to grasp their own history and criticize themselves for their failure to properly write it, which I attribute to the impossibility of historical genres to capture the quantum dynamics of the movement, they have accumulated tens of thousands of pages describing not only their experiences but their experiments with different methodologies with which they approach their own pasts. In the next sections I will take up a few of these writings in order to further elaborate what kind of humanness is imagined and constituted among the guerrillas. I will argue that under the sign of the concept of friendship, where the questions of "who are we?" and "how should we live?" most productively intersect, the guerrilla searches for ways to decolonize truth, freedom, and being in specific ways. First, however, I will talk about the naming practices that take women guerrillas out of the grammar of the current genre of humanness and introduce them to the grammar of what I would like to call the human-as-friend genre.

## Taking Up a New Name and Giving Birth to Oneself

The politics of naming in guerrilla warfare is a privileged site where names can become powerful tools that act out new imaginaries. Among the Kurdish guerrillas, name giving, name taking, and addressing each other by their assumed names are always consciously ethical choices that enact a universe of friendship that escapes the totalitarianism of state and patriarchal language.[36] This universe of friendship endows one with loyalties, responsibilities, and duties that are other to the operations of capitalism, nation state, and family.[37] The names that guerrillas take after joining the movement are also means through which those who died childless outside of kinship structures and as friends are remembered and commemorated.[38] For people outside of the guerrilla forces, the names of renowned guerrillas become "heritage, culture, tradition," and knowing these names becomes a way of belonging to the resistance.[39] For the guerrillas, on the other hand, these names, which are often compulsively repetitive, interject an otherness into the self, making the other continuously present in the individual psyche.

All movements deemed illegal, and guerrilla movements, in particular, require that their members take new names. Taking up new names has two obvious functions. First, the new name provides security and secrecy for the person and keeps her/him beyond the reach of the law. Since punishment depends on the establishment of individual identity abstracted in the name and a correspondence between that identity and crime, taking up a new name inserts an undecidability into the legal process. When a body that operates under the sign of an incognito name commits an illegal action, the burden to prove that that body also belongs to an officially registered name over which judgment can be made is transferred to the state. The political literature in Turkey is full of stories in which a revolutionary is tortured to confess the name under which he or she is registered by the state; one's resistance to do so undermines state sovereignty.[40] If a name stands for the person, mastering it is mastering death and life; denying that mastery to the state is a way in which political movements symbolically and materially escape its law and sovereignty.

A new name under whose sign one operates also protects the family and community to which the state's birth certificates have assigned one's belonging. The families of guerrilla members in Turkey who are regularly interrogated by the police can deny the involvement of their daughters and sons in the movement because they have taken up different names and as such severed their links to their original name on whose behalf their families are being harassed. Moreover, the names they disconnected themselves from can become empty signs under which actions can still be carried on in contexts of voting, poverty alleviation, property acquirement, census, and so on. In such circumstances, there is a doubling of the person's contribution to the movement. While she is fighting against the state, her birth name that she has emptied out is used to increase the number of those the state counts as oppositional.[41]

If the first reason for acquiring a new name among the guerrilla is the necessity of secrecy, indeterminacy, and invisibility, a form of voluntary absence and erasure in certain communities and relationships, the second reason leads us to questions of visibility, presence, and signature. The guerrilla chooses her own name. By assigning a new name to herself, she gives birth to herself and becomes without father and mother. Her official, registered name situates her in a relationship with her kin through her surname and with the nation-state through citizenship. By stripping herself of that name — and for a woman that name is always patriarchal — she leaves a kinship structure that puts her in an androcentric, gerontocratic, patriarchal universe. In Turkey, where women's practices of citizenship, rights, and duties are very much affected by her kinship status, the erasure of the body from the birth name for a woman is a way in which freedom is attained.[42] The emptiness that the person leaves behind is productive in two senses. First, it will inspire other young relatives to do the same; when someone from a lineage leaves for the mountains, brothers, sisters, and cousins will often follow her. Second, the family will take to themselves the task of reproducing her through pictures, stories, and a general worry and interest in where she is and how she is doing, and her erasure will be counteracted with an abundance of photographs making her ever-present in the lives of those who stayed behind, turning her into a "Real" that is more than reality.

The first name a guerrilla takes is either a commemorative name making reference to dead friends, such as Beritan, Zilan, or Bese, or a name that gives meaning to her struggle, such as Tolhildan (revenge) or Serhildan (insurgency). At times a first name can also come from Kurdish literature or Mesopotamian myths such as Zin, the main female protagonist in the famous story "Mem u Zin," written by Ahmede Xani. While in the case of the first set of names the guerrilla re-enfleshes the politically signified acts deceased people performed and interjects into her own subjectivity a responsibility to the other from whom she cannot divorce, the second set of names is a reminder of the rage that the movement encourages women to experience against the patriarchal and colonial regime. This feminine rage — taken up as a name by the guerrilla — which is constantly reanimated by the painfully combative struggle against "the enemies," becomes "the womb through which she rebirths herself."[43] The third set of names, on the other hand, brings the mythical temporality that the movement assumes have a bearing on the historical ruins from which the guerrilla's everyday and exceptional practices emerge. The second name, such as Amed, Wan, or Agiri, which the guerrilla takes as a surname, usually denotes where she is from. By taking the place of origin as their second names, the guerrillas collectively remap the unmapped Kurdish geography through their flesh and carve the forgotten names of places that were erased and renamed by the Turkish state in Turkish, on their skin.

Taking a new name is simultaneously a means by which the person inhabits a new grammar and a new genre of the human and a declaration that she is literally to be a *heval*, "friend," in the Kurdish guerrilla movement. It is through her new name that the guerrilla is present to the movement and visible to the collectivity. What she writes, how she fights, her strength, and her weaknesses will be narrated under this name, and how she responds to the call by this name will determine the friendship she displays.

## Hevalti / Friendship

The fact that the guerrilla declares herself "a friend" in general and not a friend to something or someone specific by taking up a new name and making a promise complicates what is understood by friendship, since the term "friend" in the guerrilla movement (contra Agamben) becomes a predicative term.[44] Friendship designates a position in a particular revolutionary grammar, a particular form of self-cultivation, and a specific form of attachment to public. If one constitutive feature of the guerrilla's ontology is the revolutionary time, a second feature that makes her "matter" in both senses of the word is the institution of friendship that "gives her life a rhythm," "endows her with everyday habits," and "affectively inculcates her orientation towards the world."[45] Friendship is both a push that forces the guerrilla to move beyond herself and a pull that grounds her sociality, anchors and sustains her. It is a form of being and becoming, making it close to Foucault's understanding of it as a way of life.[46]

Friends in Foucault's view "are those with whom we work on the historical conditions of our existence, and those with whom we share the practice of becoming who we are."[47] The PKK defines itself as an organization of relationships (*ilişki örgütü*) that transforms people into revolutionary subjects, and friendship — *hevalti* in Kurdish — is the name of an (in prison, in organization, and in combat) accumulated perspective and knowledge of the ways (*yol perspektifi ve bilgisi*) in which these relationships will be molded.[48] In the PKK's view, it is in the company of friends that one journeys toward collective truth and freedom. Friendship is a form of loyalty that cannot be contained within nation, property, or household. It cannot be transformed into utility and cannot be exchanged. It involves both equality and differentiation. It develops through harmony as well as conflict, recognition as well as criticism. Friendship, most importantly, puts the guerrilla in the mode of play rather than inserting her in the melodramatic or the tragic that unfolds in the familial realm, thereby making her a subject of freedom and ethics. Unauthored but played out, never fulfilled but always offered, the illegibility of the guerrilla's life as it unfolds in friendly and playful joy issues the wondrous speech of

Gültan Kışanak (which I cited in Chapter 4) and mobilizes people to act like her and talk about her in a search for meaning and symbolization.[49]

I don't think that the kinship between Foucault's understanding of friendship and that of the Kurdish Freedom Movement is accidental. First, both understandings developed under the shadow of death, where friendship as a way of life mutates into friendship as a way of death.[50] While for Foucault the AIDS crisis contextualizes his later thought on friendship, for the guerrillas the context within which their understanding of being a *heval* developed cannot be thought of as independent of the constant reality and threat of being killed in combat. Second, through the concept of "friendship," Foucault wants to give a name to the forms of pleasure, relationships, coexistences, attachments, loves, and intensities that develop outside of heteronormative encounters linking sexuality and truth.[51] In the Kurdish Freedom Movement, too, friendship becomes a name for "all those invisible affective gestures that refuse alignment along the secure axes of filiation to seek expression outside, if not against, possessive communities of belonging."[52] With their newly acquired names and their status as friends, the guerrillas who were born and raised in a strictly filial society find themselves in a state (not unlike queer communities) where they need to "invent from A to Z" the ethics by which they will relate to each other and to others. As revolutionaries, they need to enact transformative intimacies with people of the same sex or different sexes, different age groups, and different collectivities. They also must redefine their mutual dependencies and duties, "their irreducible relations of responsibility," in other words, "their "quantum entanglements," without giving up their asexuality, which delinks sexuality and truth.[53] Later, under the topics of "truth," "freedom," and being, I will discuss some of the key aspects that emerge in the life of the guerrilla as she becomes a *heval* and takes up "friendship," *hevalti*, as the main form of longing and belonging in her life. What I understand from my readings of the guerrilla's writings and my conversations with them is that decolonization of truth in the movement entails finding new laws to live and die by and forming new norms to be cited that will help the guerrilla to act and change the symbolic order supported by relations developed within capitalist modernity. Decolonizing freedom, on the other hand, is inscribing these laws and norms on the flesh of the world through motion, meaning giving, and creation. Decolonization of being, meanwhile, becomes living a form of life in the mode of play and transforming life and death into offerings, thereby initiating new communications. None of this can happen alone. Friendship as it unfolds in the intersection of the questions "Who are we?" and "How should we live?" is the ontological relationality that makes it possible to matter and give matter to the decolonized "there" and "then" that the guerrilla struggles to enflesh and that Kurdish people see as more "Real" than reality itself.

## Decolonization of Truth: Finding New Laws to Live By

A friend in the Kurdish Movement, a *heval*, in other words, defines herself first and foremost as a searcher for truth in her words and deeds. Following Öcalan's interpretations of Foucault's insights, whose ideas he uses as an inspiration in his writings, the movement believes that the greatest weapon of domination is the creation and circulation of truths and subjection of selves to such truths.[54] It is therefore of utmost important to identify first which forms of truth are detrimental to the movement, its struggle for freedom, and its members' levels of participation. While this is a collective and always ongoing process sustained through meetings, statements, reports, and debates, friendship and how friendship is ritualized in the movement are important spaces where the search for truth is realized.

Modern friendship involves the sharing of secrets and the revelation of "true" selves through such secrets. The form of friendship promoted by the Kurdish freedom movement is different; it is instead against confession and toward mutual transformation by collective labor. Such mutual transformation entails that the person embedded in relations of friendship becomes a subject against subjectification and strips herself of those aspects of herself that have been interpellated by dominant structures.[55] For the movement's understanding of true speech regarding the past, for example, consider the following quote from the notes of a meeting of women guerrillas who are debating the question of "how we should live":

> When we talk about our past, we treat it as if it is a wall of crying. We do not let go of our cries and transform the past into an experience. We only think of the past on the basis of our pain. That's how we render ourselves incapable of evaluating the future. Our approach is that we feel obligated to cry. Yes we have suffered. . . . If we know who we are, we will also decide on how we will live.[56]

The suffering that is referred to here concerns the difficult struggles women engaged in to become free and equal within the PKK, which was in the past dominated by men. Women who have been active in the movement have encountered various forms of discrimination that at times led either to their early death or to their capture by the state. This part of their history is important, since it reminds them of the costs both of becoming a women's movement and of the debt they have to their predecessors. But the quote also suggests that women guerrillas feel the need to refuse to define themselves on the basis of a "truth" revealed by retelling such stories to each other in a confessional mode. Instead, what is important is to transform the past into knowledge and experience in order to collectively enact a metamorphosis in their relationship with the future and with the movement.

The movement rejects not only "pain" but also the forms of "desire" that grant a place to the individual in the given symbolic order and lead to her capture, as the truth of the self. Instead, as Roach argues (following Foucault), friendship and friendly speech should increase the capacity to become mobilized and to act.[57] As one of the leaders of the PKK explained to me, "Truth is not whether an utterance or a position one takes is right or false. It is not about who said what and did what with what intentions and to what end. It is what that utterance or position will make that person. Whether the debate itself will help the movement towards its struggle." Consider the following excerpts from a diary written by the guerrilla Zinarin between January and September 1997, just before she died.[58] Her diary addresses another guerrilla friend, Melsa, with whom she parted ways because of their separate assignments. In the first pages of her diary Zinarin states, "I wanted you to know my inside, the depth of my heart, the projections of the painful, joyful, excited and sour moments of the struggle. I will tell you." However, as we later find out by "the depth of her heart" and "her inside," what she means is neither her secret desires (which she calls her fugitive feelings) nor her suffering. Rather, the depth of her heart refers to her struggles to increase her capacity to participate in the movement and to act collectively:

> My fugitive feelings are selfish. They eat up my sensibilities, soul, thought, fruitfulness and time. I am being exploited by my fugitive feelings. Yes, I rebel against my fugitive feelings and dreams. In order to defeat the outside I must first defeat myself. My anger at myself and at our weakness pushes me to become the opposite of me. It pushes me to become us.[59]
>
> I think and I believe that as I live in war and according to the war, I will become a more mature, deeper, and emotional person. I will become more my self and take root in my country. I hope that as I fight in the war, I will overcome the unnecessary and residual parts of myself that do not really belong to me and that women's heroism will also materialize itself in me.[60]
>
> Sometimes I feel that my emotions are waning and my material aspects are dominating. In other words, I feel like I am losing my sensitivity. . . . I think about something I did and I see that I have

approached the situation materialistically, that I haven't transferred a thought that was molded with feelings into it, that I didn't really put myself in it and that I approached it superficially: in an ordinary way. That is when my anger over myself is at its most.[61]

If you ask about me what I call difficulty and stress are actually forms of concentration. They are the emotional burdens of things I have difficulty carrying and the newness of things I have to live as I walk towards a new process in a new milieu. This is the first time that I have experienced the enemy, war, and martyrs, being always in danger of dying, and fighting the struggle of freedom and gender equality in a place where feudalism and reactionism are so strong. Suddenly, I have found my character to be poor, unprepared, and helpless. And this has stressed and nauseated me. I see it as my indispensable duty to apply the principles and the necessities of freedom under conditions of combat and reactionary feudalism. But I neither have the organization, nor the plan nor the tactic for it.[62]

Zinarin's text is intimate and powerful. It is addressed to a friend who is assumed to be going through similar troubles in order to achieve an elevated self (worthy of the women's and people's revolution) whose truth and actions are one and whose mastery of the self is accomplished. It is a text written in between two deaths, as Lacan would say, since Zinarin rejected the place given to her in the symbolic order, which is supported both by the filial attachments she left behind and the reactionism and feudalism of the people with whom she enters the war. She is now in search of new laws to give herself and new norms to perform that can be cited by other women. However, for this she needs friendships that would help her fight against her "fugitive feelings" and motivate her to act in creative ways. Zinarin's fear is that at this point she cannot be a good "friend" in the organization because she fails to "apply the principles and the necessities of freedom under conditions of combat and reactionary feudalism." Nor does she believe that others in her group are good friends because of their feudalism and reactionism, which prevents them from creating relationships that would generate collective power and joy. In Foucauldian terms the speech that Zinarin adopts in her diary is *parrhesia*. Zinarin's goal is to get rid of all that is "added to her personality." This suggests that she is struggling to change herself, to rid herself of all those disciplinary processes that subjected her and to develop alternative modes of being and becoming. Zinarin is stressed not only because she must deal with the feudalism and sexism in the organization but also because she is unable to find the capacity to engage with the people she is together with under the sign of truth.

Zinarin never loses sight of the fact that the subject is historically formed and must be de-formed and re-formed through historical (mythical and revolutionary) practice, as well. Or, as Öcalan says, in each individual the whole of history can be read and remade. Zinarin aspires to a transformation of herself and her community and is searching for the means to do that in order to become a subject of history (myth, revolution). This diary, although it is addressed to a friend, depicts Zinarin's relation to herself. More than a lack of self-knowledge, it seems that her trouble is that she fails herself in her quest for truth — for making her thoughts and deeds one. Following Foucault, Roach writes, "If the self is only a relation between subjection and subjectivation, then the true friend, the *parrhesiastes*, pushes the subject beyond historical determinants in encouraging processes of subjectivation over procedures of subjection. The friend is thus the *sine qua non* of self-transformation and immanent salvation."[63] For Zinarin, it seems, Melsa has been such a friend in the past. However, from the whole of the diary we understand that the friendship she is yearning for is not exclusive to Melsa. Rather, in her training at the *önderlik sahası*, the house of the leader Öcalan in Syria, Zinarin and others have found such a friend above all in Öcalan himself.

Öcalan displays the paramount *parrhesiatic* self in the movement; he tells it all, speaks frankly, and has no secrets. His childhood, his former marriage, his relationships with his parents and with the members of the movement are openly discussed, and he transforms them into collective contemplations of the questions of "who the guerrilla is" and "how he should live." Through his speech he activates people, creates rupture in their senses of self, and invites them to engage in relations of responsibility that are other to those dictated by capitalist modernity, specifically to conjugal affiliations. He also encourages others to talk that way and criticizes harshly those whom he feels are still subjected by familialism, capitalism, and tribalism and their laws. For women failing to free one's self from "enslavement" and for men failing to "kill the man inside one's self" are the catchwords that he and others use to describe such a situation of untruthfulness and unfreedom.[64]

In her search for truth, Zinarin eventually enters combat, despite her friends' warnings that she is not yet ready, and is killed. In the preface to her diary, Öcalan describes Zinarin as someone who owned up to her word, someone whose life and deed are the same. She is also someone who followed her desire (unintelligible to the movement at the time), and it is up to the movement to become a "response" to this desire. That is, it is up to the movement to create an environment and an organization where Zinarin's desires can be signified beyond death. Zinarin's and other women's deaths that could have been avoided (or rather delayed) and were rushed in their search for new laws must now become a basis for rethinking relationships and friendships and the capacity of the PKK to give them the means to perform new norms while living. If the decolonization of truth occurs in the movement through self-transformation, finding new laws to follow, and forming new norms to be cited in the context of friendships, freedom refers to the capacity to change the world along with the self.

## Decolonization of Freedom: Motion and Velocity

In his books that form the paradigm of the Kurdish Freedom Movement, Öcalan defines freedom as motion and energy: Freedom involves rescuing oneself from the rigidity and capture that capitalist modernity enforces on collectivities and individuals under the ideology of sovereign free choice and possessive individualism. Inspired by quantum physics, Öcalan says that free-dom entails contagious differentiations, multiplications, and pluralizations occurring in entanglements, as can be observed everywhere in the universe. Freedom, in other words, is opening oneself to unexpected relationalities and movements by making commitments and initiating communication. More-over, he adds that while life "wants" to move toward heterogeneity, it is ethics that secures such heterogeneity by linking all forms of matter to each other.[65]

For Öcalan and the movement, such ideas are not theoretical but must be constantly practiced and be inscribed to the flesh of the organization. For example, whenever he has been able to communicate with the movement, Öcalan proposes that the Kurdish freedom movement, women, and other democratic forces create new social and political bodies and that existing ones structurally transform their identities and their roles so that movement and mobility in social and political life are secured and politics will not be reduced to management and administration, dominated by habits and con-ventions. In this way those who are at the core of existing organizations will be unsettled, and the way will be cleared to open new opportunities for those at the margins.[66]

One further result of creating new organizations is non-sovereignty. The existence of a multiplicity of organizations operating in different and overlap-ping spaces and the complicated shifts in authority and in the relationships among them ensure that no single body will ever capture and monopolize the means of power and rule. To the contrary, the fact that a number of constantly changing institutions and administrators are simultaneously responsible for operating in a given field prevents each of them from remaining closed in on itself and forces all of them to remain in communication, without depriving any of them of their autonomy. It also guarantees that decisions made on the basis of the authority acquired by one organization can never be fully realized unless they are validated by the others. As such, multiplication, diversification, and differentiation — in other words, freedom — can be reproduced in a nonmechanical way.

Motion also secures an ethics of impersonality in friendship relations and encourages an anti-identitarian politics. Friendship, when personal, when not a position in life but a relationship with a significant other or others, can very easily transform into identitarian politics. Indeed, the Kurdish Freedom Movement initially suffered from such politics when coming from the same region, class, or gender was used as criteria for inclusion or exclusion from certain networks, which Zinarin calls feudal in the entries in her diary. One way in which impersonality in friendship is achieved is through assignments, which keep "friends" in the movement constantly on the move and renders them literally homeless. In the Kurdish Movement any *heval* can be assigned to anywhere (as long as she does not challenge the assignment on acceptable grounds), which makes it hard to continue personalized friendships formed in one assignment. On the contrary, she is expected to be a general friend to all, to care for them and be committed to a mutual transformation wherever she goes. An impersonal self is cultivated and secured because her assignment needs her to create and re-create new bonds with impersonal others and carry out impersonal encounters without ceasing to be a friend.

For Öcalan and the Kurdish Freedom Movement, in addition to entailing mental and physical motion, freedom is also closely related to the capacity to make and give meaning. Movement becomes freedom to the extent that people — individually and collectively — give meaning to it. In order to develop the capacity for meaning, an individual or collective must first liberate and disconnect him- or herself from the hegemonic sets of meaning. However, this alone is not enough. It is also necessary to produce explanations and stories in which an increasing number of people can recognize themselves and their experiences. For example, the historical narrative that Öcalan has developed based on the Neolithic Age provides a way for women to give meaning to their own lives, to their mothers' stories, to women's memories, myths, and tales, and to the suffering and resilience women have shown throughout history, while situating them in a holistic and sensible world.

A friend is someone who achieves freedom by the search for meaning in her activity. Rituals such as platform, where *hevals* come together to analyze each other (*çözümleme*) but also acts like *yoğunlaşma* (concentration) and *açığa çıkarma* (putting it out in the open), which involves individual and collective labor that aims at a higher quality of participation in the movement and everyday acts of making bread, cleaning, creating a fire, and exercising, are all freeing in the sense of increasing the capacity of guerrillas to be autonomous. Reading and learning, contributing to guerrilla life philosophically, participating in combat, and laboring for the sustenance of everyday life are regarded as endeavors toward freedom and truth as long as they are transformative and increase the guerrilla's capacity to be a friend. Situating freedom in such activities, as much as on the battlefield, makes the guerrilla appreciate the slow workings of guerrilla life as freeing without necessarily getting rid of the urge to be in the middle of action.

In this context I should also point to both the unique theoretical and daily vocabulary used by the Kurdish freedom movement. This vocabulary is in part created by Öcalan, and it encourages people to avoid language that will lead them to conceive of themselves in hegemonic ways. Allowing them instead to tell different stories about the universe, life, humanity, and nature, this vocabulary provides them with new ways of seeing and sensing. Having their own vocabulary for talking about different matters allows the movement and people to contribute to the production of knowledge in ways that were not previously possible.[67] Knowledge is profaned and democratized, depriving the state of one of the means of creating hegemonic structures. Freedom becomes possible when different means (including those of knowledge-making) are rescued from the hegemonic names given to them and limits imposed upon them, opening them up to multiple new names and stories.[68]

However, neither movement nor developing an autonomous capacity to create meaning is a sufficient base for freedom. Freedom also requires that people increase their power to actively build new things.[69] Freedom is not doing what one wants to do. On the contrary, it demands the immense effort and willpower that allows a person to push oneself to overcome one's limits, to go against one's habits, and to labor for and invest energy in oneself and one's relationships; that is, it involves self-care and care for others. For example, when women increase their physical capacity or acquire information and skills that are primarily the domain of men, they increase their power to "build," and they feel more joyful, independent, and free. Similarly, as Kurdish society builds its institutions and takes the means of production, reproduction, and self-defense back from the state, men, and the elite, they liberate themselves. Finally, the capacity to "build," just like the capacities of movement and meaning making, collectivizes the concept of freedom and makes clear that a person's freedom depends on the freedom and autonomy of the collective within which they live, rather than being independent from it.

## Decolonization of Being: Death Labor and Death Drive

The Kurdish Freedom Movement has lost tens of thousands of people to the war with Turkey. Some of these who died were new recruits: young, inexperienced, but heroic, nevertheless. Others were well-established names in the movement. What does it mean to have so many friends lost to the war? How to give meaning both to the death drive that animates the guerrilla and the mourning work that becomes part of the guerrilla's psyche and practice? In other words, to readdress the question with which I ended Chapter 4, what kind of a human is the guerrilla who experiences joy even, or exactly when she is under the imminent threat of death, and what does that have to do with friendship?

The guerrilla occupies three different worlds at the same time. In the world that is ruled by the war on terror, in Turkey, Iraq, and Iran and certainly in the West, where the PKK is seen to be a terrorist organization, she occupies the "zone of non-being."[70] Her ontological existence is denied; she is symbolically deadened and condemned to a "death-bound subjectivity."[71] As Derek Hook states, the zone of non-being "anonymizes and de-indivudates" her, "forecloses the need for any further knowledge about" her, and "produces an anxious need to exclude [her] from the realm of human inter-subjectivity."[72] Through the writing, speech, and action with which she addresses the global world — for example, during her resistance against ISIS — she first tries to seize access to ontology. Seizing access to ontology in this case necessitates, however, paradoxically dying in the war for an abstract "humanity" defended against ISIS, which in turn is dehumanized and de-ontologized. Ironically, as was the case after 2015, she quickly slips into the zone of non-being when she fights against the Turkish state.

Second, the guerrilla occupies the communal zone where she exists as a member of the Kurdish people. She is the one who fights for Kurdistan's freedom. Her body and flesh, her writing and action and the diplomacy she conducts with various actors (including me), initiate new articulations that link Kurdistan to the world as a space of revolution rather than as an underdeveloped zone of violence. Yet, from an everyday point of view, she is outside of Kurdistan, reentering it only as a dead body to be buried. The moment she leaves her natal home, she becomes dead-bound and perceived to be living-dead, already mourned, dead but alive, admired and loved, remembered and constitutive of the life of those she left behind. Finally, she also occupies the friendship zone where her everyday life unfolds. Here in this world, the dead and the living are together as the latter's names, memories, and stories are frantically recorded, retold, and rewritten and the desires for which they died become laws.

Addressing the question of whether there is a distinctive form of political agency that emerges from the conditions of "death-bound subjectivity," Derek Hook turns to Lacan's reconceptualization of the death drive as ethical cause and evokes his famous analyses of Antigone as a paradigmatically ethical figure. Antigone is a figure of the drive:

> Her desire is not the alienated desire of the Other; it cannot be compromised or moderated in any way ["No mediation is possible here" notes Lacan].[73] By virtue of the fact that her desire has been utterly purified, emptied of contingent ("pathological") contents or concerns, given that it has been subjected to one single activity which she is prepared to sacrifice everything for, we can say that she has crossed over from the parameters of desire to those of the (death) drive. It is in this sense that Antigone is a paradigmatically ethical figure for Lacan.[74]

For Hook the death drive is associated with the zone of non-being, where the person is symbolically dead: ejected from the social order and condemned to execution. And it is from this "condition of symbolic death ('where . . . life is already lost') that a new — and radically transformative — order of life becomes possible":

> There is, firstly, the symbolic immortality granted to such a subject if their sacrifice is witnessed, recognized, remembered, made part of history, commemorated, and afforded thus a properly historical status. And then there is, secondly, the prospect of how the existing symbolic order might itself be altered by virtue of such a sacrifice and the newness it brings into the world. So, we have, to underscore the point, the symbolic life that comes from repeatedly marking a death, firstly, and the life of a newness — a birth, a nascence — emerging by virtue of the fact that the symbolic order has been shifted.[75]

When Kurdish guerrillas say, regarding Kemal Pir, one of the founders of the PKK, who died in Diyarbakır prison in 1984 during a hunger strike, "We love the world to the extent that we would die for it," maybe this is what they mean. In the zone in which they are living as non-beings, the guerrillas respond with the creative work of their death, joyful that their death will become an event that gives rise to mobility and fidelity among their community and friends and be signified with discourse and action.

Or maybe Roach is right in arguing that friendships formed under the sign of death lead both to the appreciation of the finitude of life and estrangement from the world:

> In a time in which the death of friends is inescapable, an acceptance of death's immanence to life becomes unavoidable. Life becomes "perhaps a hundred times more appealing" when death is omnipresent and yet a clear separation between the two realms becomes a fantasy no longer sustainable. The demise of this fantasy renders friendship a relation of shared estrangement.[76]

It might be this shared estrangement and "this life becoming a hundred times more appealing" that animates the death drive of the guerrilla and makes her joyful. Or maybe it is because they live in a cosmological time where they see their death as value-producing and yet mundane labor that makes the world a more livable place, that they can sustain a war where tens of thousands have died. I shall never know. What I know is that the guerrilla wants her life to be decided on here and now and offers her life and death to be played out. She thereby becomes a historical/mythological/revolutionary subject that works on the conditions of life and forces multiple nation states to play her game instead of fulfilling her life cycle as patriarchy commands. What I further know is that writing about the Kurdish guerrilla is a difficult endeavor. Kristeva asks, "Who are you Antigone? . . . " and continues, "an outlaw, a criminal, a rebel, certainly," but she is no warrior: "You bear no relation to Joan of Arc, nor to Corneille's heroines of duty. You offer a wild resistance to tyranny, which, invariably topples the logic of the State, and perhaps even political thought in general in so far as they ignore this 'absolute individuality' in which you take up residence and which you claim your brother."[77] Antigone, one last time, is a theatrical figure: she is not real. The Kurdish woman guerrilla, on the other hand, is real, and she is a warrior. She not only offers a wild resistance to tyranny and dies doing that, but she also kills. She commits suicide bombings and assassinations. In that sense, the Kurdish woman guerrilla will never have the embrace that Antigone receives from academia and literature. Being interested in the horizon she offers, being interested in what her response to the questions "Who am I?" and "Who are we?," I run the risk of participating in the zones of illegality and unintelligibility she pushes forth. Nevertheless, I also become a friend to the Kurdish Movement. I remember with joy my chats with so many wonderful women, now dead, under the sign of truth, and I feel proud to have listened to their magical stories of snakes and bears, of deer and donkeys and trees and plants; of bleeding headscarves at home and lost diaries in war. Nudem, Delal, Leyla, and all others: know that what your names properly name will not be forgotten; your consent "not to be a single being."[78]

## Conclusion

The guerrilla, specifically the woman guerrilla, lives in between many deaths and many lives. At home she is granted a place in the social order at the expense of her social death, delivered to her by a patriarchy that renders her fungible. When she leaves home and becomes a guerrilla, she is, on the one hand, condemned to the abjected zone of non-being and to a death-bound subjectivity. On the other hand, however, she occupies the sphere of the Real for the Kurdish people, which continuously unsettles and pushes them to give her acts a meaning. She is rendered more real than anything else as people take it to themselves to give her a life crafted out from the emptiness she left behind.

In the "wildness" of the mountains, where the distinction between nature and culture collapses, the guerrilla gives herself a new name that inserts her into the revolutionary grammar, endows her with new responsibilities, and re-births herself to become a new human. Residing in the limit between the past (as someone who is destined to die childless and anti-generational) and the future (to come, which she activates through her sentient flesh), she opens up the possibility for new quantum entanglements of commitment and communication that would not be available to her had she stayed at home. Assuming friendship as a way of life and play as the mode and atmosphere of her life, she struggles to decolonize truth, freedom, and life, which unfold under the sign of colonial, patriarchal, capitalist modernity. As she performs a new ontology through the revolutionary temporality she occupies that harmonizes history and mythology, as well as the time of exception and the ordinary and, through the bond of friendship that enacts a dangerous collectivity ready to die and kill, she becomes a "stepped leader" who incites lively and deadly responses to her difference.[79] Friendship as that which interjects an otherness to the subject and forces her to go beyond herself is the context and the means by which she rescues herself from subjection to excavate new laws to live by and form new norms to cite. Öcalan's lifelong struggle to turn himself and his life into pure means so that meaning can be rescued from capture by the social and symbolic order and put in the service of contemplation is taken as an example, and women guerrillas engage in a relentless effort to give meaning to themselves and their relations through learning, writing, and debating. They also constantly "build" (inşa) new institutions, vocabularies, and relationalities, assume new fights (the fight with ISIS, for example) and new goals (not only free Kurdistan or the Middle East, but also womenkind), since freedom is a velocity inscribed in the flesh of the world. Under the constant threat and reality of death, where friendship metamorphoses from a way of life to a way of death and where mattering and re-member-ing become one, decolonization of life becomes an urgent need. Decolonization of life, if I as a friend to the Kurdish movement sense it correctly, is transforming death itself into a laborious play. Or rather as life, so does death unfold in the limit between play and labor. As life is joyful, transitory, and non-melodramatic, so is death. However, it must be heroic and produce value. In her death the guerrilla "enters the homeland of allegory" where the dead and the living share a collective cosmology.[80] Her corpse speaks for a new genre of the human and the search for new fantasies from the ruins of history. Her unfulfilled life demands a response from us, leaving the burden of further signification on the shoulders of those who remain.

# 6

# A Promise, a Letter, a Funeral, and a Wedding

Not a woman in sight. An inhabited desert, to be sure, an absolutely full absolute desert, some might even say a desert teeming with people. Yes, but men, men and more men, over centuries of war, and costumes, hats, uniforms, soutanes, warriors, colonels, generals, partisans, strategists, politicians, professors, political theoreticians, theologians. In vain would you look for a figure of a woman, a feminine silhouette, and the slightest allusion to sexual difference.

— JACQUES DERRIDA, *POLITICS OF FRIENDSHIP*

I shall talk about the question of a coming of the woman considered in her otherness and authenticity — the "otherwoman" — phrasing it in the form of a perchance. With Jacques Derrida this word "perchance" always beckons toward the unpredictability of "what happens," of what comes, the incalculable coming of the other.

— CAROLE DELY, "JACQUES DERRIDA: THE PERCHANCE
OF A COMING OF THE OTHER WOMAN"

The secret of Friend Sara's being historical and universal is that she searched for ways of being herself. She has combated breathlessly for the freedom struggle for forty years and stood against all reactionism without any calculation, She knew that other women must accompany the search for ways to become *xwebun*. Therefore, she loved women most. She believed in them most. She believed that women would together — not separately — create the free life.

— CANDA SU, "SARALARDAN ARINLERE SADELIĞIN ASIL TEMSILI"

## A Promise and a Letter

In September 2010, the then-prime minister of Turkey, Recep Tayyip Erdoğan, made a public speech in Diyarbakır, the biggest Kurdish city within Turkey's borders, which many commentators considered to be historical for its recognition of Kurdish people's memory and culture. In the beginning of his speech, Erdoğan saluted the people of Diyarbakır with a quote from a native poet and embraced them with love and sincerity:

> Poet Ahmed Arif was saying "I think of you as if you were spring. As if you were Diyarbekir." We love you with a love as great as Diyarbakır and as wide as Turkey. . . . Diyarbakır is the city of *sahabes*, knowledge, civilization and brotherhood. Those who come to this sacred city and lie will become crushed under those lies and finished. Those who come before the nation and tell what they cannot do will become crushed under those promises. Those who do not speak the language of sincerity and love, the language of heart like Yunus Emre, Mevlana, Ahmede Hani and İbrahim Gülşeni, will not be able to come before the nation and look at its face.[1]

Later in his speech, the prime minister addressed the Kurds' suffering in Turkey and recognized the Turkish state's historical wrongdoings against Kurds, something that no head of the government had done until then. Despite the fact that Erdoğan's speech followed a recent failure of a "Kurdish initiative," many considered it to anticipate a new era of peace and a solution to the "Kurdish problem," welcoming it as a rewriting of Turkey as the homeland of Turks and Kurds among others:

> We cannot forget the pain of Ape Musa that is Musa Anter. We cannot forget Orhan Miroğlu's wound. We cannot forget the suffering of Abdürrahim Semavi who was tortured for seven years in the Diyarbakır prison. We cannot disregard Şivan Perver's longing. We cannot un-remember Ahmet Kaya's death in exile. We cannot un-think Ahmede Hani's love, Faki Teryan's passion. All the 81 cities are ours. 73 million are my brothers. We love the Turkish, Kurdish, Laz, Circassian, Georgian, Roman and Arab all the same. All 73 million are my brothers. Because we love everyone that God has created. We are the grandchildren of the soldiers in the famous armies of Nurettin Zengi, Kılıçarslan and surely Selahaddin Eyyubi. We have entered Malazgirt all together in Alparslan's army. We have all together taken over Kudüs under the banner of Selahaddin Eyyubi. With the hands of Kanuni,

Yavuz Sultan Selim, Fatih we have together distributed justice to three continents. We have defended Kut'ul Amare together. In the walls of Diyarbakır the sweat of us all is engrained. In the bricks of the Mosque Süleyman exists the faith of us all. In the mortars of Mosque Ulu, Behram Paşa, Şeyh Mutahhar, Sipahiler Bazaar, Malabadi Bridge, Dicle Bridge exist our brotherhood. Zılgıt is ours, horon is ours, halay is ours, zeybek is ours. We share the same prayers; the same qibla and we walk to the same future.[2]

Appealing to the figures of Kurdish history and claiming them as his brothers and referencing to Kurdish geography and claiming it as the product of collective labor, in his speech, Erdoğan was both reciting Turkey's official narratives of the past and reconstructing them in line with a liberal Islamic multicultural ideology.[3] According to the prime minister, Turkey was a country of multiple ethnicities that shared the collective identity of Islam, a collective memory of suffering, and a collective glory grounded in the notion of "*fetih*."[4] During the secular era of the Turkish republic, the word "*fetih*" was associated with the expansion of the Ottoman Empire and its conquest of new lands, and now, as Erdoğan vernacularized it, it referred to a cycle of border crossings by means of war, centralized distribution of justice by means of law, and remaking of space by means of grandiose construction. In this new area, where Turkey's secularist law and language was being critically questioned, Erdoğan and his party had articulated a new and modern meaning for "*fetih*" by using it in the expression *gönüllerin fethi*, "*fetih* of hearts." "*Fetih* of hearts" (not lands) was his party's call, and "service" to the people was its vocation. Apparently, Erdoğan had come to Diyarbakır to conquer the hearts of the Kurdish people and to reassure them that he was as much their servant as the Turks'. Who would have guessed then that "*fetih*" would acquire a whole other meaning and show its worst face only five years later, in the very Kurdish lands where this speech was made? Then, under around-the-clock curfews, the Turkish army violently reconquered insurgent Kurdish neighborhoods and destroyed them.

The speech in Diyarbakır was part of a series of meetings Erdoğan held for a referendum that would decide changes his party proposed to the Constitution. The referendum was going to take place on September 12, 2010, the thirtieth anniversary of Turkey's last successful coup, when the current Constitution was crafted. Erdoğan, who embodied Muslim resentment toward secular bureaucratic elitism in Turkey and who was supposedly critical of the Turkish state's hierarchical and exclusionary treatment of citizens based on appearance, belief, and lifestyles, was claiming Kurds for his side in the referendum by declaring that he knew their pain and injury:

> This brother of yours has read a poem in Siirt on 12 December 1997. Because I addressed my brothers in Siirt with a poem I became prosecuted, sentenced and remained in Pınarhisar Prison. . . . We know very well the trouble of people who have been prosecuted for their ideas. We know very well the feeling of rotting in a cell just for writing, speaking, expressing ideas, reading a poem, saying "rights," saying "democracy," saying "food and jobs." We know very well to be excluded for belief, for religious practice, for wearing a headscarf. We know very well the meaning of remaining in front of the university without being allowed entrance. We know poverty, bans, repression, and being in need. We know those who have been one night killed with a bullet in the back of their head and whose murderers were never found. We know having their house raided and destroyed. We know how books are seized. We know the tortures done to villagers collected in the middle of their village; we know what forced displacement and ban of pastures are. We know very well the pain, tears, cry and the storm breaking in the heart of mothers who visit their sons in prison but won't be allowed to speak one word of Kurdish.[5]

Erdoğan's emotional speech listed the many different facets of state oppression in Turkey, forced displacement, forced disappearance, mass arrest, and executions without trial. It not only entailed a claim that Kurds and Turks shared a collective memory, but also a seductive promise that appeared in the guise of a wish: "We all want a future where each and every one of our citizens lives with dignity and honor and is regarded to be a first-class citizen. Our future is one like our past."[6] Declaring that he suffered from a similar experience with Kurds as a wronged Muslim politician who spent time in jail, his wish was his promise: As long as he remained in power, Kurds could count on the fact that their desire of being "first-class citizens" in the eyes of the state would be fulfilled. As Erdoğan anticipated, in the referendum, his Justice and Development Party was successful in the region, luring a majority of Kurds to vote "yes."[7]

There was however, one catch in Erdoğan's speech that went unnoticed. Reiterating a cliché that many peace activists have drawn upon to put the politics of mourning against the politics of sovereignty in Turkey, Erdoğan stated, "The tears of a mother from Çorum who has given her son to martyrdom, flow into my heart. The tears of a mother, who lost her son to the gangs in the mountains, to the terrorist organization; whose son is sent to a certain death, flows into my lungs."[8] With these words Erdoğan was suggesting that Kurds and Turks not only shared a history but also that they were the same in their mourning, even if they fought against each other. Moreover, they were equal, because their suffering was felt and experienced similarly by him and as closely as the fluids of his organs. This equality, however, mediated and achieved in the intimacy of the prime minister's body, was not legally but affectively granted: it was private rather than public, based on suffering rather than on struggle. It pointed to a possibility of peace and "commensuration" only as long as the integrity of Erdoğan's body and his sovereign compassion remained intact.[9]

A promising state, especially one that promises love, affection, and commensuration, is a dangerous thing, and the people of Diyarbakır, who had encountered it in many different forms, knew better. However, it is also something that one cannot not want, specifically when one is situated at the margins of the nation as a colonized people. Not long after this speech, in 2013, a peace process did indeed start in Turkey, which lasted until 2015. One of the questions that haunted the Kurdish public during this time was whether the peace process and the speeches Erdoğan made on its behalf were "sincere" and whether Erdoğan would fulfill the promises he made at the Diyarbakır meeting. Despite the Kurdish side's insistence on legal guarantees, the ruling party kept refraining from building an official framework for the process and from naming it a process of "peace." This increased Kurds' doubts and their mistrust. While the peace process failed as prophesized, I am less interested in whether Erdoğan was or has ever been sincere. On the contrary, I would argue that as with all promises, the issue has never been whether he would eventually keep his promises or not. After all, one could argue that the performative language he used at the meeting had no other purpose than to act at the moment of the utterance. The more interesting issue to me is the *scandalous* seduction manifested in Erdoğan's words and the different desires at work, which made this speech and its success possible as much as its eventual failure to bring peace inevitable.

The promise (for love), according to Shoshana Felman, is a performative speech act that is defined by the singular property of being self-referential. It refers to a reality that it constitutes itself.[10] I have explained that the reality Erdoğan constructed through his promise equated his power with that of Kurdish people's destiny — as any populist politics would have — and his body with that of a field of commensuration uniquely capable of feeling everyone's pain and suffering equally. Speaking of Don Juan's seductive promises, Felman writes:

Just as seductive discourse exploits the capacity of language to reflect itself, by means of the self-referentiality of performative verbs, it also exploits in parallel fashion the self-referentiality of the interlocutor's narcissistic desire, and his (or her) capacity to produce in turn a reflexive, specular illusion: the seducer holds out to women the narcissistic mirror of their own desire of themselves. Thus Don Juan says to Charlotte: "You are not *obliged* to me for what I say, you owe it entirely to your own beauty. . . . Your beauty is your *security*."

Whether constative or performative, seductive discourse commits and endebts; but since the debt is contracted here on the basis of narcissism, the two parties to the debt are the woman and her own self-image. "Your beauty is your security." The specular illusion of self-reference allows Don Juan to elude the status of referent. While the seducer appears to be committing himself, his strategy is to create a *reflexive, self-referential debt* that, as such, does not engage *him*.[11]

Don Juan, the lover of women, seduces them and avoids any accountability for his promises of love by delegating responsibility to their beauty. He loves them, and the guarantee of his love is their beauty. If he ceases to love them, it must be their beauty that failed them. Interestingly enough, suffering is caught up into a similar narcissistic desire. Erdoğan loves the Kurds and promises them equality; Kurds' suffering is their guarantee. After having documented, monumentalized, and publicized the events that befell them, after having repeatedly identified with their enormous suffering under the Turkish colonial state, the self-image of Kurds has primarily become their pain and injury. In a global age of truth-commissions and peace processes, trauma and reconciliation, there were even moments when they believed that this pain and injury in themselves could acquire a status of truth and qualify them for first-class citizenship.

And yet, Erdoğan is no Don Juan. Different from Don Juan, he is a believer in God and a debt-collector. In his speech, suffering is in the eye of the beholder — better yet, in the body of the beholder. While Kurds believed that the rights they deserve are owed entirely to their own suffering and struggle, Erdoğan was saying that it is him, his knowledge, and his body to which their "first-class citizenship" would be obliged. Felman thinks that the repeated promises Don Juan makes and doesn't keep testify to his desire to avoid death. Erdoğan's promise is grounded in his own body and its capacity to commensurate. His desire is to give birth to a new and homogeneous nation from within his body.

At a closer look, there are several other conclusions to be drawn from Erdoğan's speech, and based on these I argue that rather than being historical, recognizing Kurdish difference and announcing peace, Erdoğan's speech was one that was monumental, declared Kurds' destiny to be one of (an impossible sameness) to Turks, and initiated a civil war. First, an end to Kurdish suffering is an impossibility because it is suffering that secures the love and the intimacy that the state will grant to Kurds. Second, an independent Kurdish subject who does not desire or manage to communicate her suffering and to evoke the state's compassion will fail to be equal with Turks. It is, after all, not the martyr and the son who join "the terrorist organization" and find a "certain" death who bring the prime minister to tears. It is their mourning mothers who affect him.

But then, is there any place for difference proper in such a discourse to begin with? Or is it sameness, despite difference, that needs to be performed to deserve the state's love? A subtraction is needed from the Kurds' identity: their specific historical trajectories must be subtracted, to be replaced with suffering. The remainder, who suffers the pain of subtraction, can be reinserted into the community and become equal to the proper national subject only because and as long as it has the capacity to communicate its suffering without accusing the subtractor. But if that is so, the Kurd cannot be the same as the Turk, either. She is forbidden to desire to be different from the Turk, but she can also not become the same as the Turk because of the trace of state violence she carries on her body (for which she suffers), which she should not forget but also not blame anyone for.

Third, recognition is an erotic, affective, and moral process, and hence, it is associated with the household and not the public. In relation to this last point, I argue that the prime minister's extremely intimate speech in Diyarbakır was a declaration of civil war as much as an announcement of peace. Agamben states that civil war "constitutes a threshold of indifference between the *oikos* and the *polis*, between blood kinship and citizenship."[12] Civil war confuses "what pertains to the *oikos* with what is particular to the *polis*, what is intimate with the foreign."[13] In the prime minister's speech, notions of kinship (brotherhood), labor, and *fetih* (religious call) claimed the Kurds for the state-in-formation; promises for equal citizenship lured them to a common future, while his body and sovereignty were declared to protect and make them equal with Turks. His claim, his promise, and his declaration of his own bodily inevitability were inseparable and linked the past, the present, and the future as they interwove Kurds, Turks, and the state's bodies together. There was no conflict between Kurds and Turks but a misunderstanding — a miscommunication even, caused by the secular state in-passing, which could be corrected by the state-to-come that he represented and which demanded that its love for God and his creations be reciprocated with appreciation. The speech, in other words, if we follow Agamben, conflated the private and the public, the household and the political, rights and suffering, the sacred, the secular, and the erotic, along with the Kurdish, the Turkish, and the state to an extent that it redefined the Kurdish geography as a zone of civil war, "as a zone of indifference between the unpolitical space of the family and the political space of the city. In transgressing the threshold, the *oikos* is politicized; conversely, the *polis* is 'economized,' that is, it is reduced to an *oikos*."[14] The declaration of love and care and the promise for equality disguised as a wish, as seductive as they were, announced and demanded an intimacy that resonated with a patriarchal state tradition Kurds have suffered from for at least a century. The stately imperative once again commanded Kurds and Turks to be the same, as impossible as that was, and to have the same memory and desires even when it recognized difference on the surface. It thereby depoliticized the Kurds' struggle for freedom and politicized their "brotherly" loyalty to Turks

Finally, if the prime minister's speech was neither a recognition of difference but a declaration of an impossible sameness, nor an announcement of peace but one of civil war, then it also wasn't historical but "monumental."[15] That is, it cannot be dissociated from exactly where it was taking place and the discontinuity it wanted to evoke.[16] Toward the end of his speech, Erdoğan discussed the very controversial Diyarbakır Military Prison situated near the meeting area. He said:

> I always said it and I say it again in Diyarbakır: Ah if only Diyarbakır Prison had a tongue and could speak and tell all that was lived after 12th September. Ah if only that 5th cell could talk and tell those inhumane tortures and inhumane treatments. . . . Have I made a promise? Yes, we are closing the Diyarbakır Prison quickly. We will build the new prison quickly. The moment it is finished, we will demolish the infamous Diyarbakır prison. We want it not to remind our city of 12th September. God willing this will be our deed.[17]

The prime minister's depoliticization of crimes against humanity as "shame," his modern and economizing solution to political wrongs by means of erasing their traces, his understanding of the subject as primarily situated in the religious and familial realm and constituted in the navigation between the moral worlds of suffering and duty are all aspects of the new governmentality that his party aimed at instituting in Turkey and Kurdistan. But what does it really mean to say, "We want it not to remind our city of 12th September. God willing this will be our deed," when the whole speech was about proper and collective remembering?

A year before this speech the Justice and Development Party had developed a project to transform the Diyarbakır Prison into a school. However, this idea encountered fierce opposition from the people of the city. Specifically, those who stayed in the prison declared that they wanted it to become a museum as a testimony to the torture they underwent. For many inmates the Diyarbakır Prison is a sacred place, the church of the state, if you want, where sacrilege and sacrifice took stately meanings, and they didn't want it to disappear from sight. Needless to say, the idea of making the Diyarbakır Prison into a museum was inspired by the global trend of memorialization and the discourse on "facing with past truths" that was posed as a means for reconciliation and peace making.

I think that his promise to demolish the prison testifies to Erdoğan's desire that his speech would become sacred and monumental and rise on the ruins of another monument, the still operative Diyarbakır Prison, and replace it. To the extent that the prison remained in sight, in the psychic landscape of the city of Diyarbakır, it would be a reminder of a greater power than Erdoğan. His promise to give birth to a new nation would never be fulfilled, and the prison's mythical violence would reduce his reign to parody.

Eventually the Diyarbakır Prison would not be demolished; neither would it become a museum. However, Erdoğan made sure that the memories of the prison were overshadowed with his *fetih* of the city five years later. During that time, other monuments in Diyarbakır would be destroyed; on their ruins his reign and cruelty gained psychic dominion. Yet, contrary to the prime minister's assertions, actually the walls of Diyarbakır did have a tongue, and they did indeed speak. The inmates told their stories, asking for justice with no avail to this day. These stories were, however, not only about suffering but about how to become human through friendship in pain and death when one is object to subtraction.[18] This struggle of remaining human, a different genre of human, was however, not on the agenda of the prime minister and pointed to the very different understandings of peace that the PKK and the Turkish state adhere to.

Three years after Erdoğan's speech, in 2013, Diyarbakır would witness another great event. In the day of Newroz (March 21), MP Sırrı Süreyya Önder, who was one of the few people who then had the right to visit Abdullah Öcalan, read his letter, foretelling the coming peace process along with the spring:

I salute the people of the Middle East and Central Asia celebrating
this awakening, revival and resurgence day of Newroz with extraordinary participation and unity. . . . I salute all the peoples celebrating Newroz, which is the daylight and turning point of a new era,
with great enthusiasm and democratic tolerance. . . . I salute all the
travelers on this grand path toward democratic rights, freedom, and
equality. . . . I salute you, the Kurdish people, living at the Zagros and
Taurus mountain skirts and in the valleys of the Euphrates and Tigris
rivers. I salute the Kurdish people, an ancient people, dwellers in the
sacred lands of Mesopotamia and Anatolia, mother to all agricultural,
village and urban civilizations.[19]

After his salute, Öcalan, like Prime Minister Erdoğan, made reference to the
common past and culture of Turkish and Kurdish people:

Kurds have taken part in this several-thousand-year-old civilization in
friendship and accord with diverse races, religions, creeds — we have
all built it together. For Kurds the Euphrates and Tigris are the siblings
of Sakarya and Maritsa. Ararat and Judi are the friends of Kaçkars and
Erciyes. Halay and Delilo are in the family of Horon and Zeybek.

Notice that instead of brotherhood, Öcalan refers to friendship between Kurds
and Turks. Once again, it is unlikely that Öcalan read Derrida. Yet, as a leader
of a liberation movement that claims to be a women's movement, it is likely
that he was aware of the dangers that "sisters" posed to the fraternity Erdoğan
wished for and instead referred to friendship as a possibility as much as a reality that can ground a democracy to come.

Three further aspects stood out in Öcalan's letter that radically differentiated his stance toward peace from that of Erdoğan's. First, he refrained from
promises of commensuration and instead underlined that conflict would go
on even in this new era, albeit without using the means of violence:

The period of armed struggle is ending, and the door is opening to
democratic politics. We are beginning a process focused on political,
social and economic aspects; an understanding based on democratic
rights, freedoms, and equality is growing. We have sacrificed much of
our lives for the Kurdish people, we paid a high price. None of these
sacrifices, none of our struggles, were in vain. For as a consequence of
them, the Kurdish people have attained once again their identity and
their roots. We have now reached the point of "silence the weapons
and let the ideas and politics speak." The modernist paradigm that has
disregarded, excluded and denied us has been razed to the ground.

Regardless of whether it be Turkish, Kurdish, Laz or Circassian — the blood spilled is flowing from a human being and from the bosom of this land. Witnessed by the millions of people who heed my call, I say a new era is beginning; an era where politics gain prominence over weapons. We have now arrived at the stage of withdrawing our armed forces outside the borders. I believe that all those who have believed in this cause and in me are sensitive to the possible dangers of the process. This is not an end, but a new beginning. This is not abandoning the struggle — we are initiating a different struggle.

Second, Abdullah Öcalan made sure to underline that it was the people who were the guarantee of the process — not their suffering, but their search for freedom. He thereby invited people to identify themselves with their struggle instead of their suffering:

> The era of exploitative regimes, repression and denial is over. The peoples of the Middle East and those of Central Asia are awakening. They are returning to their roots. They demand a halt to the blinding and seditious wars and conflicts against one another. Those thousands, millions of people who are pouring into these arenas are burning with the passion of Newroz. They cry for peace and amity, and they are demanding a solution.

Finally, Öcalan put the responsibility for peace on the shoulders of the entire peoples of the Middle East and their capacity to become mobilized and politicized:

> I call on all oppressed peoples; on women, who are the most long-standing colonized and subjugated class; on all marginalized and excluded creeds, cults, and cultures; on the working class and all subordinated classes; on everyone who has been excluded from the system to take their rightful position in Democratic Modernity and to attain its mentality. The Middle East and Central Asia are searching for a contemporary modernity and a democratic order that befits their own history. A new model in which all can coexist peacefully and amicably has become an objective need like the need for bread and water. Inevitably, again, the geography and culture of Anatolia and Mesopotamia are guiding it to build such a model. . . . We shall unite against those who want to divide and make us fight one another. We shall join together against those who want to separate us. Those who cannot understand the spirit of the age will end up in the dustbin of history. Those who resist the current will fall into the abyss. The peoples of the

region are witnessing a new dawn. The peoples of the Middle East are weary of enmity, conflict, and war. They want to be reborn from their own roots and to stand shoulder to shoulder.

One million people, including me, attended the 2013 Newroz and listened to the letter with tears in their eyes. In the Newroz arena and later in the many small cafes and restaurants of Diyarbakır, we were all talking about transformation, hope, new beginnings, and a different future. We had joined in the fantasy of finally moving toward a civic polity where freedom, friendship, and equality would flourish. The year 2013 seemed to be one of possibility, and maybe therein lay its eventual doom. For isn't possibility and the desires that attach to it exactly what the state wants to govern over and cannot leave alone?[20]

## A Wedding and a Funeral

This was not the first time that year that I was in Diyarbakır, nor would it be the last. For the Kurdish people and their friends in Turkey, a funeral and a wedding marked the beginning and the end of 2013. The funeral belonged to three Kurdish women assassinated in Paris, and the wedding was a mass wedding attended by President Erdoğan and three Kurdish celebrities whom he personally hosted.[21] Organized by the Kurdish Movement and hosted by the government, the funeral and the mass wedding staged a competition over which metaphor would prevail for the peace process and who would master it. While the Kurdish Movement put forth an economy of gift and sacrifice, martyrdom and fidelity, where the lives lost in the war could be cherished and mourned, the government crafted a political world where "war would be transformed into peace through marriage."[22] At another level, however, the funeral and the wedding, as far as both of them originated in a state act—since soon we would learn that the women were assassinated by a member of the Turkish intelligence services—also scripted the different ways in which the feminine would be figured in the post-conflict Kurdistan as they juxtaposed the image of a future where defiant women died into citizenship with one where consenting brides married into it.

On January 9, 2013, only a few days after the possibility of a peace process was first discussed in television and newspapers, three members of the Kurdish women's movement were assassinated in Paris. One of them was Sakine Cansız, a founding member of the PKK and a much beloved figure among the Kurdish opposition. During her lifetime she had built a respectable reputation; she had remained in the notorious Diyarbakır Prison during the 1980

Figure 11. The three murdered women in Paris (Özgür Politika Archives)

military regime and resisted its torture and repression both in prison and in court. When she came out of prison in 1991, she had stayed in different PKK camps, where she organized and headed women's squads. In the mid-1990s she had moved to France to conduct diplomacy on behalf of Kurdish women and was granted asylum in 1998.

The death of the three women was both shocking and confusing. Even though by then people had made themselves familiar with comparable peace processes in the world, and the Colombian example in particular, where the government had assassinated several FARC members participating in the negotiations, it was hard to understand why it was these three women who were chosen to be the victims of peace. Whether intentionally or by chance, it seemed that a conspiratorial force had materialized itself and targeted the women's movement with a strong Alevi component — a minor and progressive religious sect — alerting people to the government's desire to transform the peace process into a patriarchal Sunni alliance between Turkish and Kurdish men.

The funeral for the three women took place eight days after their death once the government allowed a public ceremony and agreed to withhold any intervention.

Their bodies were first brought to Diyarbakır, and from there each was taken to the place they were born. Thousands attended the ceremonies and mourned their deaths against the background of laments sung by women in different Kurdish dialects. Being revolutionaries, feminists, and Alevis, the deceased were everything that the Turkish nation claimed not to be and that the Sunni, patriarchal, and now the neoliberal state abjected. The Kurds participating in the funeral crafted their identity out of that very abject-ness and formed themselves as people in their very act of mourning.

Sakine Cansız was fifty-five when she died. Kurds embraced her casket as if she were a daughter, and women carried her to the grave as if she were a sister. Adriana Cavarero notes the scarcity of sisters and daughters in the tragedy form and the abundance of mothers and brides.[23] In the Kurdish public, however, the names "daughter" and "sister" situated the deceased in the tragic genealogy of female guerrillas, who are neither brides nor mothers. Instead of wedding dresses, as is the case in single women's untimely deaths, flags in the Kurdish colors of yellow, red, and green covered the caskets of the three women, testifying to their death into a nation that only existed in imagination. It was only after their death that they could be integrated into Kurdistan's space — yet even then only as a trace, since the fact that at least two of them were PKK members (Sara and Rojbin) was systematically erased from public speech, and they were referred to as women politicians or activists.

Eleven months after the funeral, on November 16, 2013, Erdoğan came to Diyarbakır to affirm the peace process — this time in his own style. He was hosting three other men, all Kurdish: Şivan Perwer, one of the most beloved Kurdish singers whose taped songs were formative in the making of Kurdishness in Turkey during 1990s; Mesoud Barzani, the president of the Kurdish federal government in Iraq; and İbrahim Tatlıses, another world-renowned Kurdish singer, who while being popular among the Turkish and Arab publics, is less than respected among Kurdish oppositional groups, who regard him as a symbol of assimilation. In the meeting the prime minister held, Perwer and Tatlıses sang in Kurdish, testifying to the newly found multiculturalism of the Turkish republic.

There was, however, something uncanny and grotesque in the union of the three men that left the audience in Dyarbakır utterly dissatisfied. For one thing, both Barzani and Perwer were criticized for arriving as guests of Erdoğan, given the fact that they had rejected several earlier invitations extended to them by the Kurdish opposition. İbrahim Tatlıses had come to the end of a singing career that had started in the late 1970s. Throughout the 1980s and 1990s many of the songs he made popular were actually translations of

Figure 12. The funeral of Sakine Cansız (Sara), Fidan Doğan (Rojbin), and Leyla Şaylemez (Ronahî) (Özgür Politika Archives)

Kurdish traditional songs into Turkish, and he made himself sympathetic to Turkish crowds by capitalizing on his poor background and his working-class experience. Throughout his career he had accumulated many friends in the so-called deep state, and recently, he had been shot in the head by a mafia figure with whom he had a history of feuding. The occasion in Diyarbakır was the first time he appeared on stage, and, as an archaic figure representing assimilation and self-denial, he was not going to excite the public.

In the meeting of Erdoğan, Barzani, Perwer, and Tatlıses, the metaphor in operation was marriage. Their union on the stage stood for a union between Kurdish and Turkish people not as "brothers" but as "bride" and "groom" in a patriarchal marriage. The three men, although iconic in their fields, by taking the stage with Erdoğan in place of those who were the real actors of peace, injured their own reputation and hence the possibility of being qualified as equal brothers. Instead, the stage, where the injured body of Tatlıses and his disfigured voice became the dominant motif, was transformed into a pornographically charged space or, better, into a scandalous spectacle against which a kind of collective ethnic shame was felt, and it looked like Erdoğan had groomed the three Kurdish men.

Julia Lupton notes that, along with the figure of the brother, "a recurrent but less-remarked image of the citizen is that of the bride. The bride's consent to marriage both inserts a contractual element into sovereign relations and institutes a hierarchy between partners; indeed, the rites of marriage wed the contrary principles of contract and coercion, equality and difference, civility and sovereignty."[24]

If there was still any doubt about what metaphor of peace the government wanted to institute after this staged meeting, that doubt was put to rest by what followed. A ceremony where four hundred couples wed crowned the union of

Figure 13. From left to right: İbrahim Tatlıses, Recep Tayyip Erdoğan, Mesoud Barzani, Şivan Perwer (Getty Images)

the four men. While Barzani and Erdoğan became witnesses to the marriage ceremony, a duet by Perwer and Tatlıses sealed it.

The funeral and the wedding, both authored by the Turkish government, revealed the future it wanted to institute in Kurdistan through women's bodies: in peace-time death and marriage would complement each other and operate in harmony, reproducing normative life cycles and reestablishing a culture of reproductive futurity. While conflict would be relegated to the past, the sovereignty of the nation and family would be reestablished. In post-conflict, fraternal Turkey, a future for women PKK members was unimaginable.[25]

Two years later, in 2015, the peace process in Turkey collapsed for reasons easily explicable at the level of Real-politik. I, however, take the invitation Jaspir Puar extended in her *Terrorist Assemblages* and believe that such explanations should be disrupted because they refuse to take into account feminist and queer perspectives.[26] Perhaps the peace process collapsed also because the women guerrillas, women politicians, and mothers, who understood the future envisioned for them by Erdoğan and others, have opened up a tear in the straight map that the state, patriarchy, imperialism, and capitalism had drawn of the future of Turkey and Kurdistan and made visible for people to see what other potential pathways there are that could otherize the colonial, patriarchal, and neoliberal present.

## Conclusion

In her ethnography on how Black lives are affected by progressive projects, Savannah Shange writes that "Black flesh is always in excess, uncivil, and marked by its incongruity with the progressive project, to which we remain narratively central, and yet materially surplus."[27] In this chapter I have shown that so is Kurdish women's flesh. Despite being central to Erdoğan's narrative and staging of the Kurdish initiative and the peace process, Kurdish women remain materially surplus to them. Erdoğan, who claims to embody the possibility for a democratic state, cannibalizes Kurdish resistance and struggle, its flesh, its voice, and its narrative. He monumentalizes himself in place of the Diyarbakır prison, a primary sign of Kurdistan's occupation and Kurdish oppression, declaring it to be without sound. He "dematerializes" and "dematernalizes" the Kurdish voice, which relies on the inassimilable language of the mother and her songs, by turning it into a consenting masculine nod.[28] He thereby transforms the radical musical tradition of Kurdishness that screams "we will win" into the tense of "look what you have accomplished" and "domesticates freedom dreams to the realm of what's possible rather than what's necessary."[29] Meanwhile, the vision of a democratic, liberal, and progressive state is crafted by replacing friends, sisters, and daughters with happy brides and tearful mothers. The order of the public is restored by the love of the state and its *fetih* of the hearts and by killing and/or marrying women that went stray. Kurds are invited to exchange their suffering, which is now abstracted in stately speech and subtracted from sentient flesh, in return for a citizenship they should perform neither in sameness nor in difference. Occupying the threshold between "melancholia and mourning," as well as "mourning and morning," women in turn continue performing "improvisational and generative ensembles of a life in common" in the political and the social worlds, claiming a different form of universality instead of the one that is refused to them under the sign of equal citizenship.[30] This universality resides in the "screams, songs, prayers, cries and goans" of women that lament in Sakine's, Fidan's and Leyla's funeral, not only because they connect them to other women in the world but rather because it is in these sounds and voices that one can hear the different "phonic substances" that express the cut and the augementation law exercizes on women's flesh and their freedom dreams.[31]

# Conclusion

We are fugitives. From the laws of life that expected us. What is out there for a 20 years old woman like me? Here, I have relearned how to walk, how to project my voice. It is like I have newly discovered my body. Yes, there might be a peace accord. Men in PKK can lay down arms. But not us. What about the war against women? We are not laying down our weapons until we win that war.

         — FEMALE RECRUIT IN THE QANDIL MOUNTAINS

On November, 25, 2020, the Kurdish Women's Movement in Europe (TJK-E) inaugurated a campaign against the Turkish president Erdoğan.[1] The campaign, "100 Reasons to Prosecute the Dictator," listed a hundred cases in which women were killed by state officers or their direct allies; it aimed at collecting one hundred thousand signatures demanding international prosecution of Erdoğan for committing systematic femicide in Turkey and abroad. Among the murders included on the list were those of Sakine Cansız, Fidan Doğan, and Leyla Şaylemez; Ekin Wan, Taybet İnan, and Seve Demir; and Pakize Nayır and Fatma Uyar. Also included were the murders of Ceylan Önkol, Dilek Doğan, and Hevrin Khalaf (they are not mentioned in this book despite being widely publicized). Ceylan Önkol, twelve years old, died as a result of a mortar shell shot from a nearby police station in 2009. Dilek Doğan was killed in 2015 in a house raid when she asked a police officer to take off his shoes; and the Syrian-Kurdish politician Hevrin Khalaf was executed in 2019 by mercenaries during the Turkish assaults on northern Syria. When the campaign "100 Reasons to Prosecute the Dictator" was completed on March 8, 2021, TJK-E delivered the signatures to the UN as a petition asking for an investigation of Erdoğan's involvement in these murders. TJK-E also declared that the broader framework of the campaign was informed by the feminist struggle to have femicide recognized as a crime against humanity, to be treated as other war crimes and genocide.

At first sight it might seem odd that a movement whose freedom dreams point to the creation of an "otherwise" outside of the structures of capitalism, patriarchy, and the nation-state would choose the UN as an address to account for the crimes committed against it. Why would women whose very being and becoming unfold in incongruence with the law and whose entire experience repeatedly point to the impossibility of becoming full citizens in the existing international order adopt a legal language as a way of framing their struggle? For the Kurdish Women's Freedom Movement, femicide is the manifestation of a global war waged against women and society led by states, capital, and men. How come while theorizing it as such, the movement insists on the recognition of femicide as a war crime by the very structures that support it? I am asking these questions both in political and theoretical terms in the context of feminist, queer, Black, and autonomist movements that have recently almost altogether lost their hope in any formal political procedures.

A second question I would like to raise in relation to the campaign in question is whether "femicide" is the right term to categorize these murders that have been committed by the state in the context of war, often without any account of the sex of the victims. This is a question I also raised in Chapter 4. There I have argued that there is a lineage, an echo, a reverberation between the women who have been victims of femicide and those targeted by the state mediated by the work that the latter perform and the ideology within which they give meaning to their activities. Here, I would like to extend that argument by coming back to the political imagination of the Kurdish Women's Freedom Movement.

Femicide is not only a crime committed against women's right to live, which reduces it to a matter of the body. It targets the imagination and aims at capturing women as they migrate out of the imaginative and material spaces of patriarchy. These are spaces where new knowledges about the limits of the body, politics, and subjectivity can be experienced and where, following Suelly Rudnick, the decolonization of the unconscious can occur.[2] As Fred Moten would have it, these are spaces where the excess that the laws of the imagination incite can be given flesh and experimented with.[3] If we would conceptualize femicide as a war against gendered ways of being and becoming that interrupt the reproduction of the racist capitalist patriarchal order as other scholars have done, then women killed because of their participation in the Kurdish Freedom Movement cease to be considered casualties in a war.[4] Each of the deaths becomes a singular act that targets the heterogeneous ways in which women generate knowledges as they act in autonomy and contempt.[5]

The Kurdish Women's Freedom Movement, in its commitment to the generality of the word and world, as much as to the singularity of the flesh and voice, has the ambition to practice universality.[6] That is, it has the ambition of showing and telling the knowledge that it has gained through its members' insubordination and of sharing the political imagination it has developed. If universality, as Ferreira da Silva has stated, is difference without separability, both claiming that women who have been killed in war are victims of femicide and asking the UN for justice are acts in which Kurdish women resist their provincialization enacted by separating their flesh and voice from the world and word.

I have argued in this book that the political imagination of the Kurdish Women's Freedom Movement resists being One and instead unfolds in the limits between voice and language, the mythical time, the maternal time, and the time of political urgency, legality and illegality, flesh and body, past and present, and mourning and morning. To remind the reader of a quote from Berjin Haki that I used as an epigraph in the Introduction of this book, this imagination, like the tune of a flute, is neither a completed composition nor an ignorable noise; it is a unique improvisation that interpellates listeners to become — even if momentarily — awake and uncomfortable in their bodies, leading them to a journey both toward their flesh and toward transcendence.

Addressing the UN and requesting it to recognize the murders of women in the war of the Turkish state against Kurds is then not a desperate attempt to achieve a goal but a means without end that changes the music of the world and forces other rhythms and tunes to interrupt the reproduction of the present as future. It is, in the Kurdish Freedom Movement's terms, a way of self-defense, as it is only by claiming all the means that the oppressed in their struggle to survive have generated, including the utopia that once must have informed the UN, that freedom dreams can be dreamt and an imagination of universality grounded in difference-without-separability can be achieved.[7] Let me finish this book with some final words on what I called the political imagination of the Kurdish Women's Freedom Movement and revisit some of the ideas that I have tried to develop in order to contribute to its will to be understood and seen.

## The Matter of the Kurdish Women's Freedom Movement: Its Music and Flesh

I have started this book with the year 2015, when the peace process between the state and PKK collapsed, and, in its retaliation, the Turkish state has produced corpses of Kurdish women along with ruined cities to be watched and viewed by Turkish audiences. I have argued that this was not only a military response to the increased sovereignty of the Kurdish Freedom Movement in Turkey's Kurdistan but also an attempt to undo the political imagination that Kurdish women generated in the Middle East through the figures of the mother, woman politician, and woman guerrilla. This political imagination and the feminine joy associated with its performance are what the state wanted to interdict by separating bodies from their community, by transforming the Kurdish voice and language into a noise, and by collapsing time and space through reducing the places where Kurdishness breathes into rubbles. I have, however, also argued that despite all, after a literal devastation and an attempt to elimination, which to this day still continues, Kurdish women's imagination, the fantasies they generate, and their joy have survived, since the movement's greatest intervention is where psychoanalysis and politics intercept: the matter, the temporality, and the spatiality of politics, which they have carved on the flesh of the world through their lives and deaths.[8]

The Turkish state is obsessed with Kurds, even more so with Kurdish women. It constantly asks, "Yes, but what do you want?" The answer to the state's question is easy: Kurds want what is necessary for their survival. And often their survival necessitates the transformation of the entire system. Women, who have divorced themselves from patriarchy, embody this desire subjectively, struggling to make a difference and bring about a new future through their flesh and voice, body and speech.[9] Sometimes they do it with a hysterical laughter, at other times with an excited speech, sometimes with an embrace, at other times with a scarf turned into heritage, and sometimes they do it by fighting and at other times by dying.

## The Mother

The Kurdish Women's Freedom Movement unfolds beside the shriek of the mother, her maternal song, and her claim to have her sovereign love be publicly accounted for. As the Turkish state fills the frames in which Kurdishness is represented with the noise of guns, bombs, shackles, and screams and bans the mother tongue, the Kurdish mother continues singing her lullabies and laments and moans, thereby making sure that her children will remain incongruent with law as the music that falls on their ears becomes an echo that injures their relationship with words. However, this is not enough, since assimilation and elimination threaten to reduce the maternal song either into an unrepresentable and inescapable melancholic rhythm for Kurds or into a suffering objectified in mother's tears, whose representation becomes a token of exchange between the state and its liberal opposition. The language and the body of the mother are cannibalized, and, in the best scenario, as oc- curred between 2009 and 2015, Kurds are expected to exchange her suffering in return for a citizenship that they can perform neither in sameness nor in difference. The Kurdish Women's Freedom Movement, in response, theorizes motherhood anew and enacts a movement of mothers that is both always an- tecedent to the current moment and anticipatory of a not-yet. As the sovereign love of the mother erupts into the public, it challenges the sovereign law of the state, opening up new temporalities and giving rise to new fantasies about how the divine, the living, and the dead could be reassembled. The mother's shriek, her voice, her moaning become a morning: a language to come.

The flesh of the mother, ungendered by labor and pain, by patriarchy and the nation state and the generosity that this very ungendering generates, be- comes for the Kurdish Movement the ground for envisioning new loves, laws, and norms. By going back in time to mythology and by fast-forwarding to a fu- ture ruled by matrilineality (enacted by all-women organizations), the women of the movement try to bring the mother's laws that haunt them to have a bearing on politics here and now. As they are reduced in their struggle to flesh and condemned to death-bound subjectivities, they turn their voice, flesh, and lives into means without end, into overtures in quantum entanglements.

## The Politician

The speech and the narratives of the women in the Kurdish Movement, as their political performances, improvise between the need to envision other worlds and the need to connect to the world and word. Melodrama, as the genre of modernity, and play, as the genre of freedom, are both employed, leading to an oscillation between intelligibility and unintelligibility. Through melodramatic tellings of the suffering of their people, Kurdish women politi- cians address the "conscience" of people, which they hope is able to account for those lives that are rendered unintelligible by law. As they work the interval between the need of their people and the possibilities that formal politics of- fer, they improvise performances in the limits between legality and illegality, the demands not to forgive and forget and the demand to reconcile, between autonomy and citizenship, their ungendered flesh in protests and the bod- ies that are given to them as parliamentary personas. These improvisations produce new norms that can be cited and build the political tradition of the Kurdish Women's Freedom Movement that can be cited and collectivized, the purple color of the Kurdish Politics, as Gültan Kışanak calls it.[10] As Tur- key's mode of colonization of Kurdish lands changes, as the space of Kurdistan is shrunk by new technologies, and as the border between Turkey's Kurdistan are stabilized, these limits that Kurdish women occupy are thinned down, as well. The women politicians are forced toward illegality and flesh, and yet they struggle to hang in those limits even when they are jailed, isolated, or beaten and reach out to other flesh to keep remaining entangled, ensembled.

## The Guerrilla

The guerrilla is both like the mother and the politician. She is like the mother, unreproductive as she is, because as a void in Kurdistan, unrepresentable and unlivable, she is its Real. She is also like the politician because she must represent her people and fight for them at the same time as she creates a new life. The Kurdish Women's Freedom Movement, as it unfolds in between the mother's shriek and claim, the politician's laughter and speech, also happens between the void the woman guerrilla left in patriarchy in her freedom search and the freedom she promises with her death. When the guerrilla leaves her house, she refuses to be rendered flesh by patriarchy and her condemnation to nothingness as a bride; for her relatives, however, it is in that very act that she dies and her mourning begins. Between her death as a potential wife and new birth as a friend to the Kurdish people until the day she becomes a "martyr" lie the great mountains of Kurdistan. In these mountains, which are both exilic spaces and spaces from which the guerrilla reconnects Kurdistan to the world and unprovincializes it, rendering it as the birthplace of a time yet-to-come, a new genre of the human and new forms of erotics are performed. Occupying revolutionary time, where history, mythology, the slow life of reproduction, and the exceptional time of war collide, and becoming a friend to the people and nature, the guerrilla practices decolonization of truth, freedom, and life.

Truth becomes a transformation of subjectivity from subjection to subjectivization through discursive and material labor and unearthing and performing new laws and norms for women's desire. Freedom becomes a movement against capture that needs to be signified by meaning giving and rebuilding the word and the world. Meanwhile, as singular women entangled in the quantum dynamics of the movement, women guerrillas refuse to be the author of their lives and rather situate themselves in ensembles and let their lives be played out. These lives then become stepleaders, with overtures making other people move in excitement.

The imaginary and the fantasies that the Kurdish Freedom Movement produce and reproduce do not reaffirm existing communities but occupy the limits between the communal and the political, the universal and the plural and become a force within and beyond these limits. This is how the flight, the divorce, the migration from existing worlds occurs: by a constant movement in between, by owning up to homelessness experienced by women in a patriarchal society, and by an oscillation between belonging and non-belonging. This leads women to continuously organize and reorganize in many overlapping fronts and organizations.

The mother, the politician, and the guerrilla are important figures not because they should be replicated elsewhere (because of their historical content) but because there are historically specific (products of a discursive order) escaping the law and its determination.[11] Mother, politician, and guerrilla fail to be mothers, politicians, and guerrillas as we know them; they instead occupy limits and thereby produce new fantasies of the real, new imagos, and new meanings about how to live a life without being the subject of a life story. Mothers who survive matricide to ban the cruel laws and fantasies of patriarchy, politicians whose voice and flesh reach out to damned communities and risk their own condemnation, joyful guerrillas who in their life and death make new geographies and promise new futures provide the self-defense of Kurdish women, exactly because they decolonize the unconscious by becoming forces that move the Kurdish women to new utopias. These utopias in turn feed into the creation of pedagogies of love and defiance, femininities that refuse to abide by the law, all the while being deeply embedded in relationships that bring homelessness home. It is these relationships and their fantasies that survive Creon, even if he is not yet defeated. Antigone was alone. Kurdish women have friends, mothers, and representatives — theirs is a collective struggle of a different kind from hers.

As I began with the *halay*, I want to end this book with the *halay*, since it is *halay*, this extraordinary fleshly togetherness, that has no beginning and end that sets the rhythm and the tune of this book. *Halay*, as a performance of difference without separability that evokes both tradition and anticipation, promises joy both when it is danced and viewed, provides open access to anyone who wants to join it, yet allows you to be good at it only when you dance it again and again and, as a space that is both disciplined and welcomes excess, is to me the condensed materialization of the imagination I have attempted to delineate in this book. The aesthetic imagination that *halay* brings to the world also informs the radical political tradition of Kurdish women, the being and becoming that they constitute and the joy they generate, which the state tries to interdict with no avail:

That night, I have once again caught that thing, which moves towards its goal with a determination and serenity beyond human power, in the slow steps of those that were dancing the *halay*. In harmony with the monotonous rhythm of the drum, the crowd that was making the same steps with the same hand and shoulder moves as if the end would never come, was recording on the marble ground on which purple lights were playing with invisible letters: That which was to come was being expected for a long time, to stop it, to come on its way was as impossible as hindering the season's turn.[12]

# Acknowledgments

While this might appear to be a book with a single author, its tone is set by several ensembles that I have been part of, crafted at the margins of the spaces of the state, family, and capital. This book, as the life that I call mine, belongs to you all, with all its sins and merits: 10-C, 12-C, Boğaziçi, Moda, Eigenmann+g+k, the 2006 bus to Diyarbakır and all its multiple extensions, Balcı ap., ugliness studies, Hazal Ana, Eşli King, Barış Meclisi, BİKG, BAK, Massacre at Letafet Hanım's, sürgünlük, writing posse, Jin TV, International Initiative, and pis olmak.

Ayşe, Cihat, Dicle, Leyla, Nagehan, and Nejat (aka Paramaz), our complicated entanglement continues after your deaths, and this book is one way in which I respond to living with your gift and curse. "Neverland," "I wish I had the words," "there is too much pain in this world," "Is it body or flesh?," and "of course, I fall in love" are the stops I visit every day.

Nazlım, Stefan, Raoul, and Emma, thank you for always swimming in the sea with me and making coming to the shore worthwhile.

I thank the generosity and embrace of the Kurdish Movement. You brought me to where I should be. Life becomes a consent not to be a single being in your company.

Babacım, would you like this book? So many words. You preferred silence. I love you even more for it, for it is your insistence on remaining in the place of moaning that motivated me to speak words without erasing the trace of their injury. Annecim, thank you for teaching me that joy is courage. It is in between moaning and joy that I crafted this book.

I thank Gerda Henkel Stiftung Patrimonies Program, Academiy in Exile,

IIE Scholar Rescue Fund, and the Rosa Luxemburg Foundation for supporting the writing of this book.

I thank Zehra Doğan and Serpil Odaşı for their generosity and kindness in letting me use their art.

And finally, thank you, Joan Scott, for giving me a hand when I needed it most.

Some of the material in Chapter 3 appeared in a different form as "Antigone as Kurdish Politician: Gendered Dwellings in the Limit between Freedom and Peace," *History of the Present* 9, no. 1 (Spring 2019): 131–41.

# Notes

## Introduction

EPIGRAPH SOURCES: Ashon T. Crawley, *Blackpentecostal Breath: The Aesthetics of Possibility* (New York: Fordham University Press, 2017), 23; Anthony Bogues, "And What About the Human? Freedom, Human Emancipation and the Radical Imagination," *Boundary 2* 39, no. 3 (2012): 38; Sait Üçlü, *Güneş Ülkesinde Diriliş: Amara Birinci Kitap 1. Cilt* (Neuss: Mezopotamya Yayınları, 2018), 9–10; Berjin Haki, *Kavalın Ezgisi* (Istanbul: Belge Yayınları, 2014), 11.

1. Cizre is a city in Turkey's southeast and Kurdistan's north with a population of approximately 140,000 people, predominantly Kurds who were forcibly displaced from their villages in the 1990s. It is one of the cities where the Kurdish Freedom Movement is most popular and where recruitment to guerrilla forces is high.

2. See Haydar Darıcı, "Of Kurdish Youth and Ditches," *Theory & Event* 19, no. 1 Supplement (2016); Harun Ercan, "Is Hope More Precious Than Victory?: The Failed Peace Process and the Urban Warfare in the Kurdish Region of Turkey," *South Atlantic Quarterly* 118, no. 1 (2019): 111–27; and Nazan Üstündağ, "Bakur Rising: Democratic Autonomy in Kurdistan," *Roar Magazine* 6 (2017): 86–94 for discussions on how the ending of the peace process by the Justice and Development Party in government led to the building of trenches by the youth.

3. Throughout this book I will use the word "state" in the singular to denote its gendered and ethnic "policing function." In their discussion on black motherhood, Carter and Willoughby define the state this way: "We acknowledge that the state is not a singular actor, and these multiple and often competing actors that make up 'the state' do not benefit in the same ways from the state's role as a policing agent of Black motherhood. Nevertheless, we read the cultural logic and social meaning of the state solely in its gendered and raced policing function. Read in this way, the effect of the state is experienced materially, socially, discursively, and psychically

as a bundle of injuries that target black motherhood collectively. In this way, the state, is in fact, a unitary force that can and does kill"; Lashonda Carter and Tiffany Willoughby-Herard, "What Kind of Mother Is She? From Margaret Garner to Rosa Lee Ingram to Mamie Till to the Murder of Korryn Gaines," *Theory & Event* 21, no. 1 (2018): 92. Similarly, Kurds experience the Turkish state materially, socially, discursively, and psychically as a bundle of injuries that target them collectively. I would even go further and say that the Turkish public, too, recognizes the state as a unitary force by recourse to its effects on Kurds and becomes baffled and suspect "state unity" only when it is they that are targeted; Nazan Üstündağ, "Pornographic State and Erotic Resistance," *South Atlantic Quarterly* 118, no. 1 (2019): 95–110.

4. According to a UN report, 2,000 people died during the curfews, and 500,000 people were displaced. For a comprehensive list of reports prepared by different Human Rights Organizations on the curfews, see Hakikat, Adalet ve Hafıza Merkezi (Center for Truth, Justice and Memory), *Reports on Curfews in Turkey*, Hakikat, Adalet ve Hafıza Merkesi Sitesi Kaynaklar Bölümü, 2017, https://hakikatadalethafiza.org/en/kaynak_tipi/reports-on-curfews (last accessed April 7, 2021). For the ruination of whole or parts of cities during the curfews, see the example of Diyarbakır: Fırat Genç, "Governing the contested City: Geographies of displacement in Diyarbakır, Turkey," *Antipode* 53, no. 6 (2021): 1,682–1,703.

5. One of the videos leaked by the counterinsurgency squads shows tens of young men lying on the ground cuffed and with faces down as a commander walks around them yelling that they will see the power of the state of the Turkish Republic and that of the Turks and asks what the state has ever done to them: Özel Harekat Komutanı: "Türk'ün Gücünü Göreceksiniz," YouTube, August 8, 2015, https://www.youtube.com/watch?v=Yu5HLob2GwE (accessed April 7, 2021). See Banu Bargu, "Sovereignty as Erasure: Rethinking Enforced Disappearances," *Qui Parle* 23, no. 1 (2014) for a discussion of the different modes sovereignty takes when performed as erasure or as spectacularization of death. For how the exposure and defamation of the dead body is used as a form of counterinsurgency in other contexts, see Suhad Daher-Nashif, "Colonial Management of Death: To Be or Not to Be Dead in Palestine," *Current Sociology* 69, no. 7 (2021): 945–62; Nadera Shalhoub-Kevorkian, "Criminality in Spaces of Death: The Palestinian Case Study," *British Journal of Criminology* 54, no. 1 (2014): 38–52; and Randa May Wahbe, "The Politics of Karameh: Palestinian Burial Rites under the Gun," *Critique of Anthropology* 40, no. 3 (2020): 323–40. Also, for how trans bodies become sites where state and family sovereignties are produced in Turkey, see Aslı Zengin, "The Afterlife of Gender: Sovereignty, Intimacy and Muslim Funerals of Transgender People in Turkey," *Cultural Anthropology* 34, no. 1 (2019): 78–102.

6. See Saskia Sassen, "When the City Itself Becomes a Technology of War," *Theory, Culture & Society* 27, no. 6 (2010): 33–50, and Eyal Weizmann, *Hollow Land: Israel's Architecture of Occupation* (New York: Verso, 2012), for how the city itself is used as a tool for counterinsurgency in the context of asymmetrical war.

7. I borrow the expression "corpsing" from David Marriott. Inspired by theater,

Marriott uses "corpsing" to refer to the failure of living according to social roles ("Corpsing; or, the Matter of Black Life," *Cultural Critique* 94 [Fall 2016]: 33). Marriott argues that "race is the means by which corpsing comes to be a metaphor for social life" (ibid., 35). Given that black life is characterized by social death — that is, by a constant threat and exposure to injury, violence, and murder — the black person is corpsed the moment s/he claims life. The Kurdish insurgent who claims life faces the same destiny.

8. Ibid., 37.

9. Nazan Üstündağ, "After Tahir Elçi," *Jadaliyya* (2015), https://www.jadaliyya .com/Details/32784/After-Tahir-El%C3%A7i (accessed April 10, 2022).

10. The trauma of representation occurs also because no narrative can convincingly explain what has happened and why. See David Marriott, *On Black Men* (New York: Columbia University Press, 2000), 13, and Patrice Douglass, "Black Feminist Theory for the Dead and Dying," *Theory & Event* 21, no. 1 (2018): 108. The Kurdish Movement's narrative of the insurgency is that if it were not for the glorious resistance of the martyrs that also cost many lives to the Turkish security forces, the state would implement a genocidal plan in the region, which it planned all along irrespective of the declaration of autonomy and building of trenches. In my opinion the film *The End Will Be Spectacular* produced by the Rojava Film Commune narrates the events best because, instead of trying to come up with a historical narrative, it focuses on the decisions that insurgents made on the ground, letting their lives be played out, informed by a will to remain free and unaccommodating. For forced poses, see Allen Feldman, "Violence and Vision: The Prosthetics and Aesthetics of Terror," in *States of Violence*, ed. Fernando Coronil and Julie Skursky (Ann Arbor: University of Michigan Press, 2006).

11. Human rights discourse failed also because, despite the calls of Kurdish political parties on human rights organizations and European Human Rights Court, no action was taken on their part, most likely because the discourse of human is applied only to the "innocent" civilian, whose criteria Kurds fail to meet. See Haydar Darıcı and Serra Hakyemez, "Neither Civilian nor Combatant: Weaponised Spaces and Spatialised Bodies in Cizre," in *Turkey's Necropolitical Laboratory*, ed. Banu Bargu (Edinburgh: Edinburgh University Press, 2019): 71–94, for a discussion of these issues from a legal anthropological perspective.

12. See Fulden İbrahimhakkıoğlu, "'The Most Naked Phase of Our Struggle' Gendered Shaming and Masculinist Desiring Production in Turkey's War on Terror," *Hypatia* 33, no. 3 (2018): 418–33, for an interpretation of how the killing of Kurdish women constituted the Turkish state as a desiring man.

13. Marriott. "Corpsing; or, The Matter of Black Life," 16.

14. Both for Ekin Wan and Taybet İnan, I use illustrations done by women instead of real pictures, not to participate in the "trauma of representation," but to contribute to its healing through art.

15. During the curfews, the police forced those living in trenched neighborhoods out and demolished their houses in order to isolate the youth. The property rights of

Kurds indeed can easily be made obsolete by forced displacement, as has been the case many times since the foundation of the Turkish republic. See Zerrin Özlem Biner, *States of Dispossession: Violence and Precarious Coexistence in Southeast Turkey* (Philadelphia: University of Pennsylvania Press, 2020) for a discussion of the numerous ways in which Kurds are dispossessed in Turkey.

16. Crawley, *Blackpentecostal Breath*, 64–65.

17. Ibid., 72.

18. For a discussion of why states perform violence and torture on dead bodies, see Steven Miller, *War after Death: On Violence and Its Limits* (New York: Fordham University Press, 2014).

19. Calvin Warren, "Onticide Afro-Pessimism, Gay Nigger #1, and Surplus Violence," *GLQ: A Journal of Lesbian and Gay Studies* 23, no. 3 (2017): 391–418.

20. Crawley, *Blackpentecostal Breath*, 64.

21. Sylvia Wynter, "Unsettling the Coloniality of Being/Power/Truth/Freedom: Towards the Human, after Man, Its Overrepresentation — An Argument," *CR: The New Centennial Review* 3, no. 3 (2003): 257–337.

22. While there exist autonomous governments in Northeastern Syria, as well, these are yet to be recognized by the central Syrian state and the world in general.

23. For a comprehensive account of Kurdish history, see Hamit Bozarslan, Cengiz Güneş, and Veli Yadırgı, eds. *The Cambridge History of the Kurds* (Cambridge: Cambridge University Press, 2021).

24. See Hişyar Özsoy, "Between Gift and Taboo: Death and the Negotiation of National Identity and Sovereignty in the Kurdish Conflict in Turkey" (unpublished Ph.D. diss., University of Texas, 2010) and "The Missing Grave of Sheikh Said: Kurdish Formations of Memory, Place, and Sovereignty in Turkey," in *Everyday Occupations*, ed. Kamala Visweswaran (Philadelphia: University of Pennsylvania Press, 2013) for a discussion of how death, burial, and memory figure into the building of a Kurdish oppositional national identity.

25. *Partiya Karkeren Kurdistan* in Kurdish.

26. Nazan Üstündağ, "A Travel Guide to Northern Kurdistan," in *Anywhere but Now: Landscapes of Belonging in the Eastern Mediterranean*, ed. Samar Kanafani et al. (Berlin: Heinrich Boell Foundation, 2012.)

27. For the different paramilitary operations of the Turkish state against Kurds, see Yeşim Yaprak Yıldız and Patrich Baer, "Confessions without Guilt: Public Confessions of State Violence in Turkey," *Theory & Society* 50 (2021): 125–49, and Ayhan Işık, "The Emergence of Paramilitary Groups in Turkey 1980s," in *The Kurdish Question in Turkey: New Perspectives on Violence, Representation and Reconciliation*, ed. Cengiz Güneş and Welat Zeydanlıoğlu (London and New York: Routledge, 2013). For forced disappearances, see Özgür Sevgi Göral, Ayhan Işık, and Özlem Kaya, *The Unspoken Truth: Enforced Disappearances* (Istanbul: Truth, Justice, Memory Center Publications, 2013).

28. See Copjec's discussion on the distinction Freud makes between fixation and perseverance; Joan Copjec, *Imagine There's No Woman: Ethics and Sublimation*

(Cambridge, Mass.: MIT Press, 2004), 12–47. Copjec attributes the former to power and the latter to the process by which power is interrupted.

29. For a discussion of the meaning of his capture by an international alliance for the EU and wider International Law, see Norman Peach, "Öcalan, European Law, and the Kurdish Question," in *Building Free Life: Dialogues with Öcalan*, ed. International Initiative (Oakland, Calif.: PM Press, 2020).

30. The lifting of the death penalty occurred both because Turkey was in the process of accession to the European Union and because Kurds all over the world rose up to support their leader.

31. Three of these books have already been published in English: Abdullah Öcalan, *Manifesto for a Democratic Civilization: The Age of Masked Gods and Disguised Kings* (Porsgrunn, Norway: New Compass Press, 2015); *Capitalism: The Age of Unmasked Gods and Naked Kings* (Porsgrunn, Norway: New Compass Press 2018); and *Sociology of Freedom: Manifesto of the Democratic Civilization*, vol. 3 (Oakland, Calif.: PM Press, 2020).

32. See, for example, Cengiz Güneş and Çetin Gürer, "Kurdish Movement's Democratic Autonomy Proposals in Turkey," in *Democratic Representation in Plurinational States: The Kurds in Turkey*, ed. Ephraim Nimni and Elçin Aktoprak (Cham, Switzerland: Palgrave Macmillan, 2018); Mesut Yeğen, "Armed Struggle to Peace Negotiations: Independent Kurdistan to Democratic Autonomy, or the PKK in Context," *Middle East Critique* 25, no. 4 (2016): 365–83; and Ahmet Hamdi Akkaya and Joost Jongerden, "Confederalism and Autonomy in Turkey: The Kurdistan Workers Party and the Reinvention of Democracy," in Güneş and Zeydanlıoğlu, *Kurdish Question in Turkey*.

33. Cengiz Güneş. *The Kurds in a New Middle East: The Changing Geopolitics of a Regional Conflict* (Cham, Switzerland: Palgrave Macmillan, 2019).

34. Fluidity for Öcalan is a very important concept, which he uses to explain what he understands of freedom inspired by quantum physics.

35. See Dilar Dirik, "The Revolution of Smiling Women: Stateless Democracy and Power in Rojava," in *Routledge Handbook of Postcolonial Politics* (London and New York: Routledge, Kindle edition, 2018), and Dirik, "Stateless Citizenship: Radical Democracy as Consciousness Raising in the Rojava Revolution," *Identities: Global Studies in Culture and Power* 19, no. 1 (2022): 27–44. See also Michael Knapp, Anja Ayboğa, and Ercan Ayboğa, *Revolution in Rojava: Democratic Autonomy and Women's Liberation in Syrian Kurdistan*. (London: Pluto Press 2020), and Nazan Üstündağ, "Self-Defense as a Revolutionary Practice in Rojava, or How to Unmake the State," *South Atlantic Quarterly* 115, no. 1 (2019): 197–210.

36. For a recent volume compiling ethnographies of young scholars that study Kurdish subjectivites, among other topics, see Lucie Drechselova and Adnan Çelik, eds., *Kurds in Turkey: Ethnographies of Heterogenous Experiences* (London: Lexington, 2019).

37. For comprehensive accounts on the history of the Kurdish Women's Freedom Movement, see Handan Çağlayan, *Analar, Yoldaşlar, Tanrıçalar: Kürt Hareketinde*

*Kadınlar ve Kadın Kimliğinin Oluşumu*, 6th ed. (Istanbul: İletişim Yayınları, 2017), and Dilar Dirik, *The Kurdish Women's Movement: History, Theory, Practice* (London: Pluto Press, 2022).

38. Sara Aktaş, *Parçalanmış Ülkede Kürt Kadın Devriminin Gelişim Pratikleri* (manuscript in preparation).

39. This is comparable to Walter Mingolo's conceptualization of delinking from Western epistemology as necessary for decolonization. Since for Öcalan and PKK the first colony is women, it is foremost for them that they delink themselves from patriarchal knowledge to come up with a new form of decolonized knowledge and understanding of the human.

40. Ibid.

41. See Necla Açık, "Redefining the Role of Women within the Kurdish National Movement in Turkey in the 1990s," in Güneş and Zeydanlıoğlu, *Kurdish Question in Turkey*, for an account of the emergence of the Kurdish Women's Movement. See also Nisa Göksel, "Gendering Resistance: Multiple Faces of the Kurdish Women's Struggle," *Sociological Forum* 34, no. S1 (2019): 1,112–31, for the different dimensions of the women's movement and its mobilization.

42. See Gültan Kışanak, *Kürt Siyasetinin Mor Rengi* (Istanbul: Dipnot Yayınları, 2019); Umut Erel and Necla Açık, "Enacting Intersectional Multilayered Citizenship: Kurdish Women's Politics," *Gender, Place and Culture: A Journal of Feminist Geography* 27, no. 4 (2020): 479–501; and "Göksel, Gendering Resistance.

43. Feminist scholars have pointed to the lack of record and archive of women's revolutionary actions. See for example, Naghemh Sohrabi, "Writing Revolution as if Women Mattered," *Comparative Studies of South Asia, Africa and the Middle East* 42, no. 2 (2022): 546–50. Recognizing this, the Kurdish Women's Freedom Movement is especially wary of producing its own archive and records.

44. Crawley, Blackpentecostal Breath, 8.

45. For women's anti-colonial imaginaries in the Middle East, see the recent special issue published by the Beirut-based journal *Kohl*: "Anticolonial Feminist Imaginaries," *Kohl: A Journal for Body and Gender Research* 9, no. 1 (2023).

46. Deniz Duruiz, "Tracing the Conceptual Genealogy of Kurdistan as International Colony," *Middle East Report* 295 (2020).

47. Havin Güneşer, *The Art of Freedom: A Brief History of the Kurdish Liberation Struggle* (Oakland, Calif.: PM Press, 2021).

48. Fred Moten, *Stolen Life (Consent Not to Be a Single Being)* (Durham, N.C., and London: Duke University Press, 2018).

49. Bogues, "And What About the Human?," 45.

50. David Marriott, "Inventions of Existence: Sylvia Wynter, Frantz Fanon, Sociogeny, and 'the Damned,'" *New Centennial Review* 11, no. 3 (2012): 49.

51. Sina Kramer, "Outside/In: Antigone and the Limits of Politics," in *The Returns of Antigone*, ed. Tina Chanter and Sean D. Kirkland (Albany: SUNY Press, 2014), 174.

52. Liz Appel, "Itinerant Antigone," in *The Returns of Antigone*, ed. Tina Chanter and Sean D. Kirkland (Albany: SUNY Press, 2014), 188.

53. Eduardo Mendieta, "Toward a Decolonial Feminist Imaginary: Decolonizing Futurity," *Critical Philosophy of Race* 8, no. 1–2 (2020): 242.

54. Ibid., 252.

55. For how the occupation of different temporalities led to different knowledges and senses in the case of Black women, see Denise Ferreira da Silva, "Toward a Black Feminist Poetics: The Quest(ion) of Blackness toward the End of the World," *Black Scholar* 44, no. 2 (2014): 81–97.

56. Crawley, *Blackpentecostal Breath*, 8.

57. S. K. Keltner, *Kristeva: Thresholds* (Cambridge: Polity Press, 2011), 3.

58. Max Hantel, "What Is It Like to Be a Human?: Sylvia Wynter on Autopoiesis," *PhiloSOPHIA* 8, no. 1 (2018): 121–36.

59. Ibid.

60. Alain Badiou, *The True Life*, trans. Susan Spitzer (Malden, Mass.: Polity Press, 2017).

61. Ibid., 94.

62. Yannis Stavrakakis, *Lacan and the Political* (London and New York: Routledge, 2002), 6.

63. Yannis Stavrakakis, ed., *Routledge Handbook of Psychoanalytic Political Theory* (London and New York: Routledge, 2020).

64. Begona Aretxaga, *States of Terror: Begona Aretxaga's Essays* (Reno, Nev.: Center for Basque Studies, University of Nevada, 2005).

65. Cornelius Castoriadis, *Imaginary Institution of Society: Creativity and Autonomy in the Social-Historical World* (Cambridge and Malden, Mass.: Polity Press, 1997).

66. Katherine McKittrick, Frances H. O'Shaughnessy, and Kendall Witaszek, "Rhythm, or On Sylvia Wynter's Science of the Word," *American Quarterly* 70, no. 4 (2018): 867, 872, 874.

67. Ibid., 870.

68. Fred Moten, *Stolen Life*, vol. 1 of *Consent Not to Be a Single Human Being* (Durham, N.C., and London: Duke University Press, 2018), 77; Denise Ferreira da Silva, "On Difference without Separability," *32nd Bienal De Sao Paulo Art Biennial,"Incerteza Viva,"* 2016.

69. Saidiya Hartman, *Wayward Lives, Beautiful Experiments: Intimate Histories of Social Upheaval* (New York and London: W. W. Norton, 2020).

## 1. The Voice of the Maternal: Kurdish Mothers at the Intersection of Linguicide and Matricide

EPIGRAPH SOURCES: "Women sing, men speak"; Kurdish proverb. In Kurdish, "Jin dipêjin, mêr dibêjin"; Zeyneb Yaş, "Lost Voices," in *Feminist Pedagogy: Museums,*

*Memory Sites and Practices of Remembrance*, ed. Meral Akkent and Nehir S. Kovar (Istanbul: Istanbul Women's Museum Publications, 2019), 92; Mîrza Metîn, my translation; from intervew by Jînda Zekioğlu, "Mirza Metin: Kürtçe yüz yıllık bir enkazın altında," *Gazete Duvar*, April 28, 2020, https://www.gazeteduvar.com.tr/kultur-sanat/2020/04/28/mirza-metin-kurtce-yuz-yillik-bir-enkazin-altinda (accessed on April 11, 2022). The original quote is the following: "Kürtçenin Türkiye'de eğitim dili, ticaret dili veya günlük yaşam dili olmamasının yarattığı sessel bir primitiflik var. Yani Kürtçenin ses, konuşma, düşünme, yazma ve okuma kalıpları Türkçe kadar yaygın değil. Bu anlamda özgür bir dil"; Catherine Clément and Julia Kristeva, *The Feminine and the Sacred* (New York: Columbia University Press, 2003), 10; Mladen Dolar, *A Voice and Nothing More* (Cambridge and London: MIT Press, 2006), 45; Fred Moten, *In the Break: The Aesthetics of the Black Radical Tradition* (Minneapolis and London: University of Minnesota Press, 2003), 23.

1. During the 1990s, the Turkish state adopted different counterinsurgency tactics in Turkey's Kurdistan, including paramilitary organization, extrajudicial killings, mass arrest, and forced displacement and disappearance. According to official figures, 378,000 people were evacuated by the security forces from 3,165 rural settlements by the end of 1999, while other reports estimate the total number of displaced Kurdish population to be between 2.5 and 4.5 million. See Dilek Kurban et al., *Coming to Terms with Forced Migration: Post-Displacement Restitution of Citizenship Rights in Turkey* (Istanbul: TESEV, 2006), and Bilgin Ayata and Deniz Yükseker, "A Belated Awakening: National and International Responses to the Internal Displacement of Kurds in Turkey," *New Perspectives in Turkey* 32 (2005): 5–42.

2. Nazan Üstündağ, "Belonging to the Modern: Women's Suffering and Subjectivities in Urban Turkey" (Ph.D. diss., Indiana University, 2005).

3. Joan Copjec, *Imagine There's No Woman: Ethics and Sublimation* (Cambridge, Mass.: MIT Press, 2004), 23.

4. In Turkey the neoliberal transformation of the economy and the displacement of Kurds coincided with enabling businesses to freely exploit Kurdish unskilled and unsecured labor newly arrived in cities. During this time, for many young people in urban areas, including Kurds, engaging with the illegal economy proved to be more profitable than formal or informal employment. See also Deniz Yonucu, "A Story of a Squatter Neighborhood: From the Place of the 'Dangerous Classes' to the 'Place of Danger,'" *Berkeley Journal of Sociology* 52 (2008): 50–72, for a discussion of the relationship between crime, neoliberalism, and squatters.

5. In the beginning of the 2000s many displaced Kurds appealed to the European Court of Human Rights in their pursuit of justice. As a result of the increasing number of rulings that sentenced the Turkish state to paying large numbers of fines, the government passed Law 5237, which obliged the state to pay compensation to families who proved that they were forced to leave their village due to the pressures of the army. However, "proving" displacement involved a cumbersome process. For a discussion of this law and the requirement people were expected to meet

to be eligible for compensations, see Kurban et al, *Coming to Terms with Forced Migration*.

6. Bonnie Honig, *Antigone Interrupted* (Cambridge: Cambridge University Press, 2013), 137.

7. Also translated as "ordeal" or "tribulations," *çile* refers to the burdens one needs to carry and endure. Mostly inflicted by intimate others, *çile* defines a woman and grows with age.

8. Adriana Cavarero, *For More Than One Voice: Toward a Philosophy of Vocal Expression* (Stanford, Calif.: Stanford University Press, 2005), 11.

9. Despite her focus on language in the postcolonial experience, Rey Chow writes that "race is grasped and presented predominantly as a visual drama, which highlights what it is like to be seen as black in a society that treats being black with contempt, as something dirty"; Rey Chow, *Not Like a Native Speaker: On Languaging as a Postcolonial Experience* (New York and Chichester, West Sussex: Columbia University Press, 2014), 20. Colonial and postcolonial experiences of ethnicity, however, are not necessarily based on how one looks but also on how one sounds. Although "Lacan isolated the gaze and the voice as the two paramount embodiments of *objet petit a*," little attention has been given to sounds in tracing fantasies of otherness, power, and domination; Dolar, *A Voice and Nothing More*, 39.

10. Moten, *In the Break*, 6.

11. Lewis R. Gordon et al., "Afro Pessimism," *Contemporary Political Theory* 17, no. 1 (2018): 115.

12. Besides Irigaray and Kristeva, who are widely known for their reinterpretations of the mother-daughter relationship, see also Bracha L. Ettinger, "Matrixial Trans-subjectivity," *Theory, Culture & Society* 23, no. 2–3 (2006): 218–22, whose theories have influenced a new generation of researchers of the maternal.

13. For a brilliant ethnographic study of how the counterinsurgency violence of the state also led to the mass dispossession of Kurds, see Zerrin Özlem Biner, *States of Dispossession: Violence and Precarious Coexistence in Southeast Turkey* (Philadelphia: University of Pennsylvania Press, 2020).

14. Stories of forced displacement are told to many actors over and over again, including relatives, researchers, Kurdish organizations, and Turkish authorities. Elsewhere I have argued that telling these stories the same way in each of these occasions allows women a sense of emotional control over their narratives; Nazan Üstündağ, *Belonging to the Modern*.

15. Village guards (*Korucular* in Turkish) are paramilitaries recruited mostly from ethnic Kurds that act as a local militia against the PKK and assist the Turkish army's military operations in the region.

16. Despite the fact that they are continuously threatened by state violence and repression, Kurdish women and men want to be recorded in interviews. I think the explanation that Marlene Schäefers gives for the importance of recording among Kurdish women singers as an aspiration to authorship can be generalized to

include most Kurds; Schäefers, "Writing against Loss: Kurdish Women, Subaltern Authorship, and the Politics of Voice in Contemporary Turkey," *Journal of the Royal Anthropological Institute* 23, no. 3 (2017): 543–61. The feeling of being excluded from official history and the desire to generate truth lead Kurds to regard themselves, their voices, and narratives as documents of state violence to be archived.

17. Dolar, *A Voice and Nothing More*, 28.

18. In her influential essay "Mama's Baby, Papa's Maybe: An American Grammar," *Diacritics* 17, no. 2 (1987): 64–81, Hortense Spillers argues that "the American grammar fails to name [the black woman], because the subject position the symbolic order tries to name — that of black woman in the United States — confronts the radical expulsion of black women from the modern order of the human. That historical expulsion ultimately renders all signifiers equally inadequate and propels the symbolic order's need for more injurious ones. That is the case because the sign is not the performative event of a subjectivity in motion, but the extended scene of captive flesh"; quoted in Andres Fabian Henao Castro, *Antigone in the Americas: Democracy, Sexuality, and Death in the Settler Colonial Present* (Albany: SUNY Press 2022, 70). The Turkish grammar operates in a similar vein in relation to the Kurdish maternal, who is seen as anachronistic, primitive, and ultimately dysfunctional.

19. This different tension is best explained by Castro when he says that in the case of slavery and settler colonialism, "linguistic signification literally cuts the flesh of the subject"; Castro, *Antigone in the Americas*, 71–73. The imposition of Turkish on Kurds in Turkey, as I will explain in the rest of this chapter, performs a similar function as it occurs violently both at the material and psychic levels.

20. Cavarero, *For More Than One Voice*.

21. Zakkiah Iman Jackson writes, "The black mater(nal) signifies the form(lessness) of noise, and noise is produced as isomorphic to black mater(nal) reciprocally"; Jackson, "Sense of Things," *Catalyst: Feminism, Theory, Technoscience* 2, no. 2 (2016): 20. While Jackson's statement opens up a productive line of inquiry for understanding the specific relationship between the black maternal, sound, and language, I believe that it is also inspirational for inquring this relationship in other contexts.

22. Moten, *In the Break*.

23. Dolar, *A Voice and Nothing More*, 73.

24. Ibid., 39.

25. Dylan Evans, *An Introductory Dictionary of Lacanian Psychoanalysis* (London and New York: Routledge, 1996), 129.

26. Dolar, *A Voice and Nothing More*, 74.

27. Yannis Stavrakakis, *Lacan and the Political* (London and New York: Routledge, 2002), 38.

28. Ibid., 44.

29. See Clément and Kristeva, *The Feminine and the Sacred*, where they debate

many different embodiments of the sacred. Voice is one permanent theme in this debate.

30. Dolar, A Voice and Nothing More, 28.

31. Ibid., 137, 138.

32. George Shulman, "Fred Moten," Critical Theory for Political Theology 2.0 (April 13, 2021), at https://politicaltheology.com/fred-moten/.

33. Cavarero, For More Than One Voice.

34. Dolar, A Voice and Nothing More, 81.

35. See Alev Kuruoğlu and Wendelmoet Hamelink, "Sounds of Resistance: Performing the Political in the Kurdish Music Scene," in The Politics of Culture in Turkey, Greece and Cyprus: Performing the Left since the Sixties, ed. Leonidas Karakatsanis and Nikolaos Papadogiannis (London and New York: Routledge, 2017); Derya Bayır, "The Role of the Judicial System in the Politicide of the Kurdish Opposition," in The Kurdish Question in Turkey: New Perspectives on Violence, Representation and Reconciliation, ed. Cengiz Güneş and Welat Zeydanlıoğlu (London and New York: Routledge, 2013); Welat Zeydanlıoğlu, "Turkey's Kurdish Language Policy," International Journal of the Sociology of Language, no. 217 (2012): 99–125; and Vahap Çoşkun, M. Şerif Derince, and Nesrin Uçarlar, Scar of Tongue: Consequences of the Ban on the Use of Mother Tongue in Education and Experiences of Kurdish Students in Turkey (Diyarbakır: DİSA, 2012).

36. "Elimination is a process, and the loss of the mother tongue, like the loss of the traditional burial practice, and confidence in the wisdom of elder, calls attention to an ongoing colonial form of violence paradigmatically oriented toward their genocide"; Castro, Antigone in the Americas, 106.

37. See Tanıl Bora, Türkiye'nin Linç Rejimi, 3rd ed. (Istanbul: İletişim Yayınları, 2021), and Zeynep Gambetti, "'I'm No Terrorist, I Am a Kurd': Societal Violence, the State, and the Neo-Liberal Order," in Rhetorics of Insecurity: Belonging and Violence in the Neoliberal Era, ed. Zeynep Gambetti and Marcial Godoy-Anativia (New York: New York University Press, 2013).

38. See, for example, Akın and Danışman's collection, which brings together nineteen testimonies on being children in Kurdistan during 1990s; Rojin Canan Akın and Funda Danışman, Bildiğin Gibi Değil: 90'larda Güneydoğu'da Çocuk Olmak (Istanbul: Metis Yayınları, 2011).

39. Çoşkun, Derince, and Uçarlar, Scar of Tongue.

40. Jasbir K. Puar, The Right to Maim: Debility, Capacity, Disability (Durham, N.C., and London: Duke University Press, 2017).

41. Sylvia Wynter, "Towards the Sociogenic Principle: Fanon, Identity, the Puzzle of Conscious Experience, and What It Is Like to Be 'Black,'" in National Identities and Socio-Political Changes in Latin America, ed. Antonio Gomez-Moriana and Mercedes Duran-Cogan (London and New York: Routledge, 2001), 41. Kelly Oliver argues that colonization of psychic space results in debilitating alienation: "If the alienation inherent in subjectivity is the subject turning back on itself to become

self-conscious, then debilitating alienation is the subject being turned inside out to become an object for another"; Oliver, *Colonization of Psychic Space: A Psychoanalytic Social Theory of Oppression* (Minneapolis: University of Minnesota Press 2004), 7.

42. Frantz Fanon, *Black Skin, White Masks*, rev. ed. (New York: Grove Press, 2008).

43. An example I witnessed is when a friend of mine was talking on the phone in Kurdish on a bus; he was warned by a passenger that he shouldn't be speaking this language in this age.

44. For a short discussion of Kurdish and its variations, see Ergin Öpengin and Geoffrey Haig, "Regional Variation in Kurmanji: A Preliminary Classification of Its Dialects," *Kurdish Studies* 2, no. 2 (2014): 143–76.

45. Two of these widely circulating slogans are "jin, jiyan, azadi" (women, life, freedom) and "berxwedan jiyane" (resistance is life).

46. Ergin Öpengin, "Sociolinguistic Situation of Kurdish in Turkey: Sociopolitical Factors and Language Use Patterns," *International Journal of the Sociology of Language* 217 (2012): 151–80.

47. Ibid.

48. Metin Yüksel, "Dengbej, Mullah, Intelligentsia: The Survival and Revival of the Kurdish Kurmanji Language in the Middle East" (unpublished Ph.D. diss, University of Chicago, 2011).

49. See Wendelmoet Hamelink, *The Sung Home: Narrative, Morality, and the Kurdish Nation* (Leiden: Brill, 2016).

50. Şerif Derince, "A Break or Continuity? Turkey's Politics of Kurdish Language in the New Millennium," *Dialectical Anthropology* 37, no. 1 (2013): 147.

51. Ibid.

52. Welat Zeydanlıoğlu, "Repression or Reform? An Analysis of AKP's Kurdish Language Policy," in *The Kurdish Question in Turkey: New Perspectives on Violence, Representation and Reconciliation*, ed. Cengiz Güneş and Welat Zeyndanlıoğlu (London and New York: Routledge, 2013).

53. Lauren Berlant states that "recognition is the misrecognition you can bear"; Berlant, *Cruel Optimism* (Durham, N.C.: Duke University Press 2011), 26. The partial recognition enforced on Kurds was a misrecognition that many could not bear, as would be obvous in the collapse of the peace process (see Chapter 6). See also Bülent Küçük, "The Burden of Sisyphus: A Sociological Inventory of the Kurdish Question in Turkey," *British Journal of Middle Eastern Studies* 46, no. 5 (2019): 752–66, and Cuma Çiçek, "The Pro-Islamic Challenge for the Kurdish Movement," *Dialectical Anthropology* 37, no. 1 (2013): 159–63.

54. See Bülent Küçük, "What Is a Democratization Package Good For?," *Jadaliyya*, October 21, 2013, https://www.jadaliyya.com/Details/29674/What-Is-a-Democratization-Package-Good-For (accessed April 13, 2022). See also Çağrı Yoltar, "Making the Indebted Citizen: An Inquiry into State Benevolence in Turkey," *PoLAR* 43, no. 1 (2020): 153–71, and Çağrı Yoltar and Erdem Yörük, "Contentious

Welfare: The Kurdish Conflict and Social Policy as Counterinsurgency in Turkey,"
*Governance: An International Journal of Policy, Administration, and Institutions*
34, no. 2 (2021): 353–71, for an analysis of how neoliberalim and programs for
relief of poverty among Kurds went hand in hand to regulate Kurdish griveances
during this time of the opening. I also recommend İlker Cörüt's ethnography on
the transformation of health policies in a Kurdish city that shows how Kurds have
nevertheless discursively resisted seing the opening as an improvement in their lives;
Cörüt, *Failure of the Kurdish Policy of the AKP: Healthcare Provision in Hakkâri in
2003–2014* (Bern, Switzerland: Peter Lang, forthcoming).

55. Joost Jongerden. "Looking Beyond the State: Transitional Justice and the
Kurdish Issue in Turkey," *Ethnic and Racial Studies* 41, no. 4 (2018): 721–38.

56. Castro, *Antigone in the Americas*, 141.

57. For an ethnographic field study on this period from the perspective of
language activism, see Kelda Ann Jamison, "Making Kurdish Public(s): Language,
Politics and Practice in Turkey" (unpublished Ph.D. diss., University of Chicago,
2015).

58. Derince, "A Break or Continuity?," 145.

59. Dolar, *A Voice and Nothing More*, 15.

60. Ibid., 52.

61. Ibid., 85.

62. Accessed on April 26, 2020.

63. Mirza Metin, "Mirza Metin: Kürtçe yüz yıllık bir enkazın altında," interview
by Jînda Zekioğlu, *Gazete Duvar*, April 28, 2020, https://www.gazeteduvar.com.tr
/kultur-sanat/2020/04/28/mirza-metin-kurtce-yuz-yillik-bir-enkazin-altinda (accessed
on April 11, 2022).

64. Amir Hassanpour convincingly argues that the language of Kurdish is one
of the sites where patriarchy is reproduced; Hassanpour, "The (Re)production of
Patriarchy in the Kurdish Language," in *Women of a Non-State Nation*, ed. Shahrzad
Mojab (Costa Mesa, Calif.: Mazda, 2001). By using the expression "matrilineal
song," I am not questioning the patriarchal features of the language as much as
foregrounding the maternal heritage of its enunciation and performance.

65. Lia A. Roth (*Psychoanalytic Perspectives on Gaze, Body Image, Shame,
Judgment and Maternal Function: Being and Belonging* [New York and London:
Routledge, 2020]) shows how judgment of female bodies leads women to experience
trauma and shame. To get rid of this shame and achieve belonging, women feel a
need to sacrifice something intimate. I find this to resonate with the experience of
linguicide and the shame one experiences because of the Kurdish-speaking mother.

66. Dilan Yıldırım, "Kurdish Mothers and Daughters" (unpublished term paper,
Boğaziçi University, 2008).

67. Ibid.

68. Popstar Turkey, which is the Turkish version of American Idol, was
broadcast in 2003–4 on Kanal D. It was the first among many similar shows where
a jury composed of four people decided on those who would participate in the

competition. Once the competition started the jury assumed the role of trainer and commentator of the singers, with people voting for the best competitors by sending SMS messages.

69. My translation. The original lyrics are the following: İşkencede günlerce/ Özgürlük mahkumları/Sayısı on binlerce/Özgürlük mahkumları/Kelepçeli elleri/Kollarında zincir var/Haykırıyor dilleri/Zincirleri şakırdar/Akşam boş duran saha/Zindan oldu sabaha/Kimisi çocuk daha/Özgürlük mahkumlar/Sizleri tutan onlar/Onlara yakın sonlar/Peşinizde milyonlar/Özgürlük mahkumları/Vatan ağalı beyli/Mahkumlar isyan huylu/İşçi emekçi köylü/Özgürlük mahkumları.

70. *Popstar Turkey* and *That Voice Is Turkey*, which followed it, have been extremely popular in Turkey, not least as a result of the competitors' varied background. Many of the former competitors have disadvantaged and/or tragic backgrounds, and among them many are Kurds. These programs have accomplished translating political problems such as racism, colonialism, capitalism, and poverty into social and moral issues, promising to overcome them with unity, compassion, and communication. As expected, none of the Kurdish or any other competitors displayed any political views and avoided singing controversial songs in their performances. It would be interesting to follow their lives afterward, since some of these lives have become monumental examples of "cruel optimism," a term that Lauren Berlant invented to point to people's investment in hopes and dreams that are actually detrimental to their well-being and often bring destruction; Lauren Berlant, *Cruel Optimism*.

71. See Stephen Best and Saidiya Hartman's "Fugitive Justice," *Representations* 92, (2005): 9, for how inaudible voices are linked to utopian aspirations.

72. Joan Wallach Scott, *The Fantasy of Feminist History* (Durham, N.C., and London: Duke University Press, 2011), 61.

73. Ibid., 62.

74. Dolar, *A Voice and Nothing More*, 45.

75. Rosalind Mayo and Christina Moutsou, "The Maternal: An Introduction," in *The Mother in Psychoanalysis and Beyond: Matricide and Maternal Subjectivity*, ed. Rosalind Mayo and Christina Moutsou (New York and London: Routledge, 2017), 8.

76. Lisa Baraitser, *Maternal Encounters: The Ethics of Interruption* (New York: Routledge, 2009).

77. Jacqueline Rose, *An Essay on Love and Cruelty*, repr. ed. (New York: Farrar, Straus and Giroux, 2019).

78. For a conceptualization of colonialism as permanent war, see Maldonado-Torres, "On the Coloniality of Being: Contributions to the Development of a Concept," *Cultural Studies* 21, no. 2–3 (2007): 240–70.

79. Rosalind C. Morris, "The War Drive: Image Files Corrupted," *Social Text* 25, no. 2 (2007): 103–42.

80. For the forced Turkification of Kurdish mothers, see Zeynep Türkyılmaz, "Maternal Colonialism and Turkish Woman's Burden in Dersim: Educating the 'Mountain Flowers' of Dersim," *Journal of Women's History* 28, no. 3 (2016): 162–86.

81. Halide Edib Adıvar, *Kalp Ağrısı* (1924; repr. Istanbul: Can Yayınları, 2010), and *Zeyno'nun Oğlu* (1928; repr. Istanbul: Can Yayınları, 2010).

82. See Hülya Adak, *Halide Edib Adıvar ve Siyasal Şiddet: Ermeni Kırımı, Diktatörlük ve Şiddetsizlik* (Istanbul: Istanbul Bilgi Üniversitesi Yayınları, 2016); Keith David Watenpaugh, "The League of Nation's Rescue of Armenian Genocide Survivors and the Making of Modern Humanitarianism," *American Historical Review* 115, no. 1 (2010): 1,315–39; and Watenpaugh, "Are There Any Children for Sale? Genocide and the Transfer of Armenian Children (1915–1922)," *Journal of Human Rights* 12, no. 3 (2013): 283–95.

83. Audra Simpson writes, "An Indian woman's body in settler regimes such as the US, in Canada is loaded with meaning — signifying other political orders, land itself, of the dangerous possibility of reproducing Indian life and most dangerously, other political orders. Other life forms, other sovereignties, other forms of political will"; Simpson, "The State Is a Man: Theresa Spence, Loretta Saunders and the Gender of Settler Sovereignty," *Theory & Event* 19, no. 4 (2016): 7.

84. Schotten argues that the biopolitics of settler sovereignty operates "primarily at the level of desire, not biology, which establishes the distinction between life and death via the institution of temporality, not (only) security." I find this to be a compelling argument in this context, where the state attempts to undo the desires of the inmates and replace it with horror. Schotten continues, "The name for the improperly desirous, the name of all those who refuse or fail the futurist temporalization of desire and its imposition of settler sovereignty, is 'death'"; C. Heike Schotten, *Queer Terror: Life, Death, and Desire in the U.S. Settler Colony* (New York: Columbia University Press 2018), 21–22.

85. My analysis of Diyarbakır Prison is indebted to a project initiated by the Foundation of 78s, where we have collected 500 testimonies of people who were inmates in the prison between the years 1980 and 1984.

86. In Turkish: "Kamber Ateş nasılsın?" "İyiyim."

87. Nazan Üstündağ, "Pornographic State and Erotic Resistance," *South Atlantic Quarterly* 118, no. 1 (2019): 95–110.

## 2. Law(s) of the Maternal: Kurdish Mothers in Public

EPIGRAPH SOURCE: Gabeba Baderoon, "The Law of the Mother," *Meridians* 18, no. 1 (2019): 14–16.

1. At the time I was doing fieldwork the criteria for financial assistance was being unemployed and propertyless. While Gönül was both, since the criteria were applied on a household basis rather than on an individual basis, it was unlikely that she would receive any assistance.

2. This was very untypical, since children in Kurdistan usually stayed with the father. It hinted that Gönül's father was either very poor or had no larger kin.

3. One recent event concerns İpek Er, who was an eighteen-year-old Kurdish student from Batman who died on August 18, 2020, following a suicide attempt

on July 16. She claimed that she had been drugged and raped by Musa Orhan, a specialized sergeant in the Turkish army, and that he had told her that she could complain, but he would not be harmed by it. Indeed, after being questioned by authorities, Musa Orhan was released from custody. When I was writing this book, the court had yet to determine the outcome of his pending trial.

4. Elizabeth Podnieks and Andrea O'Reilly, "Introduction: Maternal Literature in Text and Tradition; Daughter-Centric, Matrilineal and Matrifocal Perspectives," in *Textual Mothers: Maternal Texts; Motherhood in Contemporary Women's Literatures*, ed. Elizabeth Podnieks and Andrea O'Reilly (Waterloo, Ontario, Canada: Wilfrid Laurier University Press, 2010), 14.

5. I use the term "gratuitous" intentionally here to put patriarchy and slavery in (an obviously uncomfortable) comparison. Orlando Patterson, *Slavery and Social Death: A Comparative Study, with a New Preface* (Cambridge, Mass.: Harvard University Press, 2018), defines three characteristics of social death under slavery: gratuitous violence, natal alienation, and general dishonor. Many women under patriarchy, patrilocality, and patrilinearity share a similar destiny, encountering random violence in marriage, and natal alienation, since their children belong to the patrilineage, and if they divorce their husbands the children stay with him. Women also experience a generalized inequality and dishonor in all spheres of life compared to men. The Kurdish leader Abdullah Öcalan therefore sees women equal to slaves under the harsh patriarchal and colonial conditions in Kurdistan and encourages women to come up with collective ways to refashion themselves to be rescued from externally forced and internalized forms of slavery. Most importantly for him, as I will explain later in this book, marriage is an institution of slavery held together by violence and law and by the affective economies of patriarchy.

6. Podnieks and O'Reilly, "Introduction," 12.

7. See, for example, Michelle Hughes Miller, Tamar Hager, and Rebecca Jaremko Bromwich, *Bad Mothers: Regulations, Representations and Resistance* (Bradford, Canada: Demeter Press, 2017).

8. I follow Lisa Baraitser in defining the maternal as "to include motherhood as an embodied and embedded relational and material practice (the very literal daily labor of raising children), through to its figural, symbolic and representational forms. As the meaning of the maternal widens, it comes to signify both as an unanswered theoretical question about the vanishing point of knowledge, and as a structural and generative dimension in human relations, politics and ethics"; Baraitser, "Maternal Publics: Time, Relationality and the Public Sphere," in *Re(Con)Figuring Psychoanalysis: Critical Juxtapositions of the Philosophical, the Sociohistorical and the Political*, ed. Aydan Gülerce (London: Palgrave Macmillan, 2012), 226.

9. For what I mean by a "feminist philosophy of history," see Alys Eve Weinbaum, *The Afterlife of Reproductive Slavery: Biocapitalism and Black Feminism's Philosophy of History* (Durham, N.C.: Duke University Press, 2019). Meanwhile, Amber Jacobs convincingly uses the plural instead of the singular in her writing on the law(s) of the mother: "What I want to stress is that the matricidal law — or law of the mother

that I am proposing — is not the one and only maternal law with a capital M; it is actually just one aspect of the laws of the mother which are yet to be theorized and will contribute to the creation of what Irigaray terms the 'yet to be female imaginaries.' The use of the plural is crucial. The Laws of the mother cannot then be reduced to or made symmetrical to the current dominant model of the singular Law of the Father (in capital letters)." They function in very different ways"; Jacobs, "Rethinking Matricide," in *The Mother in Psychoanalysis and Beyond: Matricide and Maternal Subjectivity*, ed. Rosalind Mayo and Christina Moutsou (London and New York: Routledge, 2017), 28.

10. I am aware that law(s) of the mother and mothers are different, as is the law of the Father and fathers. Nevertheless, in Gönül's particular case, she blames her mother for not having been protected from the perversities of patriarchy. What that means in terms of her psyche is beyond the purposes of this book.

11. Walter D. Mignolo and Catherine E. Walsh, *On Decoloniality: Concepts, Analytics, Praxis* (Durham, N.C.: Duke University Press, 2018).

12. Genevieve Morel, *The Law of the Mother: An Essay on the Sexual Sinthome* (London and New York: Routledge, 2019).

13. Amber Jacobs, *On Matricide: Myth, Psychoanalyses, and the Law of the Mother* (New York: Columbia University Press, 2007); Hortense J Spillers, "Mama's Baby, Papa's Maybe: An American Grammar Book," *Diacritics* 17, no. 2 (1987): 64–81; and Juliet Mitchell, "The Law of the Mother: Sibling Trauma and the Brotherhood of War," *Canadian Journal of Psychoanalysis* 21, no. 1 (2013): 145–59.

14. M. Shadee Malaklou and Tiffany Willoughby-Herard, "Notes from the Kitchen, the Crossroads, and Everywhere Else, Too: Ruptures of Thought, Word, and Deed from the 'Arbiters of Blackness Itself,'" *Theory & Event* 21, no. 1 (2018): 2–67.

15. "Captive maternal" is a term invented and conceptualized by Joy James: "The captive maternal labors to nurture the 'private realm' of family and community that seek shelter from social and state aggression and stabilize the 'public realm' of policing, presidential powers and policies that prey upon said family and community." One unintended consequence of the captive maternal is that its offspring are rebels: "From an environment of trauma, a matrix can evolve, one conducive to rebellion within the predatory Western Womb"; James, "Presidential Powers and Captive Maternals: Sally, Michelle, and Deborah," Blog of the APA, May 6, 2020, https://blog.apaonline.org/2020/05/06/presidential-powers-and-captive-maternals-sally-michelle-and-deborah/ (last accessed on June 19, 2021). See also Joy James, "The Womb of Western Theory: Trauma, Time Theft, and the Captive Maternal," *Carceral Notebooks* 12 (2016): 253–96.

16. Baraitser, "Maternal Publics."

17. Christina Sharpe, *Monstrous Intimacies: Making Post-Slavery Subjects* (Durham, N.C.: Duke University Press, 2010).

18. Catherine Clément and Julia Kristeva, *The Feminine and the Sacred* (New York: Columbia University Press, 2003).

19. Calvin Warren, "Onticide Afro-Pessimism, Gay Nigger #1, and Surplus Violence," *Glq* 23, no. 3 (2017): 391.

20. Ibid.; Jared Sexton, "'The Curtain of the Sky': An Introduction," *Critical Sociology* 36, no. 1 (2010): 11–24.

21. Adriana Cavarero, *Horrorism: Naming Contemporary Violence* (New York: Columbia University Press, 2008).

22. Miri Rozmarin, "Medea Chic: On the Necessity of Ethics as Part of the Critique of Motherhood," in Miller, Hager, and Bromwich, *Bad Mothers: Regulations, Representations and Resistance*.

23. See, for example, Lisa Baraitser, *Maternal Encounters: The Ethics of Interruption* (New York: Routledge, 2009).

24. As Saidiya Hartman states in the context of black lives, "Those of us who have been touched by the mother need acknowledge that this brilliant and formidable labor of care, paradoxically, has been produced through violent structures of slavery, anti-black racism, virulent sexism, and disposability"; Hartman, "The Belly of the World: A Note on Black Women's Labors," *Souls* 18, no. 1 (2016): 171.

25. Luisa Muraro, *The Symbolic Order of the Mother*, repr. ed. (Albany: SUNY Press, 2019).

26. Avery F. Gordon, *Ghostly Matters: Haunting and the Sociological Imagination* (Minneapolis: University of Minnesota Press, 2008).

27. Janice Radway, "Foreword," in Gordon, *Ghostly Matters*, xii.

28. Christina Sharpe, *In the Wake: On Blackness and Being* (Durham, N.C.: Duke University Press, 2016), 16.

29. Ibid.

30. Ibid., 20.

31. Jacobs, *On Matricide*, and Miri Rozmarin, "Staying Alive: Matricide and the Ethical-Political Aspect of Mother-Daughter Relations," *Studies in Gender and Sexuality* 17, no. 4 (2016): 242–53, https://doi.org/10.1080/15240657.2016.1236540.

32. See, for example, Sheila L. Cavanagh, "Antigone's Legacy: A Feminist Psychoanalytic of an Other Sexual Difference," *Studies in the Maternal* 9, no. 1 (2017): 1–33, who uses Bracha L. Ettinger's theory of matrixial for an interpretation of how the maternal figures in Antigone's actions to show that it is the feminine that is at stake in the Antigonian tragedy rather than the burial of an outlaw. See also Ettinger's own interpretation: Ettinger, "Antigone with[out] Jocasta," in *Interrogating Antigone in Postmodern Philosophy and Criticism*, ed. S. E. Wilmer and A. Zukauskaite (Oxford: Oxford University Press, 2010), and Moira Amado-Miller, "Refiguring Jocasta's Desire," *New Antigone* 1 (Spring 2005), for an interesting reading of how Jacosta's desire plays out in her interactions with Oedipus, which has resonances with what I am arguing here.

33. Baraitser, "Maternal Publics."

34. Sara Aktaş, *Parçalanmış Ülkede Kürt Kadın Devriminin Gelişim Pratikleri* (unpublished manuscript).

35. Ibid.

36. Gurminder K. Bhambra, "Postcolonial and Decolonial Dialogues," *Postcolonial Studies* 17, no. 2 (2014): 11; Hasret Çetinkaya, "Mothers as the Middle-Ground between the Mountain and the State," *Journal of International Women's Studies* 21, no. 7 (2020): 210. Although Öcalan never read Irigaray or Cixous, here I would also like to note that he combines their ideas. On the one hand, a post-patriarchal future can be envisioned at the limits of myth; Hélène Cixous, "The Laugh of the Medusa," in *Feminisms: An Anthology of Literary Theory and Criticism*, ed. Robyn R. Warhol and Diane Pierce Hendl (New Brunswick, N.J.: Rutgers University Press, 1997). On the other hand, myths need to be deconstructed, since they are historically embedded and reflect patriarchal imaginations; Luce Irigaray, "Between Myth and History: The Tragedy of Antigone," in *Interrogating Antigone in Postmodern Philosophy and Criticism*, ed. S. E. Wilmer and Audrone Zukauskaite (New York: Oxford University Press, 2010). See Vanda Zajko and Miriam Leonard, *Laughing with Medusa: Classical Myth and Feminist Thought* (Oxford and New York: Oxford University Press, 2006).

37. Zakiyyah Iman Jackson, "Sense of Things," *Catalyst: Feminism, Theory, Technoscience* 2, no. 2 (2016): 8 and 13.

38. Dickson challenges the view that "Enki and Ninhursag" is a genesis myth and puts forth the idea that it is a trickster myth based on Enki's actions; Keith Dickson, "Enki and Ninhursag: The Trickster in Paradise," *Journal of Near Eastern Studies* 66, no. 1 (2007): 1–32.

39. Ibid.

40. Ibid.

41. Ibid., 3.

42. Ibid., 4.

43. Sara Aktaş, *Parçalanmış Ülkede Kürt Kadın Devriminin Gelişim Pratikleri*.

44. Çetinkaya, "Mothers as the Middle-Ground between the Mountain and the State," 211.

45. Abdullah Öcalan, *Sociology of Freedom: Manifesto of the Democratic Civilization*, vol. 3 (Oakland, Calif.: PM Press, 2020).

46. Hortense Spillers says, "The African American woman, the mother, the daughter, becomes historically the powerful and shadowy evocation of a cultural synthesis-long evaporated — the law of the mother-only and precisely because legal enslavement removed the African-American male not so much from sight as from mimetic view as partner in the prevailing social fiction of the father's name, the father's law"; Spillers, "Mama's Baby, Papa's Maybe," 80. In the case of the Kurdish movement, the mother is a powerful and shadowy evocation of the law of the mother not so much because the Kurdish father is removed from mimetic sight by colonialism, but because the mother is removed from the effects of colonialism, particularly linguicde, and thereby carries in herself the echoes of a matrilineal culture long evaporated.

47. Sharpe, *Monstrous Intimacies*, 31, and Sarah Jane Cervenak, "Christina Sharpe: Monstrous Intimacies, Making Post-Slavery Subjects, *Women's Studies* 40 (2011): 1,121.

48. Malaklou and Willoughby-Herard, "Notes from the Kitchen," 18–19.

49. Ibid., 19.

50. Cervenak, "Christina Sharpe," 1,121.

51. I will talk about the refusal of women guerrillas to engage in sexual relationships later in the book.

52. Tiffany Lethabo King, "Black 'Feminisms' and Pessimism: Abolishing Moynihan's Negro Family," *Theory & Event* 21, no. 1 (2018): 69.

53. In the literature on kinship and motherhood, forms of fictive kinship have been an important area of inquiry for thinking of liberatory scripts. In the Kurdish movement, too, fictive kinship, whereby, for example, mothers who lost their children to state violence become "the mother of all" and politicize motherhood, point to liberatory practices; Nisa Göksel, "Losing the One, Caring for the All: The Activism of the Peace Mothers in Turkey," *Social Sciences* 7, no. 174 (2018): 1–20. Less analyzed however, is how kin, even sons and daughters, become comrades and are called "friend," replacing kinship terminologies.

54. Interestingly enough, women in the workshop speak less about their sons, and if they do, their concern is that their sons will be affected by patriarchy to the extent that their labor on them will prove itself to be futile.

55. For the activism of mothers of hunger strikers, see Çetinkaya, "Mothers as the Middle-Ground between the Mountain and the State."

56. Andres Fabian Henao Castro, *Antigone in the Americas: Democracy, Sexuality, and Death in the Settler Colonial Present* (Albany: SUNY Press 2022), 30.

57. Emine Rezzan Karaman, "Remember, S/He Was Here Once: Mothers Call for Justice and Peace in Turkey," *Journal of Middle East Women's Studies* 12, no. 3 (2016): 382, https://doi.org/10.1215/15525864-3637576.

58. Diana Taylor, *Disappearing Acts: Spectacles of Gender and Nationalism in Argentina's 'Dirty War'* (Durham, N.C.: Duke University Press, 1997), and *The Archive and the Repertoire: Performing Cultural Memory in the Americas* (Durham, N.C.: Duke University Press, 2003).

59. For a classic take on the issue, see Mary Dietz, "Citizenship with a Feminist Face: The Problem of Maternal Thinking," *Political Theory* 13, no. 1 (1985): 19–37.

60. Karaman, "Remember, S/He Was Here Once: Mothers Call for Justice and Peace in Turkey."

61. Başak Can, "How Does a Protest Law?: Rituals of Visibility, Disappearances under Custody and the Saturday Mothers in Turkey," *American Anthropologist* (forthcoming).

62. Ibid.

63. A politics of conscience in Öcalan words articulates "the truth of society"; *Sociology of Freedom: Manifesto of the Democratic Civilization*, vol. 3. I understand

this truth to refer to an affective and psychic account of bodies and events rendered unintelligeble by existing laws.

64. Çetinkaya, "Mothers as the Middle-Ground between the Mountain and the State," 209.

65. Castro, *Antigone in the Americas*.

66. Many commentaters believe that the two ISIS bombings that occurred right after the peace process collapsed, which targeted gatherings of Turkish and Kurdish activists for peace, were government conspiracies aiming to disintegrate the emerging alliance between Turks and Kurds around issues of democracy and equality. In these bombings more than 100 people were killed.

67. Nazan Üstündağ, "Belonging to the Modern: Women's Suffering and Subjectivities in Urban Turkey" (unpublished Ph.D. diss, Indiana University, 2005.

68. Nisa Göksel, "Losing the One, Caring for the All." For an analysis of masculinity in the context of forced migration, see Nil Mutluer, *Dignity and Masculinity: Kurdish Men, Internal Displacement and Memory in Everyday Istanbul* (Lanham, Md., Boulder, Colo., New York, and London: Lexington, 2023, forthcoming).

69. Hikmet Kocamaner, "Delinquent Kids, Revolutionary Mothers, Uncle Governor, and Erdoğan the Patriarch: The Gezi Park Protests and the Policy of Family," in *Resistance Everywhere: The Gezi Protests and Dissident Visions of Turkey*, ed. Anthony Alessandrini, Nazan Üstündağ, and Emrah Yıldız, *JadMag Pedagogy Publications* 1, no. 4 (2013), and Zeynep Kurtuluş Korkman and Salih Can Açıksöz, "Erdoğan's Masculinity and the Language of the Gezi Resistance," in Alessandrini, Üstündağ, and Yıldız, *Resistance Everywhere* .

70. Since 2015, the Turkish state also organizes mothers of guerrillas to orchestrate protests against the Kurdish Freedom Movement for recruiting their children. However, since such protests are provided infrastructure and aid by the state, I am not including them in my analyses.

71. Nazan Üstündağ, "Mother, Politician, and Guerilla: The Emergence of a New Political Imagination in Kurdistan through Women's Bodies and Speech," *differences* 30, no. 2 (2019): 115–45.

72. Walter Benjamin, *Reflections: Essays, Aphorisms, Autobiographical Writing* (New York: Schocken, 1986).

73. Rosalind C. Morris, "Chronicling Deaths Foretold: The Testimony of the Corpse and the Problem of Political Violence in South Africa," in *Reverberations: Violence across Time and Space*, ed. Yael Navaro et al. (Philadelphia: University of Pennsylvania Press, 2021).

74. Lisa Baraitser, *Enduring Time* (London and New York: Bloomsbery Academic, 2017).

75. Özgür Sevgi Göral, "'İmkansız Bir Talep' Olarak Adaleti Beklemek: Kaybedilenler ve Yakınları," in *Beklerken: Zamanın Bilgisi ve Öznenin Dönüşümü*, ed. Özge Biner and Zerrin Özlem Biner (İstanbul: İletişim Yayınları, 2019). For

a different conceptualization of "enforced" waiting in Kurdistan as a technology of control, see Ömer Özcan, "Curfew 'Until Further Notice': Waiting and Spatialization in a Kurdish Border Town in Turkey," *Social Anthropology* 29, no. 3 (2021): 816–30. I think our different conceptualization is rooted in our different perspectives. While Özcan shows how space is shrunk through enforced waiting, I focus on how mothers' public action, their extension of space, in other words, intercepts the progressive time of the state.

76. Elizabeth Freeman, *Time Binds: Queer Temporalities, Queer Histories* (Durham, N.C., and London: Duke University Press, 2010), and C. Heike Schotten, *Queer Terror: Life, Death, and Desire in the U.S. Settler Colony* (New York: Columbia University Press 2018).

## 3. Antigone as Kurdish Politician: Gendered Dwellings in the Limit between Freedom and Peace

EPIGRAPH SOURCES: Evrim Alataş, quoted by Yıldırım Türker, "Evrim Is Gone," *Radikal*, April 17, 2010; Hélène Cixous, "The Laugh of the Medusa," in *Feminisms: An Anthology of Literary Theory and Criticism*, ed. Robyn R. Warhol and Diane Pierce Hendl (New Brunswick, N.J.: Rutgers University Press, 1997); Lee Edelman, *No Future: Queer Theory and the Death Drive* (Durham, N.C.: Duke University Press, 2004), 106; Hortense J Spillers, "Mama's Baby, Papa's Maybe: An American Grammar Book," *Diacritics* 17, no. 2 (1987): 80; Jack Halberstam, *Skin Shows: Gothic Terror and the Technology of Monsters*, (Durham, N.C.: Duke University Press, 1995), 27.

1. *Milliyet*, "Bülent Arınç Emine Aynaya Yaratık Dedi," December 22, 2009, http://www.milliyet.com.tr/bulent-arinc-emine-ayna-ya-yaratik-dedi-siyaset-1176750/ (accessed September 19, 2018).

2. Julia Reinhard Lupton, *Citizen-Saints: Shakespeare and Political Theology* (Chicago: University of Chicago, 2014).

3. Tina Chanter, *Whose Antigone? The Tragic Marginalization of Slavery* (New York: SUNY Press, 2011), 144.

4. Sina Kramer, *Excluded W/In: The (Un)intelligibility of Radical Political Actors* (New York: Oxford University Press, 2019).

5. See, for example, Judith Butler, *Antigone's Claim: Kinship between Life and Death* (New York: Columbia University Press, 2000); Tina Chanter and Sean Kirkland eds., *The Returns of Antigone: Interdisciplinary Essays* (New York: SUNY Press, 2014); Joan Copjec, *Imagine There's No Woman: Ethics and Sublimation* (Cambridge, Mass.: MIT Press, 2004); Bonnie Honig, *Antigone Interrupted* (Cambridge: Cambridge University Press, 2013); Andres Fabian Henao Castro, *Antigone in the Americas: Democracy, Sexuality, and Death in the Settler Colonial Present* (Albany: SUNY Press, 2022); Cecilia Sjöholm, *The Antigone Complex: Ethics and the Invention of Feminine Desire* (Stanford, Calif.: Stanford University Press, 2004); Fanny Söderbäck, *Feminist Readings of Antigone* (New York:

Oxford University Press, 2010); and S. E. Wilmer and Audrone Zukauskaite, eds., *Interrogating Antigone in Postmodern Philosophy and Criticism* (New York: Oxford University Press, 2010).

6. Luce Irigaray, "Between Myth and History: The Tragedy of Antigone," in Wilmer and Zukauskaite, *Interrogating Antigone in Postmodern Philosophy and Criticism*.

7. Jacques Rancière, *The Politics of Aesthetics: The Distribution of the Sensible* (New York: Continuum International, 2004), and Rancière, *Dissensus: On Politics and Aesthetics* (New York: Bloomsbury, 2010).

8. Butler, *Antigone's Claim: Kinship Between Life and Death, Precarious Life: Power of Mourning and Violence* (2000; repr. New York: Verso, 2006); Butler, *Giving an Account of Oneself* (New York: Fordham University Press, 2005).

9. Honig, *Antigone Interrupted*.

10. Julia Kristeva, "Antigone: Limit and Horizon," in Söderbäck, *Feminist Readings of Antigone*.

11. For cases where truth movements in the aftermath of war have deadened women's memories, see Allen Feldman, *Archives of the Insensible: Of War, Photopolitics, and Dead Memory* (Chicago: Chicago University Press, 2015), and Fiona Ross, *Bearing Witness: Women and the Truth and Reconciliation Commission in South Africa* (London: Pluto Press, 2003). For the auditing cultures emerging during reconciliation, see Diane M. Nelson, *Reckoning: The Ends of War in Guatemala* (Durham, N.C.: Duke University Press, 2009).

12. For the politics of exile, see Cecilia Sjöhölm, "Naked Life: Arendt and the Exile at Colonus," in Wilmer and Zukauskaite, *Interrogating Antigone*. For body politics, see Adriana Cavarero, "On the Body of Antigone," in Söderbäck, *Feminist Readings of Antigone*.

13. Copjec, *Imagine There's No Woman*.

14. Jacques Lacan, *The Ethics of Psychoanalysis 1959–1960* (New York: Norton, 1992); Yannis Stavrakakis, "On Acts, Pure and Impure," *International Journal of Žižek Studies* 4, no. 2 (2010): 1–35; and Slavoj Žižek, *Antigone* (London and New York: Bloomsbury Academic, 2016).

15. Achille Mbembe, "The Age of Humanism is Ending," *Guardian*, December 22, 2016, https://mg.co.za/article/2016-12-22-00-the-age-of-humanism-is-ending/ (accessed September 15, 2019).

16. Honig, *Antigone Interrupted*, and Lupton, *Citizen-Saints*.

17. Lauren Berlant, *The Female Complaint: The Unfinished Business of Sentimentality in American Culture* (Durham, N.C.: Duke University Press, 2008).

18. Judith Butler, *Frames of War: When Is Life Grievable?* (New York: Verso, 2009).

19. Judith Butler, *Bodies That Matter: On the Discursive Limits of "Sex"* (London and New York: Routledge, 1993).

20. For selected publications on Kurdish women's participation in formal politics, see Handan Çağlayan, *Analar, Yoldaşlar, Tanrıçalar Kürt Hareketinde Kadınlar*

*ve Kadın Kimliğinin Oluşumu*, 6th ed. (İstanbul: İletişim Yayınları, 2017), and
Zeynep Şahin-Mencütek, "Strong in the Movement, Strong in the Party: Women's
Representation in the Kurdish Party of Turkey," *Political Studies* 64, no. 2 (2016):
470–87.

21. Honig, *Antigone Interrupted*.

22. Terry Eagleton, *Sweet Violence: The Idea of the Tragic* (Oxford and Berlin:
Blackwell, 2003).

23. Giorgio Agamben and Monica Ferrando, *The Unspeakable Girl: The Myth
and Mystery of Kore*, trans. Leland de la Durantaye (Dhaka, Bangladesh: Seagull,
2014).

24. Giorgio Agamben, *Profanations*, trans. J. Fort (New York: Zone, 2007).
Profanation is overcoming social separations and bringing all that is reified by state
and capitalism to the free use of people.

25. Kristeva, "Antigone: Limit and Horizon."

26. See Ruken Işık, "Claiming the Bodies of Kurdish Women: Kurdish Women's
Funerals in Northern Kurdistan/Turkey," *HAU: Journal of Ethnographic Theory* 12,
no. 1 (2022): 39–45.

27. Arzu Yilmaz, "Siyaset ve Kadin Kimligi" (unpublished master's thesis, 2006).
All translations are mine.

28. Ibid., 24.

29. Ibid., 22–24.

30. Yellow, red, and green are the colors that symbolize the Kurdish struggle and
free Kurdistan.

31. For a similar analysis in relation to Palestine, see Lotte Buch Segal, *No Place
for Grief: Martyrs, Prisoners, and Mourning in Contemporary Palestine* (Philadelphia:
University of Pennsylvania Press, 2016).

32. Lauren Berlant, "Slow Death (Sovereignty, Obesity, Lateral Agency)," *Critical
Inquiry* 33, no. 4 (Summer 2007): 754–80.

33. Ayça Örer, "Kadın Bu Hafta Medyada Mal Seksi Apolitik," *Bianet*, March 30,
2007, https://m.bianet.org/bianet/kadin/94028-kadin-bu-hafta-medyada-mal-seksi
-apolitik (accessed March 10, 2017). Aysel Tuğluk is today indeed in prison despite
suffering a severe case of dementia.

34. The Constitutional Court has regularly dissolved Kurdish political parties in
Turkey. The DTP (Democratic Society Party) was created in 2005 and became the
seventh party to be dissolved in 2009. Today the HDP (People's Democracy Party),
which was founded by the Kurdish Movement and the Turkish Left, is the major
legal actor that represents the Kurds. The DBP (Democratic Regional Party) is, on
the other hand, a political party that does not enter the elections but organizes itself
at the regional level in Kurdish cities. The party aims at educating and training
cadres that can take different positions and posts at different levels of the radical
democratic system the Kurds are building alongside state structures.

35. Reported by *Milliyet*, "Bülent Arınç, Emine Ayna'ya 'yaratık' dedi,"

December 22, 2009, http://www.milliyet.com.tr/bulent-arinc-emine-ayna-ya-yaratik
-dedi-siyaset-1176750/ (accessed on October 12, 2018).

36. The Kurdish initiative (*Kürt açılımı* in Turkish) is the name of the period between 2009 and 2013 when the government took steps to legalize some of the Kurdish demands, such as broadcasting and electoral propaganda in the Kurdish language. During this time government officials also made effective speeches calling for the brotherhood of Kurds and Turks. In 2013 a peace process started that involved visits to PKK leader Öcalan in Imralı prison and negotiation with Kurdish MPs, which ended in 2015.

37. Lupton, *Citizen-Saints*, 164.

38. Butler, *Antigone's Claim*, 11.

39. A comprehensive list of the PKK's ceasefires until 2011 can be found in Toplum ve Kuram, "Kürt Hareketinin Kronolojisi 1999–2011," *Toplum ve Kuram* 5 (2011): 21–51.

40. Butler, *Antigone's Claim*, 28.

41. Ibid.

42. Žižek, *Antigone*, 18.

43. See Alenka Zupančič, "Lacan's Heroines: Antigone and Synge de Coufontaine," *New Formations* 35 (1998): 108–21, where she juxtaposes the traditional forced choice of "your money or life" with the modern forced choice "your freedom or your life" and Honig's take on this in her Chapter 6 in *Antigone Interrupted*.

44. Zupančič, "Lacan's Heroines."

45. Lupton, *Citizen-Saints*, 164.

46. Žižek, Antigone, 18.

47. Her statement is available at http://www.diken.com.tr/emine-ayna-siyaseti
-biraktigini-acikladi/ (accessed October 30, 2018).

48. Butler, *Frames of War*.

49. Lupton, *Citizen-Saints*, 137.

50. Ibid.

51. In relation to his analysis of Antigone, Castro asks, "How then to bury the many Polyneices while resisting the allure of intelligibility that forces one to establish their innocence first?"; Castro, *Antigone in the Americas*, 152. This is an extremely important question that haunts the Kurdish Movement. While in the case of Roboski a discourse on innocence enabled Kurds to show that Kurdish lives do not matter to the Turkish state, it nevertheless put them in a connundrum when a couple of years later the peace process collapsed and the youth of Kurdistan rebelled against the state. This time, it was young insurgents that were killed without any accountability that could not be claimed as innocent. In such events it is usually the mothers (as I have explained in Chapter 2) that can challange the state on the basis of their motherhood rather than on the basis of the innocence of the deceased.

52. Stefano Harney and Fred Moten, "Michael Brown," *boundary2* 42, no. 4 (2015): 85, and Saidiya Hartmann, "Venus in Two Acts," *Small Axe* 26, no. 2 (2008): 12.

53. Erdoğan's statement is available here: *Sabah*, "Başbakan Erdoğan Konuşuyor," May 26, 2012, https://www.sabah.com.tr/gundem/2012/05/26/basbakan -erdogan-konusuyor (accessed on October 12, 2018). What Savannah Shange writes about the non-black affective experiences of blackness is also true for how Turks respond to Kurdishness. As can be seen in both the event that led to the interruption of the Kurdish initiative (the celebration of the return of the guerrillas from Qandil) that eventually led to Emine Ayna's laughter and Erdoğan's reaction to the unending mourning of the Roboski deaths point to "the enactment of policy" as "overdetermined by the affective experiences of" Turkish people "resulting in a pattern of *emotionally contingent politics* whereby cerebral commitments to racial justice are undermined by" Turkish "people's visceral commitment to order"; Shange, *Progressive Dystopia: Abolition, Antiblackness, Schooling in San Francisco* (Durham, N.C.: Duke University Press, 2019), 79.

54. Harney and Moten, "Michael Brown," 85.

55. Ibid.

56. Honig, *Antigone Interrupted*, 135.

57. Martel writes, "This is how the corpse is connected to allegory. Allegory represents for Benjamin a subversive trope that unmakes and ruins our attempts to project truth and ontology into the universe. It is, simply put, the site where the failure and breakdown of those projections becomes most visible; the corpse is the human being's most fundamental font of that resistance"; James R. Martel, *Bodies Unburied: Subversive Corpses and the Authority of the Dead* (Amherst, Mass.: Amherst College Press, 2018).

58. For a rare analysis of women's experience in the Diyarbakır Prison, see Berivan Kutlay Sarıkaya, "Between Silence and Resistance: Kurdish Women in Colonial Turkish Prison: Diyarbakır Military Prison 1980–1984" (unpublished Ph.D. diss., University of Toronto, 2021).

59. Kışanak's speech is available at https://www.youtube.com/watch?v =N4gc6jjLNnU (accessed on September 10, 2018).

60. Fred Moten, *In the Break: The Aesthetics of the Black Radical Tradition* (Minneapolis and London: University of Minnesota Press, 2003).

## 4. Kurdish Women Politicians at the Border between Body and Flesh

EPIGRAPH SOURCES: Mona Bhan and Haley Duschinski, "Occupations in Context — The Cultural Logics of Occupation, Settler Violence, and Resistance," *Critique of Anthropology* 40, no. 3 (2020): 285, https://doi.org/10.1177 /0308275X20929403; Frantz Fanon, *The Wretched of the Earth* (New York: Grove Press, 2014), 15; Audra Simpson, "The State Is a Man: Theresa Spence, Loretta Saunders and the Gender of Settler Sovereignty," *Theory & Event*, 19, no. 4 (2016):

10; Abdullah Öcalan, *Demokratik Uygarlık Manifestosu III. Kitap: Özgürlük Sosyolojisi Üzerine Deneme* (Abdullah Öcalan Akademisi Yayınları, 2013), 47; my translation.

1. For the discourse on honor killings in Turkey and how such discourse delegates femicide to tradition, specifically the tradition of Kurds, see Dicle Koğacıoğlu, "The Tradition Effect: Framing Honor Crimes in Turkey, *differences* 15, no. 2 (2004): 118–51. Such rendering also explains away the gendered affects of war and colonization. For an excellent reading of sexual crimes in post-apartheid South Africa that links the intimate with the state law and violence instead of tradition, see Rosalind C. Morris, "The Mute and the Unspeakable: Political Subjectivity, Violent Crime, and 'the Sexual Thing' in a South African Mining Community," in *Law and Disorder in the Postcolony*, ed. Jean Comaroff and John Comaroff (Chicago: University of Chicago Press, 2006).

2. Nazan Üstündağ, "Ayşe Gökkan Ölüm Orucunda," *Bianet*, November 5, 2013, https://bianet.org/bianet/bianet/151057-ayse-gokkan-olum-orucunda (accessed April 24, 2021). My translation.

3. Gayatri Chakravorty Spivak, "Woman in Difference: Mahasweta Devi's 'Douloti the Bountiful,'" in *Nationalisms & Sexualities*, ed. Andrew Parker et al. (London and New York: Routledge, 1991).

4. Ibid., 112.

5. Amahl Bishara, "Sovereignty and Popular Sovereignty for Palestinians and Beyond," *Cultural Anthropology* 32, no. 3 (2017): 349–58.

6. Kurdish regions in northern Syria are called "Rojava" in popular usage, which means "west" in Kurdish.

7. Avery Gordon, "Some Thoughts on Haunting and Futurity," *Borderlands E-Journal* 10, no. 2 (2011): 1–21.

8. Throughout the attacks of ISIS on Kurdish territories, suspicion that Turkey was helping ISIS spread, making the already difficult peace process between 2013 between 2015 even more fragile and unreliable.

9. The fact that border cities on the Turkish and Syrian sides are close made it possible for those on the Turkish side to protest when any city in Rojava was attacked by ISIS fighters or other jihadist groups, which gave moral support to fighters, some of whom originated from Turkey's Kurdistan. However, spectatorship also traumatized. For example, in Suruç, residents painstakingly and helplessly watched the explosions while their relatives on the other side fought ISIS. Eventually the war was won, but its death toll was high, and the fact that underneath the destroyed city of Kobane remained hundreds of dead bodies rotting haunted both cities. People in Suruç believed that dogs, which were the only ones to travel without restriction, crossed the border every night to feed off human flesh. People in Suruç stayed away from them, since they thought the dogs had now changed and gone mad. For a discussion of the border between Syria and Turkey and how it evolved into a biopolitical laboratory in recent years, see Ezgi Tuncer Gürkaş, "Border as 'Zone of Indistinction': The State of Exception and the Spectacle of Terror along Turkey's

Border With Syria," *Space and Culture* 21, no. 3 (2018): 322–35, https://doi.org/10.1177 /1206331217741080.

10. See Chapter 3 for how women politicians are blamed for being inauthentic/ putting on a show for attention.

11. For a comprehensive theorization of hunger strikes in Turkey, see Banu Bargu, *Starve and Immolate: The Politics of Human Weapons* (New York: Columbia University Press, 2014).

12. Avery F. Gordon, *Ghostly Matters: Haunting and the Sociological Imagination* (Minneapolis: University of Minnesota Press, 2008).

13. Ibid.

14. Audra Simpson, *Mohawk Interruptus: Political Life across the Borders of Settler States* (Durham, N.C., and London: Duke University Press, 2014); Circe Sturm, "Reflections on the Anthropology of Sovereignty and Settler Colonialism: Lessons from Native North America," *Cultural Anthropology* 32, no. 3 (2017): 340–48, https://doi.org/10.14506/ca32.3.03.

15. Andrés Fabián Henao Castro, "The Crack in the Mask, the Wound in the Flesh: Political Representation as Symptom," *Representation* 53, no. 1 (2017): 58, https://doi.org/10.1080/00344893.2017.1346875.

16. Katherine McKittrick, *Demonic Grounds: Black Women and the Cartographies of Struggle* (Minneapolis and London: University of Minnesota Press, 2006).

17. Castro, "The Crack in the Mask," 57.

18. Ayşe is sentenced to thirty years of imprsonment. At the news site *Gazete Karınca*, Ruşen Seydaoğlu wrote a brilliant commentary in response to this sentence by juxtaposing its stately temporality with the mythical temporality of the Kurdish Women's Freedom Movement. See Seydaoğlu, "Ayşe Gökkan: Havaya Suya Toprağa Düşen Cemre," *Gazete Karınca*, October 27, 2021, http://esitlikadaletkadin.org/ayse -gokkan-havaya-suya-topraga-dusen-cemre/ (accessed April 18, 2022).

19. In Chapter 3 I defined *Ate* as the "real" of a community, its spirit that moves it but remains unaccounted for in the symbolic order; that is, in this case, Turkish law; see Sarah De Sanctis, "From Psychoanalysis to Politics: Antigone as a Revolutionary in Judith Butler and Slavoj Žižek," *Opticon 1826* 14 (2017): 27–36.

20. Jason Glynos and Yannis Stavrakakis, "Politics and the Unconscious," *Subjectivity* 3, no. 3 (2010): 4, https://doi.org/10.1057/sub.2010.17.

21. Crawley thinks "of enfleshment as distinct from embodiment" and argues "that enfleshment is the movement to, the vibration of, liberation and this over and against embodiment that presumes a subject of theology, a subject of philosophy, a subject of history"; Ashon T. Crawley, *Blackpentecostal Breath: The Aesthetics of Possibility* (New York: Fordham University Press, 2017), 6.

22. In *Means without End: Notes on Politics*, trans. Vincenzo Binetti and Cesare Casarino (Minneapolis: University of Minnesota Press, 2000), Giorgio Agamben defines form-of-life as a life that cannot be seperated from its form and that cannot be isolated as naked life.

23. See Saidiya Hartman's Chapter 1 in *Scenes of Subjection* (New York and

Oxford: Oxford University Press, 1997), 81–87, for a critical discussion of how empathy reinforces the violence that makes the sufferer into an object.

24. Judith Butler, Zeynep Gambetti, and Leticia Sabsay eds., *Resistance in Vulnerability* (Durham, N.C.: Duke University Press, 2016).

25. Arielle Azoulay, *Civil Imagination: A Political Ontology of Photography*, repr. ed. (New York: Verso, 2015); Chiara Bottici and Benoit Challand, eds., *The Politics of Imagination* (Abingdon and New York: Birkbeck Law Press, 2011); Meg McLagan and Yates McKess, eds., *Sensible Politics: The Visual Culture of Nongovernmental Activism* (New York: Zone, 2012). See also how in Kashmir images are used to create humanitarian imaginaries: Deepti Misri, "Showing Humanity: Violence and Visuality in Kashmir," *Cultural Studies* 33, no. 3 (2019): 527–49.

26. Miriam Cooke, *Dancing in Damascus: Creativity, Resilience, and the Syrian Revolution* (London and New York: Routledge, 2016).

27. Chiara Bottici, *Imaginal Politics: Images beyond Imagination and the Imaginary* (New York: Columbia University Press, 2019).

28. Nazan Üstündağ, "Pornographic State and Erotic Resistance," *South Atlantic Quarterly* 118, no. 1 (2019): 95–110.

29. Judith Butler, *Frames of War: When Is Life Grievable?* (New York: Verso, 2009).

30. Andres Fabian Henao Castro, *Antigone in the Americas: Democracy, Sexuality, and Death in the Settler Colonial Present* (Albany: SUNY Press 2022), 72. Talking about the women in the slave ship, Spillers uses the term "ungendering" and explains it the following way: "Under these conditions we lose at least gender difference *in the outcome*, and the female body and the male body become a territory of cultural and political maneuver, not at all gender-related, gender-specific"; Hortense J Spillers, "Mama's Baby, Papa's Maybe: An American Grammar Book," *Diacritics* 17, no. 2 (1987): 67. This term is useful in this context as well, since the tear gas, the gas canister, and pressured water are also ways in which female and male bodies are made into territories "of cultural and political maneuver, not at all gender-related, gender-specific."

31. R. A. Judy, *Sentient Flesh: Thinking in Disorder, Poiesis in Black* (Durham, N.C.: Duke University Press, 2020).

32. Banu Bargu, "Human Shields," *Contemporary Political Theory* 12, no. 4 (2013): 277–95, https://doi.org/10.1057/cpt.2013.1; Bargu, "Bodies against War: Voluntary Human Shielding as a Practice of Resistance," *AJIL Unbound* 110 (2016): 299–304, https://www.jstor.org/stable/27003225.

33. Following the insurgency of the youth in Kurdistan between 2015 and 2016, the Turkish state once again changed its spatial politics, destroying and remapping cities by building apartment complexes, banning border zones to civilans, and reaching out toward the mountains in Iraq and occupying spaces by army squads, which were landed by helicopters.

34. Edward Soja, *Thirdspace: Journeys to Los Angeles and Other Real-and-Imagined Places* (Oxford: Blackwell, 1996).

35. For how occupation shrinks space, see Eyal Weizmann, *Hollow Land: Israel's Architecture of Occupation* (New York: Verso, 2007). Also see Diren Taş, "Displacing Resistance in Kurdish Regions: The Symbiosis of Neoliberal Transformation and Authoritarian State in Sur," in *Authoritarian Neoliberalims and Resistance in Turkey: Construction, Consolidation and Contestation*, ed. İmren Borsuk et al. (Singapore: Palgrave Macmillan, 2022), and Pınar Dinç, "Forest Fires in Dersim and Şırnak: Conflict and Environmental Destruction," in *Ecological Solidarity and the Kurdish Freedom Movement: Thought, Practice and Opportunities*, ed. Stephen Hunt (Lanham, Md., Boulder, Colo., New York, and London: Lexington, 2021) for discussions of how occupation unfolds in terms of the architecture and environment in Kurdistan in the last decade.

36. While some male politicians also attend those protests, it is more often women who participate in such protests. This is because usually women MPs come from the women's movement, which organizes these protests; even after the women become MPs, the agendas of the women's movement play a primary role in shaping their actions.

37. Arielle Azoulay, "Regime-Made Disaster: On the Possibility of Nongovernmental Viewing," in McLagan and McKess, *Sensible Politics*.

38. Ibid., 40.

39. Spillers, "Mama's Baby, Papa's Maybe."

40. Alexander G. Weheliye, *Habeas Viscus: Racializing Assemblages, Biopolitics, and Black Feminist Theories of the Human* (Durham, N.C., and London: Duke University Press, 2014), 39.

41. Rizvana Bradley, "Corporeal Resurfacings: Faustin Linyekula, Nick Cave and Thornton Dial" (unpublished Ph.D. diss., Duke University, 2013).

42. According to this conceptualization, the Musselman, for example, although robbed of his desire and personhood, is not only still a living being — "bare life," as Agamben would have it, but has also a thinking, feeling, "sentient" flesh with its own capacity and trajectory.

43. Lauren Berlant, "Slow Death (Sovereignty, Obesity, Lateral Agency)," *Critical Inquiry* 33, no. 4 (Summer 2007): 754–80.

44. Weheliye, *Habeas Viscus*, 39.

45. Audra Simpson, "The State Is a Man: Theresa Spence, Loretta Saunders and the Gender of Settler Sovereignty" *Theory & Event* 19, no. 4 (2016).

46. Lauren Wilcox, "Explosive Bodies and Bounded States: Abjection and the Embodied Practice of Suicide Bombing," *International Journal of Politics* 16, no. 1 (2014): 66–85. For Tereffe, abject and flesh are different to the extent that "the primary aspect of the abject upon which its existence hinges is jouissance." She argues that Kristeva "implies that victims of the abject may be 'willing ones,' finding in 'sublime alienation, a forfeited existence.'" Yet if we follow Spillers's hermeneutics of flesh, what subtends the transubstantiation of Black bodies into flesh concerns: "a theft of the body — a willful and violent (and unimaginable from this distance) severing of the captive body from its motive will, its active desire"; Selamawit D.

Terrefe, "Speaking the Hieroglyph," *Theory & Event* 21, no. 1 (2018): 128. I am not sure why stealing of desire forecloses the possibility of jouissance.

47. Julia Kristeva, *Powers of Horror: An Essay on Abjection* (New York: Columbia University Press, 1982), and Wilcox, "Explosive Bodies and Bounded States," 68.

48. Ibid.

49. Castro writes, "Inspired by Hortense Spillers' famous distinction between captive and liberated subject — positions . . . I here propose to understand the face as a category of the body, and the skin as a category of the flesh. Refusing symbolic integration, the wounded flesh only appears through the cracks of the broken mask"; Castro, "Crack in the Mask," 6.

50. For an account of how the Armenian genocide is remembered by Kurds, see Adnan Çelik, "The Armenian Genocide in Kurdish Collective Memory," *Middle East Report* 295 (2020).

51. See Tanıl Bora, *Türkiye'nin Linç Rejimi*, 3rd ed. (Istanbul: İletişim Yayınları, 2021), and Zeynep Gambetti, "'I'm No Terrorist, I am a Kurd': Societal Violence, the State, and the Neo-Liberal Order," in *Rhetorics of Insecurity: Belonging and Violence in the Neoliberal Era*, ed. Zeynep Gambetti and Marcial Godoy-Anativia (New York: New York University Press, 2013).

52. For discussions of increased authoritarianism in Turkey, see for example, Yeşim Arat and Şevket Pamuk, *Turkey between Democracy and Authoritarianism* (Cambridge: Cambridge University Press, 2019); Erol Babacan et al., eds., *Regime Change in Turkey: Neoliberal Authoritarianism, Islamism and Hegemony* (London and New York: Routledge, 2021); and Esra Özyürek, Gamze Özçelik, and Emrah Altındiş eds., *Authoritarianism and Resistance in Turkey: Conversations on Democratic and Social Challenges* (Cham, Switzerland: Springer, 2019).

53. See Haydar Darıcı, "Politics of Kurdish Children in Urban Turkey," *International Journal of Middle East Studies* 45 (2013): 775–90; Cenk Saraçoğlu, "The Changing Image of the Kurds in Turkish Cities: Middle-Class Perceptions of Kurdish Migrants in İzmir," *Patterns of Prejudice* 44, no. 3 (2010): 239–60; and Onur Günay, "In War and Peace: Shifting Narratives of Violence in Kurdish Istanbul," *American Anthropologist* 3, no. 21 (2019): 554–67, for a discussion of Kurdish lives in Adana, İzmir, and Istanbul, respectively.

54. For a discussion of all the failed peace attempts between 2005 and 2015 between the PKK and the Turkish state, see Amed Dicle, *2005–2015 Türkiye-PKK Görüşmeleri: Kürt Sorununun Çözümüne "Çözüm Süreci" Operasyonu* (Neuss: Mezopotamya Yayınları, 2016).

55. See Delal Aydın, "Mobilising the Kurds in Turkey: Newroz As A Myth," in *The Kurdish Question in Turkey*, ed. Cengiz Güneş and Welat Zeydanlıoğlu (London and New York: Routledge), for a discussion of political mobilization during Newroz, which is regarded to be the first day of spring (March 21) by Kurds.

56. İnsan Hakları Derneği, "2012 Newrozunda Yaşanan Hak İhlalleri Raporu," İHD, April 2, 2012, https://www.ihd.org.tr/2012-newrozunda-yasanan-hak-ihlalleri-raporu/ (accessed May 4, 2021).

57. Ekin Karaca, "Metin İnan: Tuncel ile Polis Arasında Tartışma Gaz Bombalarından Çıktı," *Bianet*, March 23, 2011, https://m.bianet.org/bianet/toplum/128801-metin-inan-tuncel-ile-polis-arasinda-tartisma-gaz-bombalarindan-cikti (accessed May 4, 2021).

58. BİA Haber Ajansı, "Tuncel İlk Değil Medyanın Gözü BDP'li Kadın Vekillerin Üstünde," *Bianet*, March 23, 2011, https://m.bianet.org/bianet/siyaset/128799-tuncel-ilk-degil-medyanin-gozu-bdp-li-kadin-vekillerin-ustunde (accessed May 4, 2021).

59. Ertuğrul Kürkçü, "Atılamayan Tokat ve Egemenin İncinen Gururu," *Bianet*, March 23, 2011, https://m.bianet.org/bianet/siyaset/128796-atil-a-mayan-tokat-ve-egemenin-incinen-gururu (accessed May 5, 2021).

60. Hakan Karakoca, "Bir Tokadın Anlattıkları," *Bianet*, March 26, 2011, https://m.bianet.org/bianet/toplum/128885-bir-tokadin-anlattiklari (accessed May 5, 2021).

61. Bettina Judd, "Sapphire as Praxis: Toward a Methodology of Anger," *Feminist Studies* 45, no. 1 (2019): 183, https://doi.org/10.15767/feministstudies.45.1.0178.

62. Bradley, *Corporeal Resurfacings*, 13.

63. For the difference between what is doable and what is necessary, see Savannah Shange, *Progressive Dystopia: Abolition, Antiblackness, and Schooling in San Francisco* (Durham, N.C.: Duke University Press 2019), 21. Starting in 2012, Kurds have started to more loudly express their will to create an autonomous region without changing Turkey's borders.

64. Founded in 2012, the People's Democracy Party (HDP) is a coalitional party that brought together different political parties, organizations, and individuals, including the BDP.

65. Feleknaza Uca entered the Parliament in November 2015 in the immediate aftermath of the collapse of the peace process. She is of Yazidi descent, born in Germany. She served with die Linke in the EU Parliament between 1999 and 2009. She didn't speak Turkish when she was elected as an MP from the People's Democracy Party (HDP).

66. See, for example, En Son Haber, "HDP'li Vekil Feleknas Uca'nın Son Hali," October 26, 2016, https://m.ensonhaber.com/ic-haber/hdpli-vekil-feleknas-ucanin-son-hali-2016-10-26 (accessed on May 12, 2021).

67. Stephen Sheehi, "Psychoanalyses under Occupation: Non-Violence and Dialogue Initiatives as a Psychic Extension of the Closure System," *Journal of Psychoanalysis and History* 20, no. 3 (2018): 353–69.

68. Ibid., 355. Meanwhile, see Umut Yıldırım, "Space, Loss and Resistance: A Haunted Pool-Map in South-Eastern Turkey," *Anthropological Theory* 19, no. 4 (2019): 440–69, https://doi.org/10.1177/1463499618783130, and Umut Yıldırım, "Spaced-Out States: Decolonizing Trauma in a War-Torn Middle Eastern City," *Current Anthropology* 62, no. 6 (2022), https://doi.org/10.1086/718206, for an ethnographic analysis of affects and subjectivities during this period of NGOization.

69. Stephen Sheehi, "Psychoanalyses under Occupation," 354.

70. Ibid.

71. I use here the Benjaminian concept of ruination because it captures how these images evoke a sense of a history of the flesh that is being unmade by the Turkish state's material and psychic colonization of Kurdistan under the names of security and progress. This history, however, erupts as tradition when Kurdish women continue citing it through their performances. See Walter Benjamin, *Origin of the German Trauerspiel*, annotated ed. (Cambridge, Mass: Harvard University Press, 2019).

72. Patrice Douglass, "Black Feminist Theory for the Dead and Dying," *Theory & Event* 21, no. 1 (2018): 113.

73. Ibid., 116.

74. *Cumhuriyet*, "BDP'li Kışanak'ın sarıldığı PKK'li Yeşiltaş'ı basmış," August 22, 2012, https://www.cumhuriyet.com.tr/haber/bdpli-kisanakin-sarildigi-pkkli-yesiltasi -basmis-365786 (accessed April 28, 2021).

75. *NTV*, "Gülten Kışanak: Gerekirse O Askerlerle de Kucaklaşırız," August 20, 2012, https://www.ntv.com.tr/turkiye/gultan-kisanak-o-askerlerle-de-kucaklasiriz,gR6 -IbqZxUOvwACRMxSwqw (accessed April 28, 2021).

76. Begona Aretxaga, *States of Terror: Begona Aretxaga's Essays* (Reno: Center for Basque Studies, University of Nevada Press, 2005): 166.

77. This is exactly the kind of ethical framework Hegel thought Antigone evoked in her insistence to bury her brother.

78. Demirören Haber Ajansı, "BDP'li Kışanak Gerilla Kontrol Noktalarının Olduğu Bir Bölgeye Gittiğimizi Biliyorduk," August 20, 2012, Haberler. Com, https://www.haberler.com/bdp-li-kisanak-gerilla-kontrol-noktalarinin-oldugu -3879869-haberi/ (accessed April 29, 2021).

79. Jacques Rancière, *The Politics of Aesthetics* (London and New York: Continuum International, 2004).

80. "Apoist" is one way that PKK members refer to themselves, signifying that they are ideologically followers of Abdullah Öcalan.

81. Frank B. Wilderson III, *Red, White, and Black: Cinema and the Structure of US Antagonisms* (Durham, N.C.: Duke University Press, 2010), 59; Shange, *Progressive Dystopia*, 96.

82. Weheliye, *Habeas Viscus*, 43.


## 5. Who Are We and How Must We Live? Being a Friend in the Guerrilla Movement

EPIGRAPH SOURCES: Eric A. Stanley, *Atmospheres of Violence: Structuring Antagonism and the Trans/Queer Ungovernable* (Durham, N.C.: Duke University Press, 2021), 14; José Esteban Muñoz, *Cruising Utopia: The Then and There of Queer Futurity* (Durham, N.C.: Duke University Press 2009), 1; Stefano Harney and Fred Moten, *All Incomplete* (Colchester, New York, and Port Watson: Minor Compositions, 2021), 30; Selma Doğan (c.n. Zinarin), *Zinarin'in Güncesi* (Neuss: Mezopotamya Yayınları, 1999), 148: "Savaş içimize, yani seni bana, beni sana ve daha kimlere taşımadı ki. Tanıştığımız binlerce insana götürdü, sevdirdi, bağladı görülmeyen bir şeylere. Ve sonra kopardı, alıp getirdi başka diyarlara, başka dağlara, ovalara, şehirlere, memleketlere."

1. In the Kurdish social and political imaginaries, the mountains are "exilic spaces" where people can exit state and communal regulations; Andrej Grubačić and Denis O'Hearn, *Living at the Edges of Capitalism: Adventures in Exile and Mutual Aid* (Oakland: University of California Press, 2016). A reading of the Kurdish Freedom Movement from a perspective grounded in landscape imaginaries is necessary but still lacking. For such an attempt, see Nazan Üstündağ, "A Travel Guide to Northern Kurdistan," in *Anywhere but Now: Landscapes of Belonging in the Eastern Mediterranean*, ed. Samar Kanafani et al. (Berlin: Heinrich Boell Foundation, 2012).

2. During the 1990s, when the war between the PKK and the Turkish state was intense, the guerrilla appeared and disappeared in villages at night, and their presence in the mountains was rather sensed than seen. With the kidnapping and arrest of Abdullah Öcalan in 1999, the PKK experienced inner turmoil and retreated from Turkey, declaring a cease fire. During this time people spoke of the guerrilla as a mythological figure whose absence signified corruption and ethical failure among Kurdish people. After 2006, the PKK's presence in Turkish Kurdistan became more paramount, with visits to their camps and temporary occupations of uncrowded roads and pastures by them becoming more frequent.

3. Roza Burç, *In Remaining a Society: Survival, Organization and Self-Defense* (unpublished manuscript).

4. Elizabeth A. Povinelli, "The Will to Be Otherwise/The Effort of Endurance," *South Atlantic Quarterly* 11, no. 3 (2012): 453–75.

5. Jack Halberstam, *Wild Things: The Disorder of Desire* (Durham, N.C., and London: Duke University Press, 2020), 20.

6. Karen Barad, "Nature's Queer Performativity," *Kvinder, KØn & Forskning* 1–2 (2012): 47.

7. Interestingly enough, whenever Turkey's minister of internal affairs wants to insult the guerrilla, he also says that the PKK is a women's organization.

8. While the Kurdish Freedom Movement makes no such differentiation, I make the following one between norms and laws: Whereas in my usage both laws and norms are always historically formed, the laws that the Kurdish Movement animates are those that have been lost to us — became repressed, marginalized, or altogether forgotten. Such laws are imagined to have formed the symbolic order of the Neolithic age where matrilinearity reigned, women and men enjoyed equal power, and women's labor of making the social was valued as the most important form of labor; David Graeber, "Öcalan As Thinker: On the Unity of Theory and Practice as Form of Writing," in *Building Free Life: Dialogues with Öcalan*, ed. International Initiative (Oakland, Calif.: PM Press, 2020). These laws can be reactivated by contemplations on mythology and archeology, discovered by quantum physics, which unearths the mysteries of the universe, and by the death labor of

women guerrillas. The forms of death labor that guerrilla women perform (like that of Antigone) point to the demands/desires of women to be recognized by the symbolic order to which they remain unintelligeble. It is the PKK's mission to signify these and become a "response to them." Meanwhile, norms are perfomed by women individually and collectively from within the existing social order (of the PKK and Kurdistan), and as they are cited and recited by other women, they become the tradition of the organization and women setting examples on how women should act.

9. Andres Fabian Henao Castro, *Antigone in the Americas: Democracy, Sexuality, and Death in the Settler Colonial Present* (Albany: SUNY Press, 2022), 102.

10. Ibid., 103.

11. Ibid., 86. I disagree with Castro, who thinks that subjects that are condemned to social death, who are already "objects on whose violent deanimation the social order relies," and whose "mere existence is considered a kind of transgression to begin with" can exercise fugitivity but not freedom (88). I think such a statement can only be made if we treat those subjects as isolated from each other. When together, subjects condemned to social death are perfectly capable of coming up with new ways of exercising freedom. Also, even when alone (as I will explain later) if we adopt a quantum physics perspective, their acts will create motions whose direction and velocity vary and the communications they incite are undeterminable. This, the Kurdish Movement would argue, is one definition of freedom.

12. For a lengthy discussion on sexuality and freedom among the guerrilla, see Abdullah Öcalan, *Nasıl Yaşamalı* (Weşanên Serxwebûn, 2008). While asexuality is increasingly considered to be a radically queer orientation, it is curious why scholars who work on the Kurdish Movement see the "asexuality" of the guerrillas in the PKK against compulsory sexuality as a lack at best and as evidence of their unfreedom at worst. See, for example, Nadja Al-Ali and Isabel Kaeser, "Beyond Feminism? Jineolojî and the Kurdish Women's Freedom Movement," *Politics and Gender* (2020): 1–32.

For discussions of asexuality as a queer orientation with radical potentialities, see C. J. DeLuzio Chasin, "Reconsidering Asexuality and Its Radical Potential," *Feminist Studies* 39, no. 2 (2013): 405–26; Breanne Fahs, "Radical Refusals: On the Anarchist Politics of Women Choosing Asexuality," *Sexualities* 13, no. 4 (2010): 445–61; Kristina Gupta, "Compulsory Sexuality: Evaluating an Emerging Concept," *Signs: Journal of Women in Culture and Society* 41, no. 1 (2015): 131–54; and Kristin S. Scherrer, "Coming to an Asexual Identity: Negotiating Identity, Negotiating Desire," *Sexualities* 11, no. 5 (2008): 621–41.

13. While I use the term "critical asexuality" to describe the guerrillas' sexual orientation for purposes of including them to the positionality of the queer, I hesitate that this is the best description. In his book on "wildeness," Halbestam declares that "rather than seeking out stray bodies within a history of sexuality and wrangling them into legibility, this book recognizes the motion of straying itself as a disorderly

relation to history and desire"; Halberstam, *Wild Things*, 29. The expression "the motion of straying" might be more fitting for describing the life in the mountains, which represents a form of "wildeness." While I was in the mountains I often heard stories about snakes or bears falling in love with individual guerrilla women and the difficulties such love and attachment cause in the camps. In one case, for example, women collectively told me a story where a snake that fell in love with a woman followed her from camp to camp until she forced herself to kill the snake, mourning its death to this day. The mountains where the guerrillas abstain from sexual relations while experimenting with other senses of the erotic is full of such stories, where the difference between nature and culture, human and animal, love and death are transgressed.

14. Lee Edelman, *No Future: Queer Theory and the Death Drive* (Durham, N.C.: Duke University Press, 2004).

15. The report can be found in this link: Women for Peace Initiative, "Report on the Process Resolution," January–December 2013, http://www.peacewomen.org /assets/media/baris_kadin_ingilizce_baski_2.pdf (accessed March 20, 2022).

16. Michael Taussig, "The Mastery of Non-Mastery: A Report and Reflections from Kobane," Public Seminar, August 7, 2005, https://publicseminar.org/2015/08 /the-mastery-of-non-mastery/ (accessed April 19, 2022).

17. Ibid.

18. Sylvia Wynter, "Unsettling the Coloniality of Being/Power/Truth/Freedom: Towards the Human, After Man, Its Overrepresentation — An Argument," *CR: The New Centennial Review* 3, no. 3 (2003): 257–337. The assertions I make here about Öcalan are based on his prison writings and discussions with his visitors between 1999 and 2015. Some of these discussions can be found in the following book: Abdullah Öcalan, *Demokratik Kurtuluş ve Özgür Yaşamı İnşa: İmralı Notları* (Neuss: Mezopotamya Yayınları, 2015). See also Nazan Üstündağ, "The Theology of Democratic Modernity: Labor, Truth, Freedom," in International Initiative, *Building Free Life*, 235–60.

19. Max Hantel, "Placticity and Fungibility: On Sylvia Wynter's Pieza Framework," *Social Text* 38, no. 2 (2020): 97–119.

20. Walter Mignolo, "Sylvia Wynter: What Does It Mean to Be Human?," in *Sylvia Wynter: On Being Human as Praxis*, ed. Katherine McKittrick (Durham, N.C.: Duke University Press, 2015).

21. Zimitri Erasmus, "Sylvia Wynter's Theory of the Human: Counter-, Not Post-Humanist," *Theory, Culture and Society* 37, no. 6 (2020): 47–65.

22. Hantel, "Placticity and Fungibility," 99.

23. Mignolo, "Sylvia Wynter?"

24. Hantel, "Placticity and Fungibility," 100.

25. Ibid., 104.

26. Ibid., 105.

27. The Kurdish Freedom Movement would agree with Lacan that there is no woman. Woman emerges only after a collective struggle of dissociation from being

objects of male desire and is always in the making. This might be a reason she is the site of Revolution.

28. Üstündağ, "Theology of Democratic Modernity."

29. Fréderike Geerdink, *The Fire Never Dies: One Year with the PKK* (New Delhi: Leftword, 2021).

30. See Fanny Söderbäck for a theoretical conceptualization of revolutionary time. Inspired by Kristeva and Irigaray, she situates the possibility of revolutionary change in an understanding of the present as both past (forgotten histories) and future (not yet, the new, the unforeseen) oriented; Söderbäck, *Revolutionary Time: On Time and Difference in Kristeva and Irigaray* (Albany: SUNY Press, 2020). It is by revisiting the past and creating newness out of it that revolution is achieved. Her linking of this kind of temporality to maternal beginnings resonates with the Kurdish Women's Freedom Movement's struggle. In the case of the Kurdish Movement, I think we also need to remember that such a temporality is only sustained by the repetitive everyday work of care and maintenance and by the exciting spectacularity of exceptional times that secure a sense of prophetic collectivity. As time unfolds in space, the multiple spaces that the movement constitutes in varying scales (from the entire globe to the autonomous guerrilla camp) necessitate the revolutionary temporality to give meaning to both mundane acts and heroic deeds.

31. Karen Barad, "Transmaterialities: Trans*/Matter/Realities and Queer Political Imaginings," *GLQ: A Journal of Lesbian and Gay Studies* 21, no. 2–3 (2015): 388.

32. Ashon Crawley, "On Friendship," *Full Stop: Reviews, Interviews, Marginalia*, September 8, 2021, https://www.full-stop.net/2021/09/08/features/ashon-crawley/on-friendship/ (accessed April 19, 2022).

33. When I write about the simultaneous demands of collectivization and individuation, I am thinking about Kristeva's writings on the feminine genius and the demand on each guerrilla (including men) to become a feminine genius in one's life and one's death. Krsiteva writes, "You are a genius to the extent that you are able to challenge the sociohistorical conditions of your identity"; Julia Kristeva, "Is There a Feminine Genius?," *Critical Inquiry* 30, no. 3. (2004): 504. She also argues that the genius is the one who does that in her particular way. Beritan, Zilan, Roza, and many other women commemorated by the guerrillas are known by their singular styles and individual ways in which they challenged the sociohistorical conditions of their identity of being a woman and thereby transformed the trajectory of the movement. Specifically, their self-chosen or enforced deaths have led the movement to reconsider itself and its capacity to become a "solution" for women's search for freedom and to adopt new strategies and identifications to overcome the limits it puts on women's self realization; Sara Aktaş, *Parçalanmış Ülkede Kürt Kadın Devriminin Gelişim Pratikleri* (unpublished manuscript).

34. Barad, "Transmaterialities," 398.

35. Ibid.

36. Jacques Derrida, *Politics of Friendship* (London and New York: Verso, 1997).

37. Leela Gandhi, *Affective Communities: Anticolonial Thought, Fin-de-Siècle Radicalism, and the Politics of Friendship* (Durham, N.C., and London: Duke University Press, 2006).

38. Derrida, *Politics of Friendship*.

39. Christian Moraru, "'We Embraced Each Other by Our Names': Levinas, Derrida, and the Ethics of Naming," *Names* 48, no. 1 (2000): 56.

40. Hazal Halavut, "The State, Narrative and the Body as Documents of Turkey's 1980 Military Coup" (unpublished masters thesis, Boğaziçi University, 2009.

41. I am using the expression "emptied out" intentionally for purposes of initiating speculation on the differing aspects of colonial forms of emptying out of spaces and bodies for other things to flow, which I discussed in Chapter 4, and decolonial forms of emptying out as exemplified in the case of names.

42. For the reproduction of inequality in the field of law through women's practices of citizenship in Turkey, see Dicle Koğacıoğlu, "Law in Context: Citizenship and Reproduction of Inequality in an Istanbul Courthouse" (unpublished Ph.D. diss., Stony Brook University, 2003).

43. Barad, "Transmaterialities," 393.

44. Giorgio Agamben, "Friendship," trans. Joseph Falsone, *Contretemps* 5 (2004).

45. In their interview on their use of love as a political concept, Michael Hardt and Lauren Berlant collectively discuss their different interpretations of how love transforms people and can become a basis for new social imaginaries. I am inspired by their discussion, since friendship in the guerrilla movement is the primary institutional and performative framework within which love is experienced; Berlant and Hardt, "On the Risk of a New Relationality," interview by Heather Davis and Paige Sarlin, review in *Cultural Theory* 2, no. 3 (2008), http://reviewsinculture.com /2012/10/15/on-the-risk-of-a-new-relationality-an-interview-with-lauren-berlant-and -michael-hardt/).

46. Michel Foucault, "Friendship as a Way of Life," in *The Essential Works of Foucault 1954–1984*, vol. 1, *Ethics: Subjectivity and Truth*, ed. Paul Rabinow, trans. Robert Hurley (New York: New Press, 1997).

47. David Webb, "On Friendship: Derrida, Foucault, and the Practice of Becoming," *Research Phenomenology* (2003): 33.

48. Mahsum Erdal, "Radikal Demokrasinin Politik Ontolojisi Üzerine Deneme," *Demokratik Modernite* 22 (2017): 16.

49. Inspired by Agamben, I see play as a mode of life where life becomes ethical "not when it simply submits to moral laws but when it accepts putting itself into play in its gestures, irrevocably and without reserve — even at the risk that its happiness or its disgrace will be decided once and for all"; Agamben, *Profanations*, trans. J. Fort (New York: Zone, 2007), 69. Following Benjamin, Agamben associates freedom with childhood and play, where things that have been separated from public use are made available to use and to be profaned. I would argue that friendship is a genre of humanness where the person is kept at youth and where things, bodies, and words, as well as being, are continuously profaned, offered, and opened up to

public use and contemplation. That is why the Kurdish Movement calls itself a movement of the youth as much as women, irrespective of the age of its members. Friendship and the mode of play in the movement force people to put themselves in constant risk of being decided on once and for all, and the cost is often death. However, friendship and play also keep the movement always alert, creative, and in debate, asking its members to be always 100 percent in the game with full presence, since there is no given place for them in the structures of kinship or nation where each life can claim a melodramatic content and value; Nazan Üstündağ, "Oyun, Komünizm, Bodrumlar ve Sırlar," in *Suphi Nejat Ağırnaslı'nın Komünist Israrı: Menkıbe'yi Yeniden Düşünmek*, ed. Rıza Ekinciler and Fikri Erkindik (2021), 31–58, https://archive.org/details/suphi-nejat-agirnaslinin-komunist-israri-menkibeyi -yeniden-dusunmek_202101/mode/2up). Instead, life remains "unrepresented" and "unfulfilled," without author. Agamben writes, "The author [of life played out] is the illegible someone, who makes reading possible, the legendary emptiness, from which writing and discourse issue" (Agamben, *Profanations*, 69–70). I would claim that this is a similar argument to the one I am making in relation to how the guerrilla becomes the "legendary" Real that issues constant action, thought, and discourse among Kurdish people. For more on how the genre of the play regulates the youth of the Kurdish Freedom Movement, see Haydar Darıcı, "Living in the Play State: Insurrectionary Youth Politics in Kurdish Borderlands" (unpublished Ph.D. diss., University of Michigan, 2019). See Delal Aydın, "Self-Craft of the Kurdish Youth in the Shadow of the Turkish State: The Formation of Yurtsever Subjectivity" (unpublished Ph.D. diss., Binghampton University, 2019), for how friendship has become a political subjectivity in the formation of the Kurdish Freedom Movement.

50. Tom Roach, *Friendship as a Way of Life: Foucault, AIDS and the Politics of Shared Estrangement* (Albany: SUNY Press, 2012), 12.

51. Ibid., 22.

52. Gandhi, *Affective Communities*.

53. Barad, "Nature's Queer Performativity," 46.

54. Ali Haydar Kaytan, *Yöntem ve Hakikat Rejimi* (Neuss: Mezopotamya Yayınları, 2016), and Michael Panser, "Power and Truth: Analytics of Power and Nomadic Thought as Fragments of a Philosophy of Liberation," in International Initiative, *Building Free Life*.

55. Erdal, "Radikal Demokrasinin Politik Ontolojisi Üzerine Deneme."

56. My translation."Tarihi ele alırken sanki ağlama duvarıdır. Yani ağlamalarımızı bırakmıyoruz ki bir tecrübeye dönüşsün. Tarihe bakarken sadece acı temelinde ele alıyoruz. Geleceğimizi de bundan dolayı değerlendiremiyoruz. Bunun için yöntemlerimiz yanlıştır. Aşırı duygu yoğunluğu, bu aşamalarda da, sanki ağlamamız gerekiyor yaklaşımlarımız açığa çıkmaktadır. Doğrudur çok acı çektik. . . . Kim olduğumuzu bilirsek, nasıl yaşayacağımızı da tayin edebiliriz."

57. Roach, *Friendship as a Way of Life*, 25–26.

58. For a different reading of Kurdish women guerrillas' diaries, see Esin Düzel, "Fragile Goddesses: Moral Subjectivity and Militarized Agencies in Female

Guerrilla Diaries and Memoirs," *International Feminist Journal of Politics* 20, no. 2 (2018): 137–52.

59. My translation. Doğan (c.n. Zinarin), *Zinarin'in Güncesi*, 33. "Kaçak duygularım çok bencil, bir canavar gibi hislerimi, ruhumu, düşüncemi ve bereketimi ve zamanımı yiyorlar. Sömürülüyorum kaçak duygularım tarafından. Evet isyan ettim kaçak dugularıma, hayallerime. Dışı yenmem için önce kendimi yenmem gerektiğini müthiş anlıyorum. Kendime öfkem, kendimin kendimizin ters yönlerine öfkem, beni kendimin tersi olmaya, yani kendimiz olmaya götürüyor."

60. My translation. Doğan (c.n. Zinarin), *Zinarin'in Güncesi*, 49. "Savaşta ve savaşa göre yaşadıkça daha olgun, daha derin ve daha duygulu bir insan olacağımı, daha çok özüme yaklaşacağımı ve ülkemde kökleşeceğimi düşünüyor, dahası buna inanıyorum. Kişiliğimde bana ait olmayan, gereksiz, fazlalık yanların savaştıkça aşılacağını, kadın yiğitliğinin benim şahsımda da kendini varlıklaştıracağını umuyorum."

61. My translation. Doğan (c.n. Zinarin), *Zinarin'in Güncesi*, 55. "Bazen duygularımın zayıfladığını, maddi yönümün ağır bastığını yani inceliğimi, duygusallığımı yitirdiğimi hissediyorum. . . . Yaptığım bir şeyin ardından düşünüyorum ve o yaptığım işte aslında çok kaba maddeci yaklaştığımı, duygularımla yoğrulmuş bir düşüncenin o işe aktarılmadığını, yani o işe bütün benliğimi katmadığımı, oldukça yüzeysel, sıradan yaklaşım sergilediğimi görüyorum. O an kendime olan öfkem her şeyimin üstüne çıkıyor."

62. My translation. Doğan (c.n. Zinarin), *Zinarin'in Güncesi*, 77. "Beni soracak olursan bu sıkıntı-mıkıntı dediklerimin hepsi ciddi bir yoğunlaşma. Yeni bir sürece yürürken ve yeni bir ortamın içinde, kaldıramadıklarımın, ağır bulduklarımın, yeni yaşadıklarımın duygusal yükü. Düşmanı, savaşı, şehidi, ölümle burun buruna olmayı, gericiliğin, feodallığın en yoğun yaşandığı yerde cins ve özgürlük savaşımını yürütmeyi ilk kez yaşıyorum. Kişiliğimi bütün bunlar karşısında çok zavallı, hazırlıksız, çaresiz buldum buluverdim birden. Ve bu beni sıktı. bunalttı. Bu halimle bu kadar sımsıcak savaş ortamında bu kadar gözü dönmüş geri feudal bir ortamda ilkeleri, özgürlük gereklerini uygulama zorunluluğunu karşımda vazgeçilmez bir ödev olarak görüyorum. Ama bunun ne örgütüne, ne planına, ne taktiğine sahibim."

63. Roach, *Friendship as a Way of Life*, 27.

64. See, for example, Abdullah Öcalan, *Kürt Aşkı: Nasıl Yaşamalı? Cilt III* (Weşanên Serxwebûn. 1999).

65. For a discussion of freedom from the perspective of the Kurdish Freedom Movement, see Erdal, *Demokratik Modernite*.

66. The state, on the other hand, attempts to stop this movement by "capturing" and "arresting" its participants. Ironically, arrest only causes others to mobilize in order to take up the slots that are left behind and bring about the permanent circulation of bodies, labor, and speech in society.

67. One of my favorite examples is the following: Öcalan asks a *heval*, another leader of the PKK, what he thinks about the universe, which in Turkish is called *evren*. *Evren*, however, is also the surname of the general who was the leader of the

1980 military coup in Turkey. Thinking that Öcalan initiates a conversation about politics, which is a readily available framework for the organization, the friend explains how he thinks Evren is just a tool of the United States. He becomes baffled when he understands that the conversation concerns the universe, and Öcalan insists that they also need to increase their capacity to talk about such things to become revolutionaries and defendants of freedom and truth.

68. One such example is *jineolojî* (women's science) and the vocabulary it has invented in thinking about women's history. *Jineolojî* makes it possible for women to write theoretically, conceptually, and politically outside of the academic language of women's studies and established feminist canons. On the other hand, it runs the risk of becoming an esoteric (to ordinary people) and sacred language, at times reducing people's use of this language to mere repetition — which I would argue is still a form of learning and self-expression outside of established canons.

69. Halil Dağ, "Liberalizm ve Radikal Demokrasi," in Erdal, *Demokratik Modernite* 22 (2017): 69–75.

70. Frantz Fanon, *Black Skin, White Masks*, rev. ed. (New York: Grove Press, 2008).

71. Derek Hook, "Death-Bound Subjectivity: Fanon's Zone of Nonbeing and the Lacanian Death Drive," *Subjectivity* 13, no. 4 (2020): 355–75.

72. Ibid., 360.

73. Jacques Lacan, *The Ethics of Psychoanalysis* 1959–1960 (New York: Norton, 1992), 283.

74. Ibid., 369.

75. Ibid., 370.

76. Roach, *Friendship as a Way of Life*, 41.

77. Julia Kristeva, "Antigone: Limit and Horizon," in *Feminist Readings of Antigone*, ed. Fanny Söderbäck (New York: Oxford University Press, 2010), 215.

78. Édouard Glissant, "One World in Relation: Édouard Glissant in Conversation with Manthia Diawara," trans. C. Winks, *Nka Journal of Contemporary African Art* 28 (Spring 2011): 4–19.

79. Barad, "Transmaterialities," 398.

80. Walter Benjamin, *Origin of the German Trauerspiel*, trans. Howard Elland, annotated ed. (Cambridge, Mass.: Harvard University Press, 2019).

## 6. A Promise, a Letter, a Funeral, and a Wedding

EPIGRAPH SOURCES: Jacques Derrida, *Politics of Friendship* (New York: Verso, 1994), 391; Carole Dely, "Jacques Derrida: The Perchance of a Coming of the Other Woman" September 24, 2008, https://www.eurozine.com/jacques-derrida-the -perchance-of-a-coming-of-the-otherwoman/ (accessed April 20, 2022); Canda Su, "Saralardan Arinlere Sadeliğin Asil Temsili," in *Hep Kavgaydı Yaşamım 3. Cilt*, by Sakine Cansız (Neuss: Mezopotamya Yayınları, 2015), 220–23, my translation. In Kurdish: "Kırk yıllık bir özgürlük mücadelesinin her anında soluk soluğa savaşan,

bütün geriliklerin karşısında hesapsız duran Sara arkadaşın kendisi olma arayışı
tarih olmasının, evrensel olmasının gizini taşıyordu. . . . Bu Xwebun arayışının hem
cinsiyle beraber yaratılacağının bilincindeydi. O yüzden en çok kadınları sevdi. En
çok kadınlara inandı. Kadınların tek tek deil, birlikte özgür yaşamı yaratacağına
inandı/.'"

1. All are my translations. All the quotes of Recep Tayyip Erdoğan in this chapter
are taken from the following site: Anadolu Ajansı, "Erdoğan: Faili Meçhullerin
Acısını Biliriz Diyarbakır," T24, September 3, 2010, https://t24.com.tr/haber/erdogan
-faili-mechullerin-acisini-biliriz-diyarbakir-aa,95982 (last accessed March 21, 2022):
"Ozan Ahmet Arif, 'Seni, baharmışın gibi düşünüyorum, Seni, Diyarbekir gibi'
diyordu. Biz de sizi Diyarbakır kadar büyük, Türkiye kadar engin bir muhabbetle
seviyoruz. . . . Diyarbakır sahabelerin şehri, Diyarbakır ilim şehri, medeniyet şehri.
Diyarbakır kardeşliğin şehri. Bu ulu şehre gelip de, yalan söyleyenler, o yalanın
altında ezilirler, biterler. Bu aziz milletin huzuruna çıkıp da, yapamayacaklarını
söyleyenler, vaatlerinin altında ezilirler. Burada samimiyet diliyle konuşmayanlar,
muhabbet diliyle konuşmayanlar; burada Yunus Emre'nin, Mevlana'nın, Ahmede
Hani'nin, İbrahim Gülşeni'nin gönül diliyle konuşmayanlar, milletin huzuruna
çıkamaz, milletin yüzüne bakamazlar."

2. "Ape Musa'nın, yani Musa Anter'in acısını bizler unutamayız. Orhan
Miroğlu'nun yarasını bizler unutamayız. Diyarbakır Cezaevinde 7 yıl işkence
gören Abdürrahim Semavi'nin çilesini bizler unutamayız. Şivan Perver'in hasretini
görmezden gelemeyiz. Ahmet Kaya'nın gurbette vefatını hatırımızdan çıkaramayız.
Ahmede Hani'nin aşkını, Faki Teyran'ın sevdasını bizler aklımızdan çıkaramayız.
81 vilayet bizim vilayetimizdir, 73 milyon benim öz be öz kardeşimdir. Türküyle,
Kürdüyle, Lazıyla, Çerkeziyle, Boşnağıyla, Gürcüsüyle, Romanıyla, Arabıyla
kim olursa olsun 73 milyon benim öz be öz kardeşimdir. Çünkü biz yaradılanı
Yaradan'dan ötürü seviyoruz. Biz, Nurettin Zengi'nin, Kılıçarslan'ın, elbette
ki Selahattin Eyyubi'nin şanlı ordusundaki neferlerin torunuyuz. Alparslan'ın
ordusunda Malazgirt'e biz hep birlikte girdik. Selahattin Eyyubi'nin sancağı altında
Kudüs'ü biz hep birlikte fethettik. Kanuni'nin, Yavuz Sultan Selim'in, Fatih'in eliyle
üç kıtaya biz birlikte adalet dağıttık. Kut'ul Amare'yi birlikte savunduk. Çanakkale'de
yan yana şehit düştük. İstiklal Savaşı'nı hep birlikte verdik. Şu Diyarbakır surlarında
her birimizin alınteri var. Şu Süleyman Camii'nin tuğlalarında her birimizin
sağlam inancı var.Ulu Camii'nin, Behram Paşa Camii'nin, Şeyh Mutahhar'ın,
Sipahiler Çarşısı'nın, Malabadi Köprüsü'nün, Dicle Köprüsü'nün harcında bizim
kardeşliğimiz var. Zılgıt da bizim, horon da bizim, halay da bizim, zeybek de bizim.
Bizim dualarımız ortak, bizim kıblemiz bir, hepimiz aynı geleceğe yürüyoruz."

3. For the neoliberal model that Turkey presented and its demise, see Cihan
Tuğal, *The Fall of the Turkish Model: How the Arab Uprising Brought Down Islamic
Liberalism* (New York: Verso, 2016).

4. *Fetih* means conquest for Islam.

5. "Bu kardeşiniz, 12 Aralık 1997'de Siirt'te, Siirtli kardeşlerinin arasında bir şiir
okudu. Siirt'e, Siirtli kardeşlerime bir şiirle seslendiğim için yargılandım, hüküm

giydim ve Pınarhisar Cezaevinde yattım. . . . Biz bu ülkede fikirlerinden dolayı mahkum edilen insanların derdini çok iyi biliriz. Biz bu ülkede yazı yazdığı için, konuştuğu için, fikirlerini söylediği için, şiir okuduğu için, aş-iş dediği için, hak dediği, demokrasi dediği için mahpus damlarında çürümenin nasıl bir duygu olduğunu çok iyi biliriz. İnancından dolayı, ibadetinden dolayı, başındaki örtüden dolayı dışlanmanın ne olduğunu biz çok iyi biliriz. Üniversite kapılarında boynu bükük kalmanın ne demek olduğunu çok iyi biliriz. Biz yoksulluğu biliriz, yasakların, baskıların, mahrumiyetin ne olduğunu çok iyi biliriz. Bir gece yarısı, sokak ortasında ensesine kurşun sıkılarak katledilen; katilleri gecenin karanlığında kaybolup bir daha hiç ortaya çıkmayan, çıkarılmayan faili meçhullerin acısını çok iyi biliriz. Evi basılıp tarumar edilmek nedir biliriz. Kitapların derdest edilmesini biliriz. Köy meydanına toplanan köylülere uygulanan eziyeti biliriz; köylerin boşaltılması ne demektir, meraların yasaklanması nedir biliriz. Hapisteki oğlunu ziyarete giden ama oğluyla tek kelime Kürtçe konuşamayan annenin acısını, gözyaşını, feryadını, yüreğinde kopan fırtınayı biz biliriz."

6. "Hepimiz, her bir vatandaşın haysiyetiyle, onuruyla yaşadığı, her bir vatandaşın, devlet karşısında birinci sınıf vatandaş olduğu bir gelecek istiyoruz. Nasıl tarihimiz birse istikbalimiz de bir."

7. The Kurdish political party BDP boycotted the referendum.

8. "Oğlunu şehit vermiş Çorumlu annenin gözyaşı benim yüreğime akar. Oğlunu dağda çetelere kaptırmış, terör örgütüne kaptırmış, göz göre göre ölüme yollanan oğlunu kaybetmiş ananın gözyaşı benim ciğerime akar."

9. Elizabeth Povinelli, "Radical Worlds: The Anthropology of Incommensurability and Inconceivability," *Annual Review of Anthropology* 30 (2001): 319–34.

10. Shoshana Felman, *The Scandal of the Speaking Body: Don Juan with J. L. Austin, or Seduction in Two Languages* (Stanford, Calif.: Stanford University Press, 2002), 11.

11. Ibid., 16.

12. Giorgio Agamben, *Stasis: Civil War as a Political Paradigm*, trans. Nicholas Heron, repr. ed. (Stanford, Calif.: Stanford University Press), 15.

13. Ibid.

14. Agamben, *Stasis*, 16.

15. Michel Foucault, *The Archeology of Knowledge: And the Discourse on Language* (New York: Pantheon, 1982).

16. A "monument," according to Mark Nichanian, exists only for itself: "To put it differently, with Lyotard's Kantian vocabulary: testimony as document belongs to the witness according to the fact; testimony as monument belongs to the witness according to the sign"; Nichanian, *The Historiographic Perversion* (New York: Columbia University Press 2009), 94.

17. "Bugün Diyarbakır'da bir kez daha söylüyorum; Ah şu Diyarbakır Cezaevinin bir dili olsa da konuşsa, 12 Eylül sonrasında yaşananları bir anlatsa . . . Ah şu 5. koğuş dile gelip, o insanlık dışı işkenceleri, o insanlıktan uzak muameleleri bir

söylese . . . Sözüm var mıydı? Diyarbakır Cezaevini kapatıyoruz. Yeni cezaevini süratle yapıyoruz. Biter bitmez hemen mevcut bu malum Diyarbakır Cezaevini de yıkacağız. İstiyoruz ki orası artık varlığıyla şehrimize 12 Eylül'ü hatırlatmasın. İnşallah bu da bize nasip olur."

18. Nazan Üstündağ, "Pornographic State and Erotic Resistance," *South Atlantic Quarterly* 118, no. 1 (2019): 95–110.

19. The whole statement can be found here: *Kurdistan Tribune* Editor, "Öcalan's Historical Newroz 2013 Statement," trans. International Initiative, March 21, 2013, https://kurdistantribune.com/ocalans-historical-newroz-2013-statement/ (accessed April 24, 2022).

20. Rosalind C. Morris, "Legacies of Derrida: Anthropology," *Annual Review of Anthropology* 36 (2007): 363.

21. The assassinations of women by the Turkish state continue. As I am writing this chapter my dear friend Nagehan Akarsel, who was one of the members of the Jineology Committee of the Kurdish Women's Movement and one of the most laborious people I know, has been shot and killed with twelve bullets in front of her house in Suleymaniyeh.

22. Rosalind C. Morris, "The War Drive: Image Files Corrupted," *Social Text* 25, no. 2 (2007): 117, https://doi.org/10.1215/01642472-2006-029.

23. Adriana Cavarero, "On the Body of Antigone," in *Feminist Readings of Antigone*, ed. Fanny Söderbäck (New York: SUNY Press, 2010), 52.

24. Julia Reinhard Lupton, *Citizen-Saints: Shakespeare and Political Theology* (Chicago and London: University of Chicago Press, 2005), 11.

25. Interestingly enough, the idea of marrying women or bringing them together with their families as a resolution operates also as a dominant trope in movies directed by Western directors on the resistance of Kurdish women against ISIS; Nilgün Yelpaze, "Representation of Kurdish Female Fighters in Cinema: A Frame Analysis of Fiction Films," in *Radicalization and Variations of Violence*, ed. Daniel Beck and Julia Renner-Mugano, (Berlin: Springer, forthcoming).

26. Jasbir K. Puar, *Terrorist Assemblages: Homonationalism in Queer Times* (Durham, N.C.: Duke University Press, 2007).

27. Savannah Shange, *Progressive Dystopia: Abolition, Antiblackness, and Schooling in San Francisco* (Durham, N.C.: Duke University Press, 2019), 4.

28. Fred Moten brilliantly links the materiality and maternity of phonic substances in his book *In the Break* by recourse to Marx's writings on "things"; Fred Moten, *In the Break: The Aesthetics of the Black Radical Tradition* (Minneapolis: University of Minnesota Press, 2003). See Chapter 1 for how I link these in the Kurdish case by explaining how linguicide and matricide have been historically linked.

29. I find this idea developed by Savannah Shange to be a brilliant description of the difference between liberal projects and radical projects that also summarizes the different tenses of Erdoğan's and Öcalan's speeches I quoted in this chapter: Shange, *Progressive Dystopia*, 18.

30. Moten, *In the Break*, and David Lloyd, "The Social Life of Black Things: Fred Moten's Consent Not to Be a Single Being," *Radical Philosophy* 2, no. 7 (Spring 2020).

31. Moten, *In the Break*, 186. I am here in an implicit dialogue with Fred Moten. Discussing what he calls Black Mo'nin,' which resides between melancholia and mourning and improvises their difference, Moten writes, "We've got to try to understand the connection between the resistance and political movement, locating that movement's direction toward new universalities held within the difference/s of phonic substance, in the difference of the accent that cuts and augments mourning and morning; Moten, *In the Break*, 198.

## Conclusion

EPIGRAPH SOURCE: Excerpt from an interview I conducted on the Qandil Mountains. I thank M. and W. for accompanying me.

1. "100 Reasons to Prosecute Erdoğan for His Feminicidal Policies," https://100 -reasons.org (last accessed on May 6, 2022).

2. Suely Rolnick, "Suely Rolnick Deconstructs the Colonial Unconscious," Symposium in Gugenheim, May 8, 2015, https://www.guggenheim.org/video/suely -rolnik-deconstructs-the-colonial-unconscious (accessed on May 6, 2022).

3. Fred Moten, *Stolen Life* (Durham, N.C., and London: Duke University Press, 2018), 20.

4. See Silvia Federici, "Undeclared War: Violence against Women," Artforum Summer 2017, https://www.artforum.com/print/201706/undeclared-war-violence -against-women-68680 (accessed May 6, 2022); Veronica Gago, "Is There a War 'on' the Body of Women?: Finance, Territory, and Violence," *Viewpoint Magazine*, March 7, 2018, https://viewpointmag.com/2018/03/07/war-body-women -finance-territory-violence/ (accessed May 6, 2022); and Rita Laura Segato, "A Manifesto in Four Themes," trans. Ramsey McGlazer, *Critical Times* 1, no. 1 (2018): 198–211.

5. Gago, "Is There a War?"

6. For the relationship between generality, singularity, and universality, see Moten, *Stolen Life*.

7. Denise Ferreira da Silva, "On Difference without Separability," *32nd Bienal De Sao Paulo Art Biennial*," *Incerteza Viva*, 2016.

8. While I am writing these words, both southern Kurdistan (Iraq) and western Kurdistan (Syria) are under attack from the Turkish state.

9. For this point, see Alenka Zupančič's discussion of Antigone's desire in *Let Them Rot: Antigone's Parallax* (New York: Fordham University Press, 2023).

10. Gültan Kışanak, *Kürt Siyasetinin Mor Rengi* (Istanbul: Dipnot Yayınları, 2019).

11. Joan Wallach Scott, *The Fantasy of Feminist History* (Durham, N.C., and London: Duke University Press, 2011), 12, https://doi.org/10.1515/9780822394730.

12. Ayşegül Devecioğlu, "Serçelerin Bile Başı Dönüyor," *Bianet*, August 4, 2012, https://bianet.org/cocuk/biamag/140095-sercelerin-bile-basi-donuyor (acessed May 6, 2022). My translation. In Turkish: O gece amacına doğru, insanı aşan bir sükûnet ve kararlılıkla ilerleyen şeyi, halay çekenlerin ağır adımlarında bir kez daha yakaladım. Davulun tekdüze ritmine uyarak, sonu hiç gelmeyecekmiş gibi, aynı omuz ve el hareketleriyle aynı adımları atan kalabalık, mor benekli ışıkların oynaştığı mermer zemine gözle görünmeyen harflerle kayıt düşüyordu: Gelmekte olan çok uzun bir zamandır bekleniyordu, onu durdurmak, önüne çıkmak, mevsim dönümünü engellemek kadar olanaksızdı.

# Bibliography

"100 Reasons to Prosecute Erdoğan for His Feminicidal Policies." https://100-reasons
.org. Accessed on May 6, 2022.

Açık, Necla. "Redefining the Role of Women within the Kurdish National
Movement in Turkey in the 1990s." In *The Kurdish Question in Turkey: New
Perspectives on Violence, Representation and Reconciliation*, edited by Cengiz
Güneş and Welat Zeydanlıoğlu, 114–36. London and New York: Routledge, 2013.

Adak, Hülya. *Halide Edib Adıvar ve Siyasal Şiddet: Ermeni Kırımı, Diktatörlük ve
Şiddetsizlik*. Istanbul: Istanbul Bilgi Üniversitesi Yayınları, 2016.

Adıvar, Halide Edib. *Kalp Ağrısı* [1924]. Istanbul: Can Yayınları, 2010.

———. *Zeyno'nun Oğlu* [1928]. Istanbul: Can Yayınları, 2010.

Agamben, Giorgio. "Friendship." Translated by Joseph Falsone. *Contretemps* 5
(2004).

———. *Means without End: Notes on Politics*. Translated by Vincenzo Binetti and
Cesare Casarino. Minneapolis: University of Minnesota Press, 2000.

———. *Profanations*. Translated by J. Fort. New York: Zone, 2007.

———. *Stasis: Civil War as a Political Paradigm*. Translated by Nicholas Heron.
Repr. ed. Stanford, Calif.: Stanford University Press, 2015.

Agamben, Giorgio, and Monica Ferrando. *The Unspeakable Girl: The Myth and
Mystery of Kore*. Translated by Leland de la Durantaye. Dhaka, Bangladesh:
Seagull, 2014.

Anadolu Ajansı. "Erdoğan: Faili Meçhullerin Acısını Biliriz Diyarbakır," T24.
September 3, 2010. https://t24.com.tr/haber/erdogan-faili-mechullerin-acisini
-biliriz-diyarbakir-aa,95982. Last accessed March 21, 2022.

Akın, Rojin Canan, and Funda Danışman. *Bildiğin Gibi Değil: 90'larda
Güneydoğu'da Çocuk Olmak*. Istanbul: Metis Yayınları, 2011.

Akkaya, Ahmet Hamdi, and Joost Jongerden. "Confederalism and Autonomy in
Turkey: The Kurdistan Workers Party and the Reinvention of Democracy." In

*The Kurdish Question in Turkey: New Perspectives on Violence, Representation and Reconciliation*, edited by Cengiz Güneş and Welat Zeydanlıoğlu, 186–204. London and New York: Routledge, 2013.

Aktaş, Sara. *Parçalanmış Ülkede Kürt Kadın Devriminin Gelişim Pratikleri*. Manuscript in preparation.

Al-Ali, Nadja, and Isabel Kaeser. "Beyond Feminism? Jineolojî and the Kurdish Women's Freedom Movement." *Politics and Gender* (2020): 1–32.

Amado-Miller, Moira. "Refiguring Jocasta's Desire." *New Antigone* 1 (2005): 78–89.

Appel, Liz. "Itinerant Antigone." In *The Returns of Antigone*, edited by Tina Chanter and Sean D. Kirkland, 187–204. Albany: SUNY Press, 2014.

Arat, Yeşim, and Şevket Pamuk. *Turkey between Democracy and Authoritarianism*. Cambridge: Cambridge University Press, 2019.

Aretxaga, Begona. *States of Terror: Begona Aretxaga's Essays*. Reno, Nev.: Center for Basque Studies, University of Nevada, 2005.

Ayata, Bilgin, and Deniz Yükseker. "A Belated Awakening: National and International Responses to the Internal Displacement of Kurds in Turkey." *New Perspectives in Turkey* 32 (2005): 5–42.

Aydın, Delal. "Mobilising the Kurds in Turkey: Newroz As A Myth." In *The Kurdish Question in Turkey*, edited by Cengiz Güneş and Welat Zeydanlıoğlu, 68–88. London and New York: Routledge, 2013.

——. "Self-Craft of the Kurdish Youth in the Shadow of the Turkish State: The Formation of Yurtsever Subjectivity." Unpublished Ph.D. diss., Binghampton University, 2019.

Azoulay, Arielle. *Civil Imagination: A Political Ontology of Photography*. Repr. ed. New York: Verso, 2015.

——. "Regime-Made Disaster: On the Possibility of Nongovernmental Viewing." In *Sensible Politics: The Visual Culture of Nongovernmental Activism*, edited by Meg McLagan, and Yates McKess, 29–42. New York: Zone, 2012.

Babacan, Erol, Melehat Kutun, Ezgi Pınar, and Zafer Yılmaz, eds. *Regime Change in Turkey: Neoliberal Authoritarianism, Islamism and Hegemony*. London and New York: Routledge, 2021.

Baderoon, Gabeba. "The Law of the Mother." *Meridians* 18, no. 1 (2019): 14–16. https://doi.org/10.1215/15366936-7297136.

Badiou, Alain. *The True Life*. Translated by Susan Spitzer. Malden, Mass.: Polity Press, 2017.

Barad, Karen. "Nature's Queer Performativity." *Kvinder, Køn & Forskning* 1–2 (2012): 25–53.

——. "Transmaterialities: Trans*/Matter/Realities and Queer Political Imaginings." *GLQ: A Journal of Lesbian and Gay Studies* 21, no. 2–3 (2015): 387–422.

Baraitser, Lisa. *Enduring Time*. London and New York: Bloomsbery Academic, 2017.

——. *Maternal Encounters: The Ethics of Interruption*. New York: Routledge, 2009.

——. "Maternal Publics: Time, Relationality and the Public Sphere." In *Re(Con) Figuring Psychoanalysis: Critical Juxtapositions of the Philosophical, the*

*Sociohistorical and the Political*, edited by Aydan Gülerce, 221–40. London: Palgrave Macmillan, 2012. https://doi.org/10.1057/9780230373303_13.

Bargu, Banu. "Bodies against War: Voluntary Human Shielding as a Practice of Resistance." *AJIL Unbound* 110 (2016): 299–304. https://www.jstor.org/stable /27003225.

———. "Human Shields." *Contemporary Political Theory* 12, no. 4 (2013): 277–95. https://doi.org/10.1057/cpt.2013.1.

———. "Sovereignty as Erasure: Rethinking Enforced Disappearances." *Qui Parle* 23, no. 1 (2014): 35–75.

———. *Starve and Immolate: The Politics of Human Weapons*. New York: Columbia University Press, 2014.

Bayır, Derya. "The Role of the Judicial System in the Politicide of the Kurdish Opposition." In *The Kurdish Question in Turkey: New Perspectives on Violence, Representation and Reconciliation*, edited by Cengiz Güneş and Welat Zeydanlıoğlu, 21–46. London and New York: Routledge, 2013.

Benjamin, Walter. *Origin of the German Trauerspiel*. Translated by Howard Elland. Annotated ed. Cambridge, Mass.: Harvard University Press, 2019.

———. *Reflections: Essays, Aphorisms, Autobiographical Writing*. New York: Schocken, 1986.

Berlant, Lauren. *Cruel Optimism*. Durham, N.C.: Duke University Press, 2011.

———. *The Female Complaint: The Unfinished Business of Sentimentality in American Culture*. Durham, N.C.: Duke University Press, 2008.

———. "Slow Death (Sovereignty, Obesity, Lateral Agency)." *Critical Inquiry* 33, no. 4 (Summer 2007): 754–80.

Berlant, Lauren, and Michael Hardt. "On the Risk of a New Relationality." Interview by Heather Davis and Paige Sarlin. Review in *Cultural Theory* 2, no. 3 (2008). http://reviewsinculture.com/2012/10/15/on-the-risk-of-a-new-relationality -an-interview-with-lauren-berlant-and-michael-hardt/.

Best, Stephen, and Saidiya Hartman. "Fugitive Justice." *Representations* 92 (2005): 1–15.

Bhambra, Gurminder K. "Postcolonial and Decolonial Dialogues." *Postcolonial Studies* 17, no. 2 (2014): 115–21. https://doi.org/10.1080/13688790.2014.966414.

Bhan, Mona, and Haley Duschinski. "Occupations in Context—The Cultural Logics of Occupation, Settler Violence, and Resistance." *Critique of Anthropology* 40, no. 3 (2020): 285–97. https://doi.org/10.1177/0308275X20929403.

BİA Haber Ajansı. "Tuncel İlk Değil Medyanın Gözü BDP'li Kadın Vekillerin Üstünde." *Bianet*, March 23, 2011. https://m.bianet.org/bianet/siyaset/128799 -tuncel-ilk-degil-medyanin-gozu-bdp-li-kadin-vekillerin-ustunde. Accessed May 4, 2021.

Biner, Zerrin Özlem. *States of Dispossession: Violence ad Precarious Coexistence in Southeast Turkey*. Philadelphia: University of Pennsylvania Press, 2020.

Bishara, Amahl. "Sovereignty and Popular Sovereignty For Palestinians and Beyond." *Cultural Anthropology* 32, no. 3 (2017): 349–58. https://doi.org/10.14506 /ca32.3.04.

Bogues, Anthony. "And What about the Human? Freedom, Human Emancipation and the Radical Imagination." *Boundary 2* 39, no. 3 (2012): 867–74.

Bora, Tanıl. *Türkiye'nin Linç Rejimi.* 3rd ed. Istanbul: İletişim Yayınları, 2021.

Bottici, Chiara. *Imaginal Politics: Images beyond Imagination and the Imaginary.* New York: Columbia University Press, 2019.

Bottici, Chiara, and Benoit Challand, eds. *The Politics of Imagination.* Oxon and New York: Birkbeck Law Press, 2011.

Bozarslan, Hamit, Cengiz Güneş, and Veli Yadırgı. *The Cambridge History of Kurds.* Cambridge: Cambridge University Press, 2021.

Bradley, Rizavana. "Corporeal Resurfacings: Faustin Linyekula, Nick Cave and Thornton Dial." Unpublished Ph.D. diss., Duke University, 2013.

Burç, Roza. *In Remaining a Society: Survival, Organization and Self-Defense.* Unpublished manuscript. 2021.

Butler, Judith. *Antigone's Claim: Kinship between Life and Death.* New York: Columbia University Press, 2000.

———. *Bodies That Matter: On the Discursive Limits of "Sex."* London and New York: Routledge, 1993.

———. *Frames of War: When Is Life Grievable?* New York: Verso, 2009.

———. *Giving an Account of Oneself.* New York: Fordham University Press, 2005.

———. *Precarious Life: Power of Mourning and Violence.* Repr. ed. New York: Verso, 2006.

Butler, Judith, Zeynep Gambetti, and Leticia Sabsay, eds. *Resistance in Vulnerability.* Durham, N.C.: Duke University Press, 2016.

Çağlayan, Handan. *Analar, Yoldaşlar, Tanrıçalar: Kürt Hareketinde Kadınlar ve Kadın Kimliğinin Oluşumu.* 6th ed. Istanbul: İletişim Yayınları, 2017.

Can, Başak. "How Does a Protest Law?: Rituals of Visibility, Disappearances under Custody and the Saturday Mothers in Turkey." *American Anthropologist.* Forthcoming.

Cavarero, Adriana. *For More Than One Voice: Toward a Philosophy of Vocal Expression.* Stanford, Calif.: Stanford University Press, 2005.

———. *Horrorism: Naming Contemporary Violence.* New York: Columbia University Press, 2008.

———. "On the Body of Antigone." In *Feminist Readings of Antigone,* edited by Fanny Söderbäck. New York: Oxford University Press, 2010.

Carter, Lashonda, and Tiffany Willoughby-Herard. "What Kind of Mother Is She? From Margaret Garner to Rosa Lee Ingram to Mamie Till to the Murder of Korryn Gaines." *Theory & Event* 21, no. 1 (2018): 88–105.

Castoriadis, Cornelius. *Imaginary Institution of Society: Creativity and Autonomy in the Social-Historical World.* Translated by Kathleen Blamey. Cambridge and Malden, Mass.: Polity Press, 1997.

Castro, Andrés Fabián Henao. *Antigone in the Americas: Democracy, Sexuality, and Death in the Settler Colonial Present.* Albany: SUNY Press, 2022.

———. "The Crack in the Mask, the Wound in the Flesh: Political Representation

as Symptom." *Representation* 53, no. 1 (2017): 55–65. https://doi.org/10.1080
/00344893.2017.1346875.

Cavanagh, Sheila L. "Antigone's Legacy: A Feminist Psychoanalytic of an Other Sexual Difference." *Studies in the Maternal* 9, no. 1 (2017): 1–33.

Çelik, Adnan. "The Armenian Genocide in Kurdish Collective Memory." *Middle East Report* 295 (2020).

Cervenak, Sarah. "Christina Sharpe: Monstrous Intimacies; Making Post-Slavery Subjects." *Women's Studies* 40 (2011): 1,120–24.

Çetinkaya, Hasret. "Mothers as the Middle-Ground between the Mountain and the State." *Journal of International Women's Studies* 21, no. 7 (2020): 207–24.

Chanter, Tina. *Whose Antigone? The Tragic Marginalization of Slavery.* New York: SUNY Press, 2011.

Çiçek, Cuma. "The Pro-Islamic Challenge for the Kurdish Movement." *Dialectical Anthropology* 37, no. 1 (2013): 159–63.

Chanter, Tina, and Sean Kirkland, eds. *The Returns of Antigone: Interdisciplinary Essays.* New York: SUNY Press, 2014.

Chasin, C. J. DeLuzio. "Reconsidering Asexuality and Its Radical Potential." *Feminist Studies* 39, no. 2 (2013): 405–26.

Chow, Rey. *Not Like a Native Speaker: On Languaging as a Postcolonial Experience.* New York and Chichester, West Sussex: Columbia University Press, 2014.

Cixous, Hélène. "The Laugh of the Medusa." In *Feminisms: An Anthology of Literary Theory and Criticism*, edited by Robyn R. Warhol and Diane Pierce Hendl. New Brunswick, N.J.: Rutgers University Press, 1997.

Clément, Catherine, and Julia Kristeva. *The Feminine and the Sacred.* New York: Columbia University Press, 2003.

Cooke, Miriam. *Dancing in Damascus: Creativity, Resilience, and the Syrian Revolution.* London and New York: Routledge, 2016.

Copjec, Joan. *Imagine There's No Woman: Ethics and Sublimation.* Cambridge, Mass.: MIT Press, 2004.

Çoşkun, Vahap, M. Şerif Derince, and Nesrin Uçarlar. *Scar of Tongue: Consequences of the Ban on the Use of Mother Tongue in Education and Experiences of Kurdish Students in Turkey.* Diyarbakır: DİSA, 2012.

Cörüt, İlker. *Failure of the Kurdish Policy of the AKP: Healthcare Provision in Hakkâri in 2003–2014.* Bern, Switzerland: Peter Lang, forthcoming.

Crawley, Ashon T. *Blackpentecostal Breath: The Aesthetics of Possibility.* New York: Fordham University Press, 2017.

———. "On Friendship." *Full Stop: Reviews, Interviews, Marginalia.* September 8, 2021. https://www.full-stop.net/2021/09/08/features/ashon-crawley/on-friendship/. Accessed April 19, 2022.

*Cumhuriyet.* "BDP'li Kışanak'ın sarıldığı PKK'li Yeşiltaş'ı basmış." August 22, 2012. https://www.cumhuriyet.com.tr/haber/bdpli-kisanakin-sarildigi-pkkli-yesiltasi -basmis-365786. Accessed April 28, 2021.

Dağ, Halil. "Liberalizm ve Radikal Demokrasi." *Demokratik Modernite* 22 (2017): 69–75.

Daher-Nashif, Suhad. "Colonial Management of Death: To Be or Not to Be Dead in Palestine." *Current Sociology* 69, no. 7 (2021): 945–62.

Darıcı, Haydar. "Living in the Play State: Insurrectionary Youth Politics in Kurdish Borderlands." Unpublished Ph.D. diss., University of Michigan, 2019.

———. "Of Kurdish Youth and Ditches." *Theory & Event* 19, no. 1 Supplement (2016).

———. "Politics of Kurdish Children in Urban Turkey." *International Journal of Middle East Studies* 45 (2013): 775–90.

Darıcı, Haydar, and Serra Hakyemez. "Neither Civilian nor Combatant: Weaponised Spaces and Spatialised Bodies in Cizre." In *Turkey's Necropolitical Laboratory*, edited by Banu Bargu. Edinburgh: Edinburgh University Press, 2019: 71–94.

Dely, Carole. "Jacques Derrida: The Perchance of a Coming of the Other Woman." *Eurozine.* September 24, 2008. https://www.eurozine.com/jacques-derrida-the -perchance-of-a-coming-of-the-otherwoman. Accessed April 20, 2022.

Demirören Haber Ajansı. "BDP'li Kışanak Gerilla Kontrol Noktalarının Olduğu Bir Bölgeye Gittiğimizi Biliyorduk." August 20, 2012. Haberler. Com, https://www .haberler.com/bdp-li-kisanak-gerilla-kontrol-noktalarinin-oldugu-3879869-haberi/. Accessed April 29, 2021.

*Demokratik Modernite* 23 (2018).

Derince, Şerif. "A Break or Continuity? Turkey's Politics of Kurdish Language in the New Millennium." *Dialectical Anthropology* 37, no. 1 (2013): 145–52.

Derneği, İnsan Hakları. "2012 Newrozunda Yaşanan Hak İhlalleri Raporu." *İHD*, April 2, 2012. https://www.ihd.org.tr/2012-newrozunda-yasanan-hak-ihlalleri -raporu/. Accessed May 4, 2021.

Derrida, Jacques. *Politics of Friendship.* London and New York: Verso, 1997.

De Sanctis, Sarah. "From Psychoanalysis to Politics: Antigone as a Revolutionary in Judith Butler and Slavoj Žižek." *Opticon 1826* 14 (2012): 27–36.

Dickson, Keith. "Enki and Ninhursag: The Trickster in Paradise." *Journal of Near Eastern Studies* 66, no. 1 (2007): 1–32. https://www.jstor.org/stable/10.1086/512211.

Dicle, Amed. *2005–2015 Türkiye-PKK Görüşmeleri: Kürt Sorununun Çözümüne "Çözüm Süreci" Operasyonu.* Neuss: Mezopotamya Yayınları, 2016.

Dietz, Mary. "Citizenship with a Feminist Face: The Problem of Maternal Thinking." *Political Theory* 13, no. 1 (1985): 19–37.

*Diken.* "DBP liderlerinden Emine Ayna, siyaseti bıraktı: Cizre Son Dama Oldu." January 1, 2016. http://www.diken.com.tr/emine-ayna-siyaseti-biraktigini-acikladi/. Accessed October 30, 2018.

Dinç, Pınar. "Forest Fires in Dersim and Şırnak: Conflict and Environmental Destruction." In *Ecological Solidarity and the Kurdish Freedom Movement: Thought, Practice and Opportunities*, edited by Stephen Hunt, 263–78. Lanham, Md., Boulder, Colo., New York, and London: Lexington, 2021.

Dirik, Dilar. *The Kurdish Women's Movement: History, Theory, Practice.* London: Pluto Press, 2022.

——. "The Revolution of Smiling Women: Stateless Democracy and Power in Rojava." In *Routledge Handbook of Postcolonial Politics*, 222–38. London and New York: Routledge, Kindle edition. 2018.

——. "Stateless Citizenship: Radical Democracy as Consciousness Raising in the Rojava Revolution." *Identities: Global Studies in Culture and Power* 19, no. 1 (2022): 27–44.

Doğan, Selma (c.n. Zinarin). *Zinarin'in Güncesi*. Neuss: Mezopotamya Yayınları, 1999.

Dolar, Mladen. *A Voice and Nothing More*. Cambridge, Mass., and London: MIT Press, 2006.

Douglass, Patrice. "Black Feminist Theory for the Dead and Dying." *Theory & Event* 21, no. 1 (2018): 106–23.

Drechselova, Lucie, and Adnan Çelik. *Kurds in Turkey: Ethnographies of Heterogenous Experiences*. London: Lexington, 2019.

Duruiz, Deniz. "Tracing the Conceptual Genealogy of Kurdistan as International Colony." *Middle East Report* 295 (2020).

Düzel, Esin. "Fragile Goddesses: Moral Subjectivity and Militarized Agencies in Female Guerrilla Diaries and Memoirs." *International Feminist Journal of Politics* 20, no. 2 (2018): 137–52.

Eagleton, Terry. *Sweet Violence: The Idea of the Tragic*. Oxford and Berlin: Blackwell, 2003.

Edelman, Lee. *No Future: Queer Theory and the Death Drive*. Durham, N.C.: Duke University Press, 2004.

*The End Will Be Spectacular*. Rojava Film Commune. Director: Ersin Çelik. Writers: Aysun Genç and Ersin Çelik. 2019.

En Son Haber. "HDP'li Vekil Feleknas Uca'nın Son Hali," October 26, 2016. https://m.ensonhaber.com/ic-haber/hdpli-vekil-feleknas-ucanin-son-hali-2016-10 -26. Accessed on May 12, 2021.

Erasmus, Zimitri. "Sylvia Wynter's Theory of the Human: Counter-, Not Post-Humanist." *Theory, Culture and Society* 37, no. 6 (2020): 47–65.

Ercan, Harun. "Is Hope More Precious Than Victory?: The Failed Peace Process and the Urban Warfare in the Kurdish Region of Turkey." *South Atlantic Quarterly* 118, no. 1 (2019): 111–27.

Erdal, Mahsum. "Radikal Demokrasinin Politik Ontolojisi Üzerine Deneme." *Demokratik Modernite* 22 (2017): 10–21.

Erel Umut, and Necla Açık. "Enacting Intersectional Multilayered Citizenship: Kurdish Women's Politics." *Gender, Place and Culture: A Journal of Feminist Geography* 27, no. 4 (2020): 479–501.

Ettinger, Bracha L. "Antigone with(out) Jacosta." In *Interrogating Antigone in Postmodern Philosophy and Criticism*, edited by S. E. Wilmer and Audrone Zukauskaite. Oxford: Oxford University Press, 2010.

——. "Matrixial Trans-Subjectivity." *Theory, Culture & Society* 23, no. 2–3 (2006): 218–22.

——. "Toward a Black Feminist Poethics: The Quest(ion) of Blackness toward the End of the World," *Black Scholar* 44, no. 2 (2014): 81–97.

Evans, Dylan. *An Introductory Dictionary of Lacanian Psychoanalysis*. London and New York: Routledge, 1996.

Fahs, Breanne. "Radical Refusals: On the Anarchist Politics of Women Choosing Asexuality." *Sexualities* 13, no. 4 (2010): 445–61.

Fanon, Franz. *Black Skin, White Masks*. Rev. ed. New York: Grove Press, 2008.

——. *The Wretched of the Earth*. New York: Grove Press, 2014

Federici, Silvia. "Undeclared War: Violence against Women." *Artforum*, Summer 2017. https://www.artforum.com/print/201706/undeclared-war-violence-against -women-68680. Accessed May 6, 2022.

Feldman, Allen. *Archives of the Insensible: Of War, Photopolitics, and Dead Memory*. Chicago: Chicago University Press, 2015.

——. "Violence and Vision: The Prosthetics and Aesthetics of Terror." In *States of Violence*, edited by Fernando Coronil and Julie Skursky, 425–68. Ann Arbor: University of Michigan Press, 2006.

Felman, Shoshana. *The Scandal of the Speaking Body: Don Juan with J. L. Austin, or Seduction in Two Languages*. Stanford, Calif.: Stanford University Press, 2002.

Ferreira da Silva, Denise. "On Difference without Separability." *32nd Bienal De Sao Paulo Art Biennial, "Incerteza Viva,"* 2016.

Foucault, Michel. *The Archeology of Knowledge: And the Discourse on Language*. New York: Pantheon, 1982.

——. "Friendship as a Way of Life." In *The Essential Works of Foucault 1954–1984*, vol. 1, *Ethics: Subjectivity and Truth*, edited by Paul Rabinow, translated by Robert Hurley, 135–40. New York: New Press, 1997.

Freeman, Elizabeth. *Time Binds: Queer Temporalities, Queer Histories*. Durham, N.C., and London: Duke University Press, 2010.

Gago, Veronica. "Is There A War 'On' the Body of Women?: Finance, Territory, and Violence." *Viewpoint Magazine*, March 7, 2018. https://viewpointmag.com/2018 /03/07/war-body-women-finance-territory-violence/. Accessed May 6, 2022.

Gambetti, Zeynep. "'I'm No Terrorist, I Am a Kurd': Societal Violence, the State, and the Neo-Liberal Order." In *Rhetorics of Insecurity: Belonging and Violence in the Neoliberal Era*, edited by Zeynep Gambetti and Marcial Godoy-Anativia. New York: New York University Press, Kindle ed., 2013.

Gandhi, Leela. *Affective Communities: Anticolonial Thought, Fin-de-Siècle Radicalism, and the Politics of Friendship*. Durham, N.C., and London: Duke University Press, 2006.

Geerdink, Fréderike. *The Fire Never Dies: One Year with the PKK*. New Delhi: Leftword, 2021.

Genç, Fırat. "Governing the Contested City: Geographies of Displacement in Diyarbakır, Turkey." *Antipode* 53, no. 6 (2021): 1,682–1,703.

Glissant, Édouard. "One World in Relation: Édouard Glissant in Conversation with

Manthia Diawara." Translated by C. Winks. *Nka Journal of Contemporary African Art* 28 (Spring 2011): 4–19.

Glynos, Jason, and Yannis Stavrakakis. "Politics and the Unconscious." *Subjectivity* 3, no. 3 (2010): 225–30. https://doi.org/10.1057/sub.2010.17.

Gordon, Avery F. *Ghostly Matters: Haunting and the Sociological Imagination*. Minneapolis: University of Minnesota Press, 2008.

———. "Some Thoughts on Haunting and Futurity." *Borderlands E-Journal* 10, no. 2 (2011): 1–21.

Göksel, Nisa. "Gendering Resistance: Multiple Faces of the Kurdish Women's Struggle." *Sociological Forum* 34, no S1 (2019): 1,112–31.

———. "Losing the One, Caring for the All: The Activism of the Peace Mothers in Turkey." *Social Sciences* 7, no. 174 (2018): 1–20. https://doi.org/10.3390/socsci7100174.

Göral, Özgür Sevgi. "'İmkansız Bir Talep' Olarak Adaleti Beklemek: Kaybedilenler ve Yakınları." In *Beklerken: Zamanın Bilgisi ve Öznenin Dönüşümü*, edited by Özge Biner and Zerrin Özlem Biner. İstanbul: İletişim Yayınları 2019: 45–86.

Göral, Özgür Sevgi, Ayhan Işık, and Özlem Kaya. *The Unspoken Truth: Enforced Disappearances*. Istanbul: Truth, Justice, Memory Center Publications, 2013.

Gordon, Lewis R., Annie Menzel, George Schulmann, and Jasmine Syedullah. "Afro Pessimism." *Contemporary Political Theory* 17 (2018): 105–37.

Graeber, David. "Öcalan As Thinker: On the Unity of Theory and Practice as Form of Writing." In *Building Free Life: Dialogues with Öcalan*, edited by International Initiative, 167–90. Oakland, Calif.: PM Press 2020.

Grubačić, Andrej, and Denis O'Hearn. *Living at the Edges of Capitalism: Adventures in Exile and Mutual Aid*. Oakland: University of California Press, 2016.

Gupta, Kristina. "Compulsory Sexuality: Evaluating and Emerging Concept." *Signs: Journal of Women in Culture and Society* 41, no. 1 (2015): 131–54.

Günay, Onur. "In War and Peace: Shifting Narratives of Violence in Kurdish Istanbul." *American Anthropologist* 3, no. 21 (2019): 554–67.

Güneş, Cengiz. *The Kurds in a New Middle East: The Changing Geopolitics of a Regional Conflict*. London: Palgrave Macmillan, 2019.

Güneş, Cengiz, and Çetin Gürer. "Kurdish Movement's Democratic Autonomy Proposals in Turkey." In *Democratic Representation in Plurinational States: The Kurds in Turkey*, edited by Ephraim Nimni and Elçin Aktoprak, 159–75. London: Palgrave Macmillan, 2018.

Güneşer, Havin. *The Art of Freedom: A Brief History of the Kurdish Liberation Struggle*. Oakland, Calif.: PM Press, 2021.

Gürkaş, Ezgi Tuncer. "Border as 'Zone of Indistinction': The State of Exception and the Spectacle of Terror Along Turkey's Border With Syria." *Space and Culture* 21, no. 3 (2018): 322–35. https://doi.org/10.1177/1206331217741080.

Hakikat, Adalet ve Hafıza Merkezi. *Reports on Curfews in Turkey*. Hakikat, Adalet ve Hafıza Merkesi Sitesi Kaynaklar Bölümü, 2017. https://hakikatadalethafiza.org/en/kaynak_tipi/reports-on-curfews. Last accessed April 7, 2021.

Halavut, Hazal. *The State, Narrative and the Body as Documents of Turkey's 1980 Military Coup*. Unpublished Masters thesis, 2009.

Halberstam, Jack. *Skin Shows: Gothic Terror and the Technology of Monsters*. Durham, N.C.: Duke University Press, 1995.

———. *Wild Things: The Disorder of Desire*. Durham, N.C.: Duke University Press, 2020.

Hamelink,Wendelmoet. *The Sung Home: Narrative, Morality, and the Kurdish Nation*. Leiden: Brill, 2016.

Haki, Berjin. *Kavalın Ezgisi*. Istanbul: Belge Yayınları, 2014.

Hantel, Max. "Placticity and Fungibility: On Sylvia Wynter's Pieza Framework." *Social Text* 38, no. 2 (2020): 97–119.

———. "What Is It Like to Be a Human?: Sylvia Wynter on Autopoiesis." *PhiloSOPHIA* 8, no. 1 (2018): 121–36.

Harney, Stefano, and Fred Moten. *All Incomplete*. Colchester, New York, Port Watson. Minor Compositions, 2021.

———. "Michael Brown." *boundary2* 42, no. 4 (2015): 85.

Hartman, Saidiya. "The Belly of the World: A Note on Black Women's Labors." *Souls* 18, no. 1 (2016): 166–73. https://doi.org/10.1080/10999949.2016.1162596.

———. *Scenes of Subjection*. New York and Oxford: Oxford University Press, 1997.

———. "Venus in Two Acts." *Small Axe*, 12, no. 2 (2008): 1–14.

———. *Wayward Lives, Beautiful Experiments: Intimate Histories of Social Upheaval*. New York and London: W. W. Norton, 2020.

Hassanpour, Amir. "The (Re)production of Patriarchy in the Kurdish Language." In *Women of a Non-State Nation*, edited by Shahrzad Mojab, 227–63. Costa Mesa, Calif.: Mazda, 2001.

Honig, Bonnie. *Antigone Interrupted*. Cambridge: Cambridge University Press, 2013.

Hook, Derek. "Death-Bound Subjectivity: Fanon's Zone of Nonbeing and the Lacanian Death Drive." *Subjectivity* 13, no. 4 (2020): 355–75.

İbrahimhakkıoğlu, Fulden. "'The Most Naked Phase of Our Struggle': Gendered Shaming and Masculinist Desiring Production in Turkey's War on Terror." *Hypatia* 33, no. 3 (2018). 418–33.

Irigaray, Luce. "Between Myth and History: The Tragedy of Antigone." In *Interrogating Antigone in Postmodern Philosophy and Criticism*, edited by S. E. Wilmer and Audrone Zukauskaite. New York: Oxford University Press, 2010.

Işık, Ayhan. "The Emergence of Paramilitary Groups in Turkey in the 1980s." In *The Kurdish Question in Turkey: New Perspectives on Violence, Representation and Reconciliation*, edited by Cengiz Güneş and Welat Zeydanlıoğlu, 59–80. London and New York: Routledge, 2013.

Isik, Ruken. "Claiming the bodies of Kurdish women: Kurdish women's funerals in Northern Kurdistan/Turkey." *HAU: Journal of Ethnographic Theory* 12, no. 1 (2022): 39–45.

Jackson, Zakkiah Iman. "Sense of Things." *Catalyst: Feminism, Theory, Technoscience* 2, no. 2 (2016): 1–48.

Jacobs, Amber. *On Matricide: Myth, Psychoanalyses, and the Law of the Mother*. New York: Columbia University Press, 2007.

——. "Rethinking Matricide." In *The Mother in Psychoanalysis and Beyond: Matricide and Maternal Subjectivity*, edited by Rosalind Mayo and Christina Moutsou, 23–37. London and New York: Routledge, 2017.

James, Joy. "Presidential Powers and Captive Maternals: Sally, Michelle, and Deborah." Blog of the APA, May 6, 2020. https://blog.apaonline.org/2020/05/06/presidential-powers-and-captive-maternals-sally-michelle-and-deborah/. Last accessed on June 19, 2021.

——. "The Womb of Western Theory: Trauma, Time Theft, and the Captive Maternal." *Carceral Notebooks* 12 (2016): 253–96.

Jamison, Kelda Ann. "Making Kurdish Public(s): Language, Politics and Practice in Turkey." Unpublished Ph.D. diss., University of Chicago, 2015.

Jongerden, Joost. "Looking Beyond the State: Transitional Justice and the Kurdish Issue in Turkey." *Ethnic and Racial Studies* 41, no. 4 (2018): 721–38.

Judd, Bettina. "Sapphire as Praxis: Toward a Methodology of Anger." *Feminist Studies* 45, no. 1 (2019): 178–208. https://doi.org/10.15767/feministstudies.45.1.0178.

Judy, R. A. *Sentient Flesh: Thinking in Disorder, Poiesis in Black*. Durham, N.C.: Duke University Press, 2020.

Karaca, Ekin. "Metin İnan: Tuncel ile Polis Arasında Tartışma Gaz Bombalarından Çıktı." *Bianet*, March 23, 2011. https://m.bianet.org/bianet/toplum/128801-metin-inan-tuncel-ile-polis-arasinda-tartisma-gaz-bombalarindan-cikti. Accessed May 4, 2021.

Karakoca, Hakan. "Bir Tokadın Anlattıkları." *Bianet*, March 26, 2011. https://m.bianet.org/bianet/toplum/128885-bir-tokadin-anlattiklari. Accessed May 5, 2021.

Karaman, Emine Rezzan. "Remember, S/He Was Here Once: Mothers Call for Justice and Peace in Turkey." *Journal of Middle East Women's Studies* 12, no. 3 (2016): 382–410. https://doi.org/10.1215/15525864-3637576.

Kaytan, Ali Haydar. *Yöntem ve Hakikat Rejimi*. Neuss: Mezopotamya Yayınları, 2016.

Keltner, S. K. *Kristeva: Thresholds*. Cambridge, Mass.: Polity Press, 2011.

Kışanak, Gültan. "Gültan Kışanak'ın tarihi Roboski konuşması." https://www.youtube.com/watch?v=N4gc6jjLNnU. Accessed on September 10, 2018.

——. *Kürt Siyasetinin Mor Rengi*. Istanbul: Dipnot Yayınları, 2019.

King, Tiffany Lethabo. "Black 'Feminisms' and Pessimism: Abolishing Moynihan's Negro Family." *Theory & Event* 21, no. 1 (2018): 68–87.

Kocamaner, Hikmet. "Delinquent Kids, Revolutionary Mothers, Uncle Governor, and Erdoğan the Patriarch: The Gezi Park Protests and the Policy of Family." In *Resistance Everywhere: The Gezi Protests and Dissident Visions of Turkey*, edited by Anthony Alessandrini, Nazan Üstündağ, and Emrah Yıldız. *JadMag Pedagogy* 1, no. 4 (2013).

Koğacıoğlu, Dicle. "Law in Context: Citizenship and Reproduction of Inequality in an Istanbul Courthouse." Unpublished Ph.D. diss., Stony Brook University, 2003.

——. "The Tradition Effect: Framing Honor Crimes in Turkey." *differences* 15, no. 2 (2004): 118–51.

Korkman, Zeynep Kurtuluş, and Salih Can Açıksöz, "Erdoğan's Masculinity and the Language of the Gezi Resistance." In *Resistance Everywhere: The Gezi Protests and Dissident Visions of Turkey*, edited by Anthony Alessandrini, Nazan Üstündağ and Emrah Yıldız. *JadMag Pedagogy* 1, no. 4 (2013).

Knapp, Michael, Anja Flach, and Ercan Ayboğa. *Revolution in Rojava: Democratic Autonomy and Women's Liberation in Syrian Kurdistan*. London: Pluto Press, 2020.

Kramer, Sina. *Excluded W/in: The (Un)intelligibility of Radical Political Actors*. New York: Oxford University Press, 2019.

——. "Outside/In: Antigone and the Limits of Politics." In *The Returns of Antigone*, edited by Tina Chanter and Sean D. Kirkland, 173–86. Albany: SUNY Press, 2014.

Kristeva, Julia. "Antigone: Limit and Horizon." In *Feminist Readings of Antigone*, edited by Fanny Söderbäck. New York: Oxford University Press, 2010.

——. "Is There a Feminine Genius?" *Critical Inquiry* 30, no. 3 (2004): 493–504.

——. *Powers of Horror: An Essay on Abjection*. New York: Columbia University Press, 1982.

Kurban, Dilek, Deniz Yükseker, Ayşe Betül Çelik, Turgay Ünalan, and A. Tamer Eker. *Coming to Terms with Forced Migration: Post-displacement Restitution of Citizenship Rights in Turkey*. Istanbul: TESEV, 2006.

*Kurdistan Tribune* Editor. "Öcalan's Historical Newroz 2013 Statement." Translated by the International Initiative, March 21, 2013. https://kurdistantribune.com /ocalans-historical-newroz-2013-statement/. Accessed April 24, 2022.

Kuruoğlu, Alev, and Wendelmoet Hamelink. "Sounds of Resistance: Performing the Political in the Kurdish Music Scene." In *The Politics of Culture in Turkey, Greece and Cyprus: Performing the Left since the Sixties*, edited by Leonidas Karakatsanis and Nikolaos Papadogiannis, 103–21. London and New York: Routledge, 2017.

Küçük, Bülent. "The Burden of Sisyphus: A Sociological Inventory of the Kurdish Question in Turkey." *British Journal of Middle Eastern Studies* 46, no. 5 (2019): 752–66.

——. "What Is a Democratization Package Good For?" *Jadaliyya*, October 21, 2013. https://www.jadaliyya.com/Details/29674/What-Is-a-Democratization-Package -Good-For. Accessed April 13, 2022.

Kürkçü, Ertuğrul. "Atılamayan Tokat ve Egemenin İncinen Gururu." *Bianet*, March 23, 2011. https://m.bianet.org/bianet/siyaset/128796-atil-a-mayan-tokat-ve -egemenin-incinen-gururu. Accessed May 5, 2021.

Lacan, Jacques. *The Ethics of Psychoanalysis 1959–1960*. New York: Norton, 1992.

Lloyd, David. "The Social Life of Black Things: Fred Moten's Consent Not to Be a Single Being." *Radical Philosophy* 2, no. 7 (Spring 2020).

Lupton, Julia Reinhart. *Citizen-Saints: Shakespeare and Political Theology*. Chicago: University of Chicago, 2014.

Malaklou, M Shadee, and Tiffany Willoughby-Herard. "Notes from the Kitchen, the

Crossroads, and Everywhere Else, Too: Ruptures of Thought, Word, and Deed from the 'Arbiters of Blackness Itself.'" *Theory & Event* 21, no. 1 (2018): 2–67.

Maldonado-Torres, Nelson. "On the Coloniality of Being: Contributions to the Development of a Concept." *Cultural Studies* 21, no. 2–3 (2007): 240–70.

Marriott, David. "Corpsing; or, the Matter of Black Life." *Cultural Critique* 94 (Fall 2016): 32–64.

———. "Inventions of Existence: Sylvia Wynter, Frantz Fanon, Sociogeny, and 'the Damned.'" *New Centennial Review* 11, no. 3 (2012): 45–89.

———. *On Black Men*. New York: Columbia University Press, 2000.

Martel, James R. *Bodies Unburied: Subversive Corpses and the Authority of the Dead*. Amherst, Mass.: Amherst College Press, 2018.

Mayo, Rosalind, and Christina Moutsou. "The Maternal: An Introduction." In *The Mother in Psychoanalysis and Beyond: Matricide and Maternal Subjectivity*, edited by Rosalind Mayo and Christina Moutsou, 1–20. New York and London: Routledge, 2017.

Mbembe, Achille. "The Age of Humanism Is Ending." *Guardian*, December 22, 2016. https://mg.co.za/article/2016-12-22-00-the-age-of-humanism-is-ending/. Accessed September 15, 2019.

McKittrick, Katherine. *Demonic Grounds: Black Women and the Cartographies of Struggle*. Minneapolis and London: University of Minnesota Press, 2006.

McKittrick, Katherine, Frances H. O'Shaughnessy, and Kendall Witaszek. "Rhythm, or On Sylvia Wynter's Science of the Word." *American Quarterly* 70, no. 4 (2018): 867–74.

McLagan, Meg, and Yates McKess, eds. *Sensible Politics: The Visual Culture of Nongovernmental Activism*. New York: Zone, 2012.

Mendieta, Eduardo. "Toward a Decolonial Feminist Imaginary: Decolonizing Futurity." *Critical Philosophy of Race* 8, no. 1–2 (2020): 237–64. https://doi.org/10.5325/critphilrace.8.1-2.0237.

Metin, Mirza. "Mirza Metin: Kürtçe yüz yıllık bir enkazın altında." Interview by Jînda Zekioğlu. *Gazete Duvar*, April 28, 2020. https://www.gazeteduvar.com.tr/kultur-sanat/2020/04/28/mirza-metin-kurtce-yuz-yillik-bir-enkazin-altinda. Accessed on April 11, 2022.

Miller, Michelle Hughes, Tamar Hager, and Rebecca Jaremko Bromwich. *Bad Mothers: Regulations, Representations and Resistance*. Bradford, Canada: Demeter Press, 2017.

Miller, Steven. *War after Death: On Violence and Its Limits*. New York: Fordham University Press, 2014.

Mignolo, Walter D. "Sylvia Wynter: What Does It Mean to Be Human?" In *Sylvia Wynter: On Being Human as Praxis*, edited by Katherine McKittrick. Kindle ed. Durham, N.C.: Duke University Press, 2015.

Mignolo, Walter D., and Catherine E. Walsh. *On Decoloniality: Concepts, Analytics, Praxis*. Durham, N.C.: Duke University Press, 2018.

*Milliyet*. "Bülent Arınç Emine Aynaya Yaratık Dedi." December 22, 2009. http://www

.milliyet.com.tr/bulent-arinc-emine-ayna-ya-yaratik-dedi-siyaset-1176750/. Last accessed October 12, 2018.

Mitchell, Juliet. "The Law of the Mother: Sibling Trauma and the Brotherhood of War." *Canadian Journal of Psychoanalysis* 21, no. 1 (2013): 145–59.

Misri, Deepti. "Showing Humanity: Violence and Visuality in Kashmir." *Cultural Studies* 33, no. 3 (2019): 527–49.

Moraru, Christian. "'We Embraced Each Other by Our Names': Levinas, Derrida, and the Ethics of Naming." *Names* 48, no. 1 (2000): 49–58.

Morel, Genevieve. *The Law of the Mother: An Essay on the Sexual Sinthome.* London and New York: Routledge, 2019.

Morris, Rosalind C. "Chronicling Deaths Foretold: The Testimony of the Corpse and the Problem of Political Violence in South Africa." In *Reverberations: Violence across Time and Space*, edited by Yael Navaro, Zerrin Özlem Biner, Alice von Bieberstein, and Seda Altuğ, 33–62. Philadelphia: University of Pennsylvania Press, 2021.

———. "Legacies of Derrida: Anthropology." *Annual Review of Anthropology* 36 (2007): 355–89.

———. "The Mute and the Unspeakable: Political Subjectivity, Violent Crime, and 'the Sexual Thing' in a South African Mining Community." In *Law and Disorder in the Postcolony*, edited by Jean Comaroff and John Comaroff. Chicago: University of Chicago Press, 2006.

———. "The War Drive: Image Files Corrupted." *Social Text* 25, no. 2 (2007): 103–42. https://doi.org/10.1215/01642472-2006-029.

Moten, Fred. *In the Break: The Aesthetics of Black Radical Tradition.* Minneapolis and London: University of Minnesota Press, 2003.

———. *Stolen Life.* Vol. 1 of *Consent Not to Be a Single Being.* Durham, N.C., and London: Duke University Press, 2018.

Muñoz, José Esteban. *Cruising Utopia: The Then and There of Queer Futurity.* Durham, N.C.: Duke University Press, 2009.

Muraro, Luisa. *The Symbolic Order of the Mother.* Repr. ed. Albany: SUNY Press, 2019.

Mutluer, Nil. *Dignity and Masculinity: Kurdish Men, Internal Displacement and Memory in Everyday Istanbul.* Lanham, Md., Boulder, Colo., New York, and London: Lexington, forthcoming.

Nelson, Diane M. *Reckoning: The Ends of War in Guatemala.* Durham, N.C.: Duke University Press, 2009.

Nichanian, Mark. *The Historiographic Perversion.* New York: Columbia University Press 2009.

NTV. "Gülten Kışanak: Gerekirse O Askerlerle de Kucaklaşırız." August 20, 2012. https://www.ntv.com.tr/turkiye/gultan-kisanak-o-askerlerle-de-kucaklasiriz,gR6 -IbqZxUOvwACRMxSwqw. Accessed April, 28 2021.

Oliver, Kelly. *Colonization of Psychic Space: A Psychoanalytic Social Theory of Oppression.* Minneapolis: University of Minnesota Press, 2004.

Öcalan, Abdullah. *Capitalism: The Age of Unmasked Gods and Naked Kings.* Porsgrunn, Norway: New Compass Press, 2018.

———. *Demokratik Kurtuluş ve Özgür Yaşamı İnşa: İmralı Notları.* Neuss: Mezopotamya Yayınları, 2015.

———. *Demokratik Uygarlık Manifestosu III. Kitap: Özgürlük Sosyolojisi Üzerine Deneme.* Abdullah Öcalan Akademisi Yayınları, 2013.

———. *Kürt Aşkı: Nasıl Yaşamalı? Cilt III.* Weşanên Serxwebûn. 1999.

———. *Manifesto for a Democratic Civilization: The Age of Masked Gods and Disguised Kings.* Porsgrunn, Norway: New Compass Press, 2015.

———. *Nasıl Yaşamalı.* Weşanên Serxwebûn. 2008.

———. *Sociology of Freedom: Manifesto of the Democratic Civilization.* Vol. 3. Oakland, Calif.: PM Press, 2020.

Öpengin, Ergin. "Sociolinguistic Situation of Kurdish in Turkey: Sociopolitical Factors and Language Use Patterns." *International Journal of the Sociology of Language* 217 (2012): 151–80.

Öpengin, Ergin, and Geoffrey Haig. "Regional Variation in Kurmanji: A Preliminary Classification of Its Dialects." *Kurdish Studies* 2, no. 2 (2014): 143–76.

Örer, Ayça. "Kadın Bu Hafta Medyada Mal Seksi Apolitik." *Bianet*, March 30, 2007, https://m.bianet.org/bianet/kadin/94028-kadin-bu-hafta-medyada-mal-seksi-apolitik. Accessed March 10, 2017.

Özcan, Ömer. "Curfew 'Until Further Notice': Waiting and Spatialization in a Kurdish Border Town in Turkey." *Social Anthropology* 29, no. 3 (2021): 816–30.

Özel Harekat Komutanı. "Türk'ün Gücünü Göreceksiniz." YouTube, August 8, 2015. https://www.youtube.com/watch?v=Yu5HLob2GwE. Accessed April 7, 2021.

Özsoy, Hişyar. "Between Gift and Taboo: Death and the Negotiation of National Identity and Sovereignty in the Kurdish Conflict in Turkey." Unpublished Ph.D. diss., University of Texas, 2010.

———. "The Missing Grave of Sheikh Said: Kurdish Formations of Memory, Place, and Sovereignty in Turkey." In *Everyday Occupations*, edited by Kamala Visweswaran, 191–220. Philadelphia: University of Pennsylvania Press, 2013.

Özyürek, Esra, Gamze Özçelik, and Emrah Altındiş, eds. *Authoritarianism and Resistance in Turkey: Conversations on Democratic and Social Challenges.* Cham, Switzerland: Springer, 2019.

Panser, Michael. "Power and Truth: Analytics of Power and Nomadic Thought as Fragments of a Philosophy of Liberation." In *Building Free Life: Dialogues with Öcalan*, edited by International Initiative, 261–67. Oakland, Calif.: PM Press, 2020.

Patterson, Orlando. *Slavery and Social Death: A Comparative Study, with a New Preface.* Cambridge, Mass.: Harvard University Press, 2018.

Peach, Norman. "Öcalan, European Law, and the Kurdish Question." In *Building Free Life: Dialogues with Öcalan*, edited by the International Initiative, 11–18. Oakland, Calif.: PM Press, 2020.

Podnieks, Elizabeth, and Andrea O'Reilly. "Introduction: Maternal Literature in

Text and Tradition; Daughter-Centric, Matrilineal and Matrifocal Perspectives."
In *Textual Mothers: Maternal Texts; Motherhood in Contemporary Women's Literatures*, edited by Elizabeth Podnieks and Andrea O'Reilly. Waterloo, Ontario, Canada: Wilfrid Laurier University Press, 2010.

Povinelli, Elizabeth A. "Radical Worlds: The Anthropology of Incommensurability and Inconceivability." *Annual Review of Anthropology*: 30 (2001): 319–34.

———. "The Will to Be Otherwise/The Effort of Endurance." *South Atlantic Quarterly* 11, no. 3 (2012): 453–75.

Puar, Jasbir K. *The Right to Maim: Debility, Capacity, Disability*. Durham, N.C., and London: Duke University Press, 2017.

———. *Terrorist Assemblages: Homonationalism in Queer Times*. Durham, N.C.: Duke University Press, 2007.

Radway, Janice. "Foreword." In *Ghostly Matters: Haunting and the Sociological Imagination*, by Avery F. Gordon, vii–xiv. Minneapolis: University of Minnesota Press, 2008.

Rancière, Jacques. *Dissensus: On Politics and Aesthetics*. New York: Bloomsbury, 2010.

———. *The Politics of Aesthetics: The Distribution of the Sensible*. New York: Continuum International, 2004.

Roach, Tom. *Friendship as a Way of Life: Foucault, AIDS and the Politics of Shared Estrangement*. Albany: SUNY Press, 2012.

Rolnick, Suely. "Suely Rolnick Deconstructs the Colonial Unconscious." Symposium in Gugenheim, May 8, 2015. https://www.guggenheim.org/video /suely-rolnik-deconstructs-the-colonial-unconscious. Accessed on May 6, 2022.

Rose, Jacqueline. *Mothers: An Essay on Love and Cruelty*. Repr. ed. New York: Farrar, Straus and Giroux, 2019.

Ross, Fiona. *Bearing Witness: Women and the Truth and Reconciliation Commission in South Africa*. London: Pluto Press, 2003.

Roth, Lia A. *Psychoanalytic Perspectives on Gaze, Body Image, Shame, Judgment and Maternal Function: Being and Belonging*. New York and London: Routledge, 2020.

Rozmarin, Miri. "Medea Chic: On the Necessity of Ethics as Part of the Critique of Motherhood." In *Bad Mothers: Regulations, Representations and Resistance*, edited by Michelle Hughes Miller, Tamar Hager, and Rebecca Jaremko Bromwich, 321–37. Bradford, Canada: Demeter Press, 2017.

———. "Staying Alive: Matricide and the Ethical-Political Aspect of Mother-Daughter Relations." *Studies in Gender and Sexuality* 17, no. 4 (2016): 242–53. https://doi.org/10.1080/15240657.2016.1236540.

*Sabah*. "Başbakan Erdoğan Konuşuyor." May 26, 2012. https://www.sabah.com.tr /gundem/2012/05/26/basbakan-erdogan-konusuyor. Accessed October 12, 2018.

Şahin-Mencütek, Zeynep. "Strong in the Movement, Strong in the Party: Women's Representation in the Kurdish Party of Turkey." *Political Studies* 64, no. 2, (2016): 470–87.

Sajed, Alina, and Sara Salem. "Anticolonial Feminist Imaginaries: Past Struggles and Imagined Futures." In *Kohl: A Journal for Body and Gender Research* 9, no. 1 (2023): 1–8.

Saraçoğlu, Cenk. "The Changing Image of the Kurds in Turkish Cities: Middle-Class Perceptions of Kurdish Migrants in İzmir." *Patterns of Prejudice* 44, no. 3 (2010): 239–60.

Sarıkaya, Berivan Kutlay. "Between Silence and Resistance: Kurdish Women in Colonial Turkish Prison: Diyarbakır Military Prison 1980–1984." Unpublished Ph. D. Thesis, University of Toronto, 2021.

Sassen, Saskia. "When the City Itself Becomes a Technology of War." *Theory, Culture & Society* 27, no. 6 (2010): 33–50.

Schäefers, Marlene. "Writing against Loss: Kurdish Women, Subaltern Authorship, and the Politics of Voice in Contemporary Turkey." *Journal of the Royal Anthropological Institute* 23, no. 3 (2017): 543–61.

Scherrer, Kristin S. "Coming to an Asexual Identity: Negotiating Identity, Negotiating Desire." *Sexualities* 11, no. 5 (2008): 621–41.

Schotten, C. Heike. *Queer Terror: Life, Death, and Desire in the U.S. Settler Colony.* New York: Columbia University Press, 2018.

Scott, Joan Wallach. *The Fantasy of Feminist History.* Durham, N.C., and London: Duke University Press, 2011. https://doi.org/10.1515/9780822394730.

Segal, Lotte Buch. *No Place for Grief: Martyrs, Prisoners, and Mourning in Contemporary Palestine.* Philadelphia: University of Pennsylvania Press, 2016.

Segato, Rita Laura. "A Manifesto in Four Themes." Translated by Ramsey McGlazer. *Critical Times* 1, no. 1 (2018): 198–211.

Sexton, Jared. "'The Curtain of the Sky': An Introduction." *Critical Sociology* 36, no. 1 (2010): 11–24. https://doi.org/10.1177/0896920509347136.

Seydaoğlu, Ruşen. "Ayşe Gökkan: Havaya Suya Toprağa Düşen Cemre." *Gazete Karınca*, October 27, 2021. http://esitlikadaletkadin.org/ayse-gokkan-havaya-suya -topraga-dusen-cemre/. Accessed April 18, 2022.

Shalhoub-Kevorkian, Nadera. "Criminality in Spaces of Death: The Palestinian Case Study." *British Journal of Criminology* 54, no. 1 (2014): 38–52.

Shange, Savannah. *Progressive Dystopia: Abolition, Antiblackness, and Schooling in San Francisco.* Durham, N.C.: Duke University Press, 2019.

Sharpe, Christina. *In the Wake: On Blackness and Being* (Durham, N.C.: Duke University Press, 2016.

———. *Monstrous Intimacies: Making Post-Slavery Subjects.* Durham, N.C.: Duke University Press, 2010.

Sheehi, Stephen. "Psychoanalyses Under Occupation: Non-Violence and Dialogue Initiatives as a Psychic Extension of the Closure System." *Journal of Psychoanalysis and History* 20, no. 3 (2018): 353–69.

Shulman, George. "Fred Moten." *Critical Theory for Political Theology* 2.0 (April 13, 2021). https://politicaltheology.com/fred-moten/

Simpson, Audra. *Mohawk Interruptus: Political Life Across the Borders of Settler States.* Durham, N.C., and London: Duke University Press, 2014.

———. "The State Is a Man: Theresa Spence, Loretta Saunders and the Gender of Settler Sovereignty." *Theory & Event* 19, no. 4 (2016).

Sjöhölm, Cecilia. *The Antigone Complex: Ethics and the Invention of Feminine Desire*. Stanford, Calif.: Stanford University Press, 2004.

———. "Naked Life: Arendt and the Exile at Colonus." In *Interrogating Antigone in Postmodern Philosophy and Criticism*, edited by S. E. Wilmer and Audrone Zukauskaite. New York: Oxford University Press, 2010.

Sohrabi, Naghemh. "Writing Revolution as if Women Mattered." *Comparative Studies of South Asia, Africa and the Middle East* 42, no. 2 (2022): 546–50.

Söderbäck, Fanny. *Feminist Readings of Antigone*. New York: Oxford University Press, 2010.

———. *Revolutionary Time: On Time and Difference in Kristeva and Irigaray*. Albany: SUNY Press. 2020.

Soja, Edward. *Thirdspace: Journeys to Los Angeles and Other Real-and-Imagined Places*. Oxford: Blackwell, 1996.

Spillers, Hortense J. "Mama's Baby, Papa's Maybe: An American Grammar Book." *Diacritics* 17, no. 2 (1987): 64–81.

Spivak, Gayatri Chakravorty. "Woman in Difference: Mahasweta Devi's Douloti the Bountiful." In *Nationalisms & Sexualities*, edited by Andrew Parker, Mary Russo, Doris Sommer, and Patricia Yaeger. London and New York: Routledge, 1991.

Stanley, Eric A. *Atmospheres of Violence: Structuring Antagonism and the Trans/ Queer Ungovernable*. Durham, N.C.: Duke University Press 2021.

Stavrakakis, Yannis. *Lacan and the Political*. London and New York: Routledge, 2002.

———. "On Acts, Pure and Impure." *International Journal of Žižek Studies* 4, no. 2 (2010): 1–35.

———, ed. *Routledge Handbook of Psychoanalytic Political Theory*. London and New York: Routledge, 2020.

Sturm, Circe. "Reflections on the Anthropology of Sovereignty and Settler Colonialism: Lessons from Native North America." *Cultural Anthropology* 32, no. 3 (2017): 340–48. https://doi.org/10.14506/ca32.3.03.

Su, Canda. "Saralardan Arinlere Sadeliğin Asil Temsili." In Sakine Cansız, *Hep Kavgaydı Yaşamım 3. Cilt*, 220–23. Neuss: Mezopotamya Yayınları, 2015.

Taş, Diren. "Displacing Resistance in Kurdish Regions: The Symbiosis of Neoliberal Transformation and Authoritarian State in Sur." In *Authoritarian Neoliberalims and Resistance in Turkey: Construction, Consolidation and Contestation*, edited by İmren Borsuk, Pınar Dinç, Sinem Kavak, and Pınar Sayan, 81–104. London: Palgrave Macmillan, 2022.

Taussig, Michael. "The Mastery of Non-Mastery: A Report and Reflections from Kobane." Public Seminar, August 7, 2005. https://publicseminar.org/2015/08/the -mastery-of-non-mastery/. Accessed April 19, 2022.

Taylor, Diana. *The Archive and the Repertoire: Performing Cultural Memory in the Americas*. Durham, N.C.: Duke University Press, 2003.

————. *Disappearing Acts: Spectacles of Gender and Nationalism in Argentina's "Dirty War."* Durham, N.C.: Duke University Press, 1997.

Terrefe, Selamawit D. "Speaking the Hieroglyph." *Theory & Event* 21, no. 1 (2018): 124–47.

*Toplum ve Kuram.* "Kürt Hareketinin Kronolojisi 1999–2011." *Toplum ve Kuram* 5 (2011): 21–51.

Tuğal, Cihan. *The Fall of the Turkish Model: How the Arab Uprising Brought Down Islamic Liberalism.* New York: Verso, 2016.

Türker, Yıldırım. "Evrim Gitti." *Radikal*, April 17, 2010.

Türkyılmaz, Zeynep. "Maternal Colonialism and Turkish Woman's Burden in Dersim: Educating the 'Mountain Flowers' of Dersim." *Journal of Women's History* 28, no. 3 (2016): 162–86.

Üçlü, Sait. *Güneş Ülkesinde Diriliş: Amara Birinci Kitap 1. Cilt.* Neuss: Mesopotamian Verlag, 2018.

Üstündağ, Nazan. "After Tahir Elçi." *Jadaliyya*, 2015. https://www.jadaliyya.com /Details/32784/After-Tahir-El%C3%A7i. Accessed April 10, 2022.

————. "Ayşe Gökkan Ölüm Orucunda." *Bianet*, November 5, 2013. https://bianet .org/bianet/bianet/151057-ayse-gokkan-olum-orucunda. accessed April 24, 2021.

————. "Bakur Rising: Democratic Autonomy in Kurdistan." *Roar Magazine* 6 (2017): 86–94.

————. "Belonging to the Modern: Women's Suffering and Subjectivities in Urban Turkey." Unpublished Ph.D. diss., Indiana University, 2005.

————. "Mother, Politician, and Guerilla: The Emergence of a New Political Imagination in Kurdistan through Women's Bodies and Speech." *differences* 30, no. 2 (2019): 115–45.

————. "Oyun, Komünizm, Bodrumlar ve Sırlar." In *Suphi Nejat Ağırnaslı'nın Komünist Israrı: Menkıbe'yi Yeniden Düşünmek*, edited by Rıza Ekinciler and Fikri Erkindik. (2021), 31–58. https://archive.org/details/suphi-nejat-agirnaslinin -komunist-israri-menkibeyi-yeniden-dusunmek_202101/mode/2up.

————. "Pornographic State and Erotic Resistance." *South Atlantic Quarterly* 118, no. 1 (2019): 95–110.

————. "Self-Defense as a Revolutionary Practice in Rojava, or How to Unmake the State." *South Atlantic Quarterly* 115, no. 1 (2019): 197–210.

————. "The Theology of Democratic Modernity: Labor, Truth, Freedom." In *Building Free Life: Dialogues with Öcalan*, edited by International Initiative, 235–60. Oakland, Calif.: PM Press, 2020.

————. "A Travel Guide to Northern Kurdistan." In *Anywhere but Now: Landscapes of Belonging in the Eastern Mediterranean*, edited by Samar Kanafani, Munira Khayyat, Rasha Salti, and Layla Al-Zubaidi, 95–114. Berlin: Heinrich Boell Foundation, 2012.

Wahbe, Randa May. "The Politics of Karameh: Palestinian Burial Rites under the Gun." *Critique of Anthropology* 40, no. 3 (2020): 323–40.

Warren, Calvin. "Onticide Afro-Pessimism, Gay Nigger #1, and Surplus Violence."

*GLQ: A Journal of Lesbian and Gay Studies* 23, no. 3 (2017): 391–418. https://doi
.org/10.1215/10642684-3818465.

Watenpaugh, Keith David. "Are There Any Children for Sale? Genocide and the
Transfer of Armenian Children (1915–1922)." *Journal of Human Rights* 12, no. 3
(2013): 283–95.

———. "The League of Nation's Rescue of Armenian Genocide Survivors and the
Making of Modern Humanitarianism, 1920–1927." *American Historical Review*
115, no. 5 (2010): 1,315–39.

Webb, David. "On Friendship: Derrida, Foucault, and the Practice of Becoming."
*Research Phenomenology* 33 (2003): 119–40.

Weheliye, Alexander G. *Habeas Viscus: Racializing Assemblages, Biopolitics, and
Black Feminist Thories of the Human.* Durham, N.C., and London: Duke
University Press, 2014.

Weinbaum, Alys Eve. *The Afterlife of Reproductive Slavery: Biocapitalism and Black
Feminism's Philosophy of History.* Durham, N.C.: Duke University Press 2019.

Weizmann, Eyal. *Hollow Land: Israel's Architecture of Occupation.* New York: Verso,
2012.

Wilcox, Lauren. "Explosive Bodies and Bounded States: Abjection and the
Embodied Practice of Suicide Bombing." *International Journal of Politics* 16, no. 1
(2014): 66–85.

Wilderson, Frank B., III. *Red, White, and Black: Cinema and the Structure of US
Antagonisms.* Durham, N.C.: Duke University Press, 2010.

Wilmer, S. E., and Audrone Zukauskaite, eds. *Interrogating Antigone in Postmodern
Philosophy and Criticism.* Oxford: Oxford University Press, 2010.

Women for Peace Initiative. "Report on the Process Resolution, January–December
2013. http://www.peacewomen.org/assets/media/baris_kadin_ingilizce_baski_2
.pdf. Accessed March 20, 2022.

Wynter, Sylvia. "Towards the Sociogenic Principle: Fanon, Identity, the Puzzle of
Conscious Experience, and What It Is Like to Be 'Black.'" In *National Identities
and Socio-Political Changes in Latin America,* edited by Antonio Gomez-Moriana
and Mercedes Duran-Cogan, 30–66. London and New York: Routledge, 2001.

———. "Unsettling the Coloniality of Being/Power/Truth/Freedom: Towards the
Human, after Man, Its Overrepresentation — An Argument." *CR: The New
Centennial Review* 3, no. 3 (2003): 257–337.

Yaş, Zeyneb. "Lost Voices." In *Feminist Pedagogy: Museums, Memory Sites and
Practices of Remembrance,* edited by Meral Akkent and Nehir S. Kovar, 92–112.
Istanbul: Istanbul Women's Museum Publications, 2019.

Yeğen, Mesut. "Armed Struggle to Peace Negotiations: Independent Kurdistan to
Democratic Autonomy, or the PKK in Context." *Middle East Critique* 25, no. 4
(2016): 365–83.

Yelpaze, Nilgün. "Representation of Kurdish Female Fighters in Cinema: A Frame
Analysis of Fiction Films." In *Radicalization and Variations of Violence,* edited by
Daniel Beck and Julia Renner-Mugano. Berlin: Springer. Forthcoming.

Yıldırım, Dilan. "Kurdish Mothers and Daughters." Unpublished term paper, 2008.

Yıldırım, Umut. "Space, Loss and Resistance: A Haunted Pool-Map in South-Eastern Turkey." *Anthropological Theory* 19, no. 4 (2019): 440–69. https://doi.org /10.1177/1463499618783130.

———. "Spaced-Out States: Decolonizing Trauma in a War-Torn Middle Eastern City." *Current Anthropology* 62, no. 6 (2022). https://doi.org/10.1086/718206.

Yıldız, Yeşim Yaprak, and Patrick Baert. "Confessions without Guilt: Public Confessions of State Violence in Turkey." *Theory & Society* 50 (2021): 125–49.

Yılmaz, Arzu. "Siyaset ve Kadin Kimligi." Unpublished master's thesis, 2006.

Yoltar, Çağrı. "Making the Indebted Citizen: An Inquiry into State Benevolence in Turkey." *PoLAR: Political and Legal Anthropology Review* 43, no. 1 (2020): 153–71.

Yoltar, Çağrı, and Erdem Yörük. "Contentious Welfare: The Kurdish Conflict and Social Policy as Counterinsurgency in Turkey." *Governance: An International Journal of Policy, Administration, and Institutions* 34, no. 2 (2021): 353–71.

Yonucu, Deniz. "A Story of a Squatter Neighborhood: From the Place of the 'Dangerous Classes' to the 'Place of Danger.'" *Berkeley Journal of Sociology* 52 (2008): 50–72.

Yüksel, Metin. "Dengbej, Mullah, Intelligentsia: The Survival and Revival of the Kurdish Kurmanji Language in the Middle East." Unpublished Ph.D. diss., University of Chicago, 2011.

Zajko, Vanda, and Miriam Leonard. *Laughing with Medusa: Classical Myth and Feminist Thought.* Oxford and New York: Oxford University Press, 2006.

Zengin, Aslı. "The Afterlife of Gender: Sovereignty, Intimacy and Muslim Funerals of Transgender People in Turkey." *Cultural Anthropology* 34, no. 1 (2019): 78–102.

Zeydanlıoğlu, Welat. "Repression or Reform? An Analysis of AKP's Kurdish Language Policy." In *The Kurdish Question in Turkey: New Perspectives on Violence, Representation and Reconciliation*, edited by Cengiz Güneş and Welat Zeydanlıoğlu, 162–85. London and New York: Routledge, 2013.

———. "Turkey's Kurdish Language Policy." *International Journal of the Sociology of Language*, no. 217 (2012): 99–125.

Žižek, Slavoj. *Antigone.* London and New York: Bloomsbury Academic, 2016.

Zupančič, Alenka. "Lacan's Heroines: Antigone and Synge de Coufontaine." *New Formations* 35 (1998): 108–21.

———. *Let Them Rot: Antigone's Parallax.* Fordham University Press, 2023.

# Index

**Nazan Üstündağ** is an Independent Scholar. Between 2020 and 2023, she was a Patri-monies Program Fellow at the Gerda Henkel Foundation. Between 2005 and 2018, she worked as an Assistant Professor of Sociology at Boğaziçi University, Turkey. She was subsequently an Academy in Exile and IIE–Scholar Rescue Fund Fellow at the Forum Transregionale Studien.

www.ingramcontent.com/pod-product-compliance
Lightning Source LLC
Chambersburg PA
CBHW020534030426
42337CB00013B/852